TRANSMITTING A TEXT THROUGH THREE LANGUAGES:

THE FUTURE HISTORY OF GALEN'S *PERI ANOMALOU DYSKRASIAS*

Gerrit Bos

Michael McVaugh

Joseph Shatzmiller

Transactions of the
American Philosophical Society
Held at Philadelphia
For Promoting Useful Knowledge
Volume 104, Part 5

ISBN: 978-1-60618-045-7
US ISSN: 0065-9746

Library of Congress Cataloging-in Publication Data

Bos, Gerrit, 1948- , author.
  Transmitting a text through three languages : the future history of Galen's Peri
anomalou dyskrasias / Gerrit Bos, Michael McVaugh, Joseph Shatzmiller.
      p. ; cm. -- (Transactions of the American Philosophical Society,
ISSN 0065-9746 ; volume 104, part 5)
  Future history of Galen's Peri anomalou dyskrasias
  Includes bibliographical references and index.
  Includes text in Arabic, Greek, Latin and Hebrew.
  ISBN 978-1-60618-045-7 (alk. paper)
  I. McVaugh, M. R. (Michael Rogers), 1938- , author. II. Shatzmiller, Joseph,
author. III. Title. IV. Title: Future history of Galen's Peri anomalou dyskrasias.
V. Series: Transactions of the American Philosophical Society ; v. 104, pt. 5.
0065-9746
  [DNLM: 1. Galen. De inaequali intemperie. 2. Manuscripts, Medical. 3. History,
Ancient. 4. Translations. WZ 290]
  R135
  610.938--dc23
                              2014046281

TABLE OF CONTENTS

PREFACE

One of the most remarkable features of the European Middle Ages is the process by which, in the twelfth and thirteenth centuries, Western Europe became possessed of Latin versions of most of the works of Greco-Arabic science and philosophy: these included works by Aristotle, Euclid, Ptolemy, and Galen, which were originally written in Greek and subsequently translated into Arabic, as well as works composed in Arabic by Christian, Muslim, and Jewish scholars, such as Avicenna, Averroes, and Maimonides. The new material intensified a passion for study in the twelfth-century schools and helped create the new universities of the thirteenth century, in the process transforming the foundations of medieval thought. The broad outline of these developments is well established: an early interest in astronomical and mathematical texts developed into a fascination with medicine and natural philosophy more generally in the second half of the twelfth century. The centers of translation were Spain for material in Arabic, and Sicily and Constantinople for material from Greek. Many of the translators are well known, and a few—such as Gerard of Cremona (d. 1187) or Burgundio of Pisa (d. 1193)—were particularly productive. The bulk of the translation effort was over by 1200, but significant additions to Latin knowledge were still being made in the century that followed by such men as Michael Scot, William of Moerbeke, and Armengaud Blaise.

To single out medicine for a closer look, the translations from Arabic by Constantine the African just before 1100 mark the beginning of the transmission process. They fused with Greek–Latin translations made in southern Italy into the collection of works loosely known as the *ars medicine* (later, *articella*) that soon became the nucleus for a loose system of medical teaching at Salerno. Translations by Burgundio and Gerard in the second half of the twelfth century greatly expanded the number of Galenic works available in Latin (e.g., *De ingenio sanitatis, De simplici medicina, De complexionibus, De crisi*) and added to them the great authorities of the Arabic-language tradition, including Avicenna, Abulcasis, and Rhazes. In the thirteenth century, the medical faculties of the newly established universities, Paris and especially Montpellier, also began to incorporate these authors, as well as Aristotle, into their teaching and created an increasingly sophisticated system of medical theory that would persist down through early modern times. Of course, in the end, the theory was shaped by the linguistic decisions made long before by the twelfth-century translators, who had varied widely in their ability to work with a second language: Burgundio could read Greek himself, whereas (at least at the beginning of his career) Gerard had had to work with a collaborator who translated the Arabic into a romance vernacular, which Gerard then put into Latin.

It is quite surprising that in this history that centers on the transmission of texts, the texts themselves should have received so little close study. Most of the new Latin texts of the twelfth century have never been carefully edited, and scholars have to read them in corrupt sixteenth-century editions, which often deform the translator's original linguistic decisions. The mechanics of translation are all the harder to get at because the few editions that exist have not always been compared with the Arabic or Greek sources from which they were taken. Indeed, even more of the Arabic originals lack careful modern editions than do their Latin translations. Of the seventy-odd works translated by Gerard of Cremona, for example, fewer than a third have been given modern Latin editions, and most of those fail to compare the Latin systematically with the Arabic text on which they were based.

This means that the core of the transmission process remains to be studied and understood. The technique of the translators, their proficiency, their word choices, their achievements, and their limitations—with all the consequences that these entailed for meaning and for the content of future European intellectual life—cannot be known until the texts themselves have been carefully edited and compared. We have begun to understand something of the lives and broad social contexts of individual translators like Gerard of Cremona or Stephen of Antioch, but only when we study their translations in detail and comprehensively, against the framework of the works they are translating, will we be able to get into their minds and identify the technical devices that stamp a particular translation as their own. Obvious difficulties stand in the way, of course: knowledge of and access to the relevant Arabic, Greek, and Latin manuscripts; a facility in all the necessary languages; and not least, time, energy, and commitment. Text editing seems a relatively unappealing and unrewarding activity to many scholars.

The study that follows is in part a contribution to this lacuna in translation studies and results from a three-way collaboration. It focuses on a short Galenic text, *Peri anomalou dyskrasias*, whose Greek text has recently been edited by Elsa García Novo. One of us (GB) has prepared an edition of the Arabic translation made of that work in ninth-century Baghdad by Ḥunayn ibn Isḥāq, basing it on the five known Arabic manuscripts studied in the light of the García Novo edition, and has accompanied it with an English translation of the Arabic. A second member of our group (MM) has prepared an edition of the Latin translation of that Arabic version, a Latin translation made in the twelfth century by Gerard of Cremona (the Latin version was often taught in the medieval universities, and some eighty manuscripts survive). Each of these editions is accompanied by an introduction that provides a look at the translator's technique as apparent in that work, whether from Greek to Arabic or from Arabic to Latin, and our various glossaries will help map out the details of their knowledge.

But there is more to the study offered here than these two editions, just as there was more to the process of medieval intercultural transmission than a movement from Greek to Arabic to Latin. Another ingredient in the process was Hebrew. Jews in eleventh-century Spain had read Arabic, but those who fled the repressive Almohads and settled in Languedoc or Provence in the twelfth century began to lose contact with that language, and a few Jewish scholars in these new territories began to translate Arabic-language philosophical and scientific works into Hebrew, beginning the creation of a new technical Hebrew vocabulary as they did so. Maimonides' *Guide to the Perplexed* was translated from its original Arabic to Hebrew well before his death in 1204, and Arabic–Hebrew translations of scientific and medical literature continued to be produced down to the end of the thirteenth century. But by 1300 the transformation of medieval Latin thought and the social prestige of European academic institutions had begun to make Latin academic medicine seem desirable to the Jews of Provence, and throughout the fourteenth century (and beyond) we find works of Latin scholastic medicine—both original works by medieval Latin authors and Latin translations from the Greco-Arabic tradition—being rendered into Hebrew for a non-Latinate Jewish audience.

One of these latter was *Peri anomalou dyskrasias*, whose Latin translation from Arabic had borne the title *De malitia complexionis diverse*. Around 1305, David Caslari of Besalú in Catalunya chose to translate Gerard's Latin version into Hebrew, probably motivated by its contemporary interest to European medical faculties. One manuscript of this translation survives, which the third member of our collaboration (JS) has edited by comparing its transcription against late manuscripts of Gerard's text.[1] In this third instance, our introduction to the edition comments not merely on these differences, and on Caslari's approach to translation, but also on the extent to which Hebrew had developed a technical medical vocabulary by the beginning of the fourteenth century. Again, the relevant glossaries will reinforce our conclusions.

Anyone who reads our study is sure to be continually sensitive to the Greek text lurking unseen in the background to the three translations edited here. We had originally planned to reproduce Kühn's version of *Peri anomalou dyskrasias* in an appendix, for consultation by those who might want to explore the translation of particular terms or passages over time, but the recent exemplary edition of that work by García Novo has made it unthinkable to direct the reader to any other version of the Greek. Her edition has explored the later history of Galen's text for what it may contribute to establishing his original language; she has pursued that history not only over the three translations that concern us, but over other medieval and Renaissance Latin versions, providing an overview of the work's history down to relatively modern times that surveys a much longer period of time than we cover here. In addition, her edition provides the reader with an English translation of the Greek as well as a detailed commentary on the language, structure, and content of the treatise.[2] Her study thus allows students to explore Galen's own thought in exacting detail. Ours, we trust, will allow students to appreciate just what three subsequent cultures—Arabic, Latin, and Hebrew—made of it.

Short though it is, Galen's *Peri anomalou dyskrasias* (*De malitia complexionis diverse*, *De inaequali temperie*[3]) has never been easy for readers to summarize. Jean de St. Amand, one of its first expositors at the University of Paris in the late thirteenth century, gave a remarkably vague summary of it to his students:

> In this book *On the evil of an unbalanced complexion* [Galen] considers generally an evil complexion as distinct from a natural complexion. It has two chapters: in the first . . . , he considers in how many ways an unbalanced complexion can arise, since it is either throughout the whole body or in a single part, and if it is in a single part, it is an aposteme arising either from blood or from choler or from phlegm or from melancholy. And he shows how it arises in different parts of the body, and how they are affected according to the diversity of the condition, and how pain arises in those members as they are changed. In the second . . . he shows how it occurs in a putrid fever. And what he says is clear.[4]

---

[1]Late because, during the thirteenth century, an accumulation of scribal errors had evidently presented Caslari with a text somewhat different from the one Gerard had originally made from the Arabic.

[2]*Galen, On the Anomalous Dyskrasia*, ed. Elsa García Novo (Madrid: Editorial Complutense, 2010). García Novo's focus is of course on Galen's original version, but she has also looked attentively at its later history and its Arabic, Latin, and Hebrew translations for the help they may provide in establishing the Greek, and her work has been of inestimable value to our study. Another recent English translation of the work (under the title "On Uneven Bad Temperament"), based on Kühn's text, is included in Mark Grant, ed., *Galen on Food and Diet* (London: Routledge, 2000), 37–45.

[3]This last title did not come into use until the sixteenth century in the Greek–Latin translation of the work by Thomas Linacre (1549). It is often today used to refer to the work, but because of its relative modernity we have avoided using it in our study.

[4]"In isto libro de malicia complexionis diversae determinat in generali de complexione mala alia a complexione naturali et sunt in eo duo capitula. In 1° capitulo quod incipit 'malicia complexionis diversae etc.' determinat de complexione diversa quot modis fit quia aut est in toto corpore aut in parte et si fit in parte, aut est apostema sanguineum aut colericum aut flegmaticum aut melancolicum ostendens quomodo fit in diversis partibus et quomodo secundum passionis diversitatem patiuntur et quomodo fit dolor in istis membris dum fit transmutatio. . . . In 2°capitulo quod incipit 'redeamus ergo ad species maliciae complexionis diversae etc.' ostendit quomodo fit in febre putrida et patet quod dicit"; Georg Matern, "Aus dem Revocativum memoriae des Johannes de Sancto Amando (XIII. Jahrhundert): Drei Bücher des Galen über die Temperamente," inaug.-diss., Berlin, 1894, 22.

John Redman Coxe gave an only slightly less vague account of it in the mid-nineteenth century:

> By *intemperies*, Galen apparently means that unseasonable or unfit state of some individual part of the body, or of the whole system, which predisposes to disease, if it be not actually disease itself. He makes four varieties of it—simple, compound, equal, and unequal. A number of affections are mentioned, seemingly as coming within the scope of this division. The modes of origin of this unequal *intemperies* are described; a concise view of his division of the body is given; and some particulars, as by what means inflammation arises and terminates in any part. Sundry anomalies are explained of this temperament, such as the sense of heat and cold at the same time, and of rigors not followed by fever, etc.[5]

Neither is of much help to a modern scholar interested in understanding Galenic thought, but their difficulties in summarizing the work are excusable, for the text is disordered, digressive, and elliptical. It is no wonder, perhaps, that medieval readers mined it for its specific contentions and failed to understand it synthetically. Its argument is best understood by reading the ending first to appreciate what Galen thought he had said, and then going back to study earlier elements from the text in the light of that account. When we do this, we find that the work is what we might think of as a Galenic nosology—a way to classify, through their causes, the majority of diseases from which humankind suffers.

Reconstructing Galen's thought in this way, we have arrived at the following succinct interpretation of his views in *Peri anomalou dyskrasias*. Many diseases, perhaps most, Galen says here, are caused by a complexional imbalance or dyscrasia—that is, an excess of one or more of the four primary qualities (the hot, cold, dry, or moist). Such a dyscrasia can arise from an external cause; for example, exercise or climate can overheat the body as a whole. It can also come from an internal cause, as when a humoral residue dominated by one or more of the four qualities flows into one of the fundamental constituents of the body, the homoiomerous members (that is, those composed of one and the same type of material: bones and muscles and veins and flesh and skin and fat, rather than the hand or finger built up from those simplest members). Dyscrasias vary in kind, depending not only on the nature of the inflowing humoral qualities, but also on the member into which they flow. Along with a qualitative dyscrasia, such humoral influxes also typically produce a swelling in the member, such as phlegmon or cancer or erysipelas, and different influxes produce different kinds of swellings; for example, phlegmon arises from hot blood.

Local hot dyscrasias (which can arise not only from humoral influxes but also from localized humoral putrefaction, which does not entail swelling) are the causes of fevers. In such cases, the dyscrasia is not universally distributed throughout the member, but is "unequal," heterogeneous: most intense at the site of the humoral influx, weaker at the periphery of the member, and weaker still in the simple members with which the originally affected member is connected (as muscles communicate with veins). In fact, it is this heterogeneity or unequal intensity that we perceive as pain; thus, the pain of the fever called "epiala" arises out of the juxtaposition of cold and hot in the body. If a hot dyscrasia should succeed in extending itself throughout the whole body, so that the body is fully and perfectly heated, a hectic fever is the result, in which the patient feels no pain since all parts of his body are equally hot. In this way, although not as systematically expressed as here, Galen has in this little treatise unified different pathological conditions, both fevers and swellings (including tumors and abscesses), within a single explanatory framework.

---

[5]John Redman Coxe, *The Writings of Hippocrates and Galen. Epitomised from the Original Latin Translations* (Philadelphia: Lindsay and Blakiston, 1846), 583–584.

I. INTRODUCTIONS

A. The Arabic Translation from Greek by Ḥunayn ibn Isḥāq (d. 873)

1. Introduction: Ḥunayn ibn Isḥāq and his setting[1]

When the Abbasids came to power in 749, they initiated the translation into Arabic of virtually the whole nonliterary scientific output of the ancient Greeks. Their efforts encompassed astrology and alchemy and the rest of the occult sciences; arithmetic, geometry, astronomy, and the theory of music; metaphysics, ethics, physics, zoology, botany, and logic; and medicine, pharmacology, and veterinary science. This translation activity, centered in Baghdad, the newly founded capital of the empire, was unique in its scope and scale and lasted for more than two hundred years, until the end of the tenth century. It was helped greatly by the availability of paper, which was introduced into the Muslim world shortly after the capture of Samarkand in 704. The enterprise involved the entire elite of Abbasid society—caliphs, princes, civil servants and military leaders, merchants and bankers, and scholars and scientists. Syriac, the language of the Christian population, played a major early role in the process, because until translators were available who could translate directly from Greek into Arabic, many works were translated first into Syriac and into Arabic only later. The vast majority of these translators were Syriac-speaking Christians who knew Greek as a liturgical language and sometimes also as a scientific language.[2]

Foremost among the translators was Ḥunayn ibn Isḥāq al-ʿIbādī (809–873). Later known as Johannitius in the West, Ḥunayn was a Nestorian Christian hailing from al-Ḥīra (in modern-day Iraq), who was nicknamed the "Prince of Translators." Bilingual in Arabic and Syriac, he is said to have studied medicine in Baghdad under the renowned physician and translator Yuḥannā ibn Māsāwayh. He then left the capital for three years to study Greek, and after returning to Baghdad he began his career as court physician and professional translator, enjoying the support and sponsorship of the Banū Mūsā, a wealthy family who patronized learning during this period.[3] His activity, along with that of his associates, is of paramount importance because it led to new initiatives beyond the field of translation proper, including the composition of original scientific works in

---

[1]This introduction is adapted from the one in V. Nutton with G. Bos, *Galen on Problematical Movements, Cambridge Classical Texts and Commentaries 47* (Cambridge: Cambridge University Press, 2011), 20–22, 85–87.
[2]See the fundamental studies by D. Gutas, *Greek Thought, Arabic Culture: The Graeco-Arabic Translation Movement in Baghdad and Early ʿAbbasid Society (2nd–4th/8th–10th centuries)* (London: Routledge, 1998); and P. E. Pormann and E. Savage-Smith, *Medieval Islamic Medicine* (Edinburgh: Edinburgh University Press, 2007), 28–29. For Syriac, see S. P. Brock, "The Syriac Background to Ḥunayn's Translation Techniques," *Aram* 3 (1991): 139–162; and P. E. Pormann, *The Oriental Tradition of Paul of Aegina's Pragmateia* (Leiden, Netherlands: Brill, 2004).
[3]See F. Micheaud, "Mécènes et médecins à Bagdad au IIIᵉ–IXᵉ siècle: Les commanditaires des traductions de Galien par Hunayn ibn Ishaq," in *Les voies de la science grecque: Études sur la transmission des textes de l'Antiquité au dix-neuvième siècle*, ed. D. Jacquart (Geneva: Droz, 1997), 147–180, on 167–170.

1

Arabic, and it helped to establish an open intellectual climate in which the major questions posed by the transmitted knowledge were hotly debated. Ḥunayn himself composed a number of original works, mainly in medicine, but also in philosophy, meteorology, zoology, and linguistics.[4]

Ḥunayn is traditionally credited with a great number of translations of works on medicine, as well as on mathematics, philosophy, magic, and even oneiromancy, although recent scholarship has shown that many of these ascriptions are false, such as that of the famous dream book of Artemidorus.[5] We are especially well informed about his translation activities in medicine thanks to his *Risāla ilā 'Alī ibn Yaḥyā* . . . (*Epistle* . . . *Concerning the Translations of Galen's Works*), a detailed survey of the various translations of Galen's works as available in his time.[6] In the *Risāla*, which survives in two different versions,[7] Ḥunayn lists a total of 129 Galenic works, of which he had translated about a hundred, either into Syriac for his Christian colleagues, or into Arabic for Muslim sponsors of his work like the Banū Mūsā, or into both. He employed two members of his family—his son Isḥāq and his nephew Ḥubayš ibn al-Ḥasan al-A'sam—and another student, 'Īsā ibn Yaḥyā. Neither Ḥubayš nor 'Īsā translated from the original Greek, as their knowledge of that language was too poor, but rather from Ḥunayn's Syriac translations, and in a few cases they employed Ḥunayn's Arabic version as the basis for a translation into Syriac. These translations are often a valuable tool for reconstructing a corrupt Greek text, since the Greek manuscripts that were used were often several centuries older and less corrupt than the ones we possess today.

2. Ḥunayn's Arabic text: *Fī sū' al-mizāǧ al-muḫtalif*

Ḥunayn translated Galen's *Peri anomalou dyskrasias* (*On the Anomalous Dyscrasia*) under the title *Fī sū' al-mizāǧ al-muḫtalif* sometime between 856 and 873. About its translation, Ḥunayn remarks in his *Risāla*: "It [i.e., Galen's *Peri anomalou dyskrasias*] was translated [into Syriac] by Ayyūb.[8] I had a manuscript of this text in Greek, but I

---

[4]See M. Ullmann, *Die Medizin im Islam*, Handbuch der Orientalistik I, Ergänzungsband VI, 1 (Leiden/Cologne: Brill, 1970), 115–119; G. Strohmaier, "Der syrische und arabische Galen," *Aufstieg und Niedergang der römischen Welt*, ii.37.2 (1987–2017); repr. in idem, *Hellas im Islam: Interdisziplinäre Studien zur Ikonographie, Wissenschaft und Religionsgeschichte*, Diskurse der Arabistik, vol. 6, ed. H. Bobzin and A. Neuwirth (Wiesbaden: Harrassowitz, 2003), 85–106.

[5]See M. Ullmann, "War Hunain der Übersetzer von Artemidors Traumbuch?" *Die Welt des Islams* 13 (1971): 204–211; Gutas, *Greek Thought*, 145.

[6]See G. Bergsträsser, *Ḥunain ibn Isḥāq: Über die syrischen und arabischen Galen-Übersetzungen*, Abhandlungen für die Kunde des Morgenlandes 17.2 (Leipzig: Brockhaus, 1925); idem, *Neue Materialien zu Ḥunain ibn Isḥāq's Galen-Bibliographie*, Abhandlungen für die Kunde des Morgenlandes 19.2 (Leipzig: Brockhaus, 1932); F. Käs, "Eine neue Handschrift von Ḥunain ibn Isḥāqs Galenbibliographie," *Zeitschrift für Geschichte der Arabischen-Islamischen Wissenschaften* 19 (2010–2011): 135–193.

[7]See Bergsträsser, *Neue Materialien*.

[8]Ayyūb ar-Ruhāwī al-Abraš (d. 835), the author of an encyclopedia on the natural sciences entitled "Book of Treasures": see *Encyclopaedia of Philosophical and Natural Sciences as Taught in Baghdad about A.D. 817 or Book of Treasures by Job of Edessa*, Syriac text ed. and trans. with a critical apparatus by A. Mingana (Cambridge: Heffer, 1935). He was a translator of Galen into Syriac for Ǧibrīl ibn Baḫtīšū' (d. 827) and for his son Baḫtīšū' ibn Ǧibrīl. On Ǧibrīl ibn Baḫtīšū' and his son see Ullmann, *Medizin im Islam*, 109–110; and Strohmaier, "Der syrische und arabische Galen," 94.

did not yet have time to read it. Subsequently, I translated it into Arabic for Abū l-Ḥasan ibn Mūsā."[9]

Galen had not divided his little work into chapters, and Hunayn seems not to have introduced divisions into his translation either. In order to provide a standard frame of reference for our study, therefore, we have introduced chapter breaks into our edition of Hunayn's text that correspond to the nine chapters into which the work is divided in Kühn's Greek edition, chapters that we have further divided editorially into smaller units. When we refer in these introductions to specific passages in the text, we will identify them in the form "§3.1" or, in the many cases when there can be no confusion as to the text in question, simply as "3.1."

The Arabic text is extant in the following manuscripts:[10]

1. Istanbul, Ayasofya 3593 (**A**), fols. 49a–52b, Maġribi script, A.H. 400–600 (A.D. 1000–1200).[11] The manuscript has not only some marginal corrections but also some explanatory notes, as in §3.1, explaining the kind of disease resulting from a flux of hot superfluities to the muscles: namely, hot tumor.
2. Madrid, Biblioteca Nacional 5011 (**B**) (formerly 130/3), Maġribi script, early fifteenth century, no foliation.[12] The text (which is partly illegible due to severe staining) was studied in Jewish circles; see, e.g., the note in Judeo–Arabic that the pulsating and nonpulsating vessels do not belong to the homoiomerous parts (§2.2).
3. El Escorial, Real Biblioteca del Monasterio 848/2 (**E**), fols. 48b–53b, Maġribi script, fourteenth century.[13] The manuscript suffers from several omissions.
4. El Escorial, Real Biblioteca del Monasterio 879/2 (**C**), fols. 41b–46a, Maġribi script, thirteenth century.[14] The manuscript suffers from several corruptions and omissions, some of which have been corrected in the margins. Parts of the last lines in the inner lower sections of the text are hard to read due to fading of the ink.

---

[9]Bergsträsser, *Ḥunain ibn Isḥāq*, no. 52. In the subsequent Arabic medical tradition the text is known from quotations by the Arab physician Abū Bakr Muḥammad ibn Zakariyā' al-Rāzī in his medical notebook entitled *K. al-Ḥāwī fī l-ṭibb* (see F. Sezgin, *Geschichte des arabischen Schrifttums*, vol. 3: *Medizin-Pharmazie-Zoologie-Tierheilkunde bis ca. 430 H.* [Leiden: Brill, 1970], 109); and by the Jewish physician Mūsā ibn Maymūn (Moses Ben Maimon), who summarized §1.1–2 in his *K. al-fuṣūl fī l-ṭibb* (Medical Aphorisms) 3.27 (see Maimonides, *Medical Aphorisms*, Treatises 1–5, a parallel Arabic-English edition ed., trans., and annot. G. Bos [Provo: Brigham Young University Press, 2004], 39–40), and a section from §8 about the "reason why in some fevers a sensation of heat and cold occurs simultaneously" in his *K. al-fuṣūl fī l-ṭibb* (Medical Aphorisms) 10.36 (Maimonides, *Medical Aphorisms*, Treatises 10–15, a parallel Arabic–English edition ed., trans., and annot. G. Bos [Provo: Brigham Young University Press, 2010], 11).

[10]See the extensive discussion in E. García Novo, *Galen, On the Anomalous Dyskrasia (De inaequali intemperie)* (Madrid: Editorial Complutense, 2010), 26–29.

[11]See H. Ritter and R. Walzer, "Arabische Übersetzungen griechischer Ärzte in Stambuler Bibliotheken," *Sitzungsberichte der Preussischen Akademie der Wissenschaften*, Jahrgang 1934, Philosophisch-historische Klasse (Berlin, 1935), 813, 838; Sezgin, *Geschichte*, 109; and García Novo, *Galen, On the Anomalous Dyskrasia*, 27.

[12]See F. Guillen Roblés, *Catálogo de los manuscritos Árabes existentes en la Biblioteca Nacional de Madrid* (Madrid, 1889), no. CIII, 65; H. Derenbourg, *Notes critiques sur les manuscrits arabes de la Bibliothèque Nationale de Madrid* (Paris, 1904), 20–21; Sezgin, *Geschichte*, 109; and García Novo, *Galen, On the Anomalous Dyskrasia*, 28.

[13]See H. P. J. Renaud, *Les manuscrits Arabes de l'Escurial décrits d'après les notes de H. Derenbourg*, vol. 2, facs. 2–3 (Paris: Geuthner, 1941), 55; Ullmann, *Die Medizin im Islam*, 39; Sezgin, *Geschichte*, 109; and García Novo, *Galen, On the Anomalous Dyskrasia*, 27.

[14]See Renaud, *Les manuscrits Arabes*, 91; Ullmann, *Die Medizin im Islam*, 39; and García Novo, *Galen, On the Anomalous Dyskrasia*, 27. We thank Cristina Alvarez Millán for providing us with photocopies of the manuscript.

5. Lisbon, Academia das Ciencias, Vermelho 292–293 (**L**), fols. 45r–50v; Oriental script, fourteenth century.[15] The manuscript starts at §2.3: أن نقصد قصد.[16] It suffers from omissions and vocalization mistakes, as in 3.2, where it has القرحة instead of الفرجة, and in 3.4, where it has ايضاله instead of اتّصاله. It has a unique correct reading, namely يبلغ in 3.4, where the other manuscripts have ينبغي for Greek ἀφίξεται.

6. Paris, Bibliothèque Nationale ar. 2847 (**P**), fols. 106a–114b; A.H. 614 (A.D. 1217).[17] The manuscript contains Ḥunayn's translation in an elaboration by Abū Djafar Aḥmad ibn Muḥammad ibn abī l-Aš'aṭ, who died in A.D. 970. Ibn abī l-Aš'aṭ copied Ḥunayn's translation, divided the text into six chapters, and added small introductory sentences to each section, while Chapter 4 has some summarizing sentences featuring the text itself. For instance, the introduction to the first chapter goes as follows: "In this chapter he [i.e., Galen] states that an anomalous dyscrasia may happen in the entire body, in some parts, or in one part, and [explains] why he called it an 'anomalous dyscrasia.' He also [explains] the difference between an anomalous dyscrasia and a dyscrasia in general, and how many kinds there are, both simple and compound." According to the introduction on fol. 106a and the colophon on fol. 114b, he considered this treatise to be the fourth treatise of Galen's "On the Temperament." The manuscript suffers from occasional scribal omissions and corruptions.

A summary of the Arabic translation by Thābit ibn Qurra is extant in Istanbul, Süleymaniye 3631, fols. 34a–38b.[18]

The manuscripts listed previously can be divided into two families:

1. **ALP** (of which **AP** are closely related, versus **L**)
2. **BCE** (of which **BE** are closely related, versus **C**)

Our edition is based on **A**, since it is the oldest manuscript and its readings are generally correct. In the case of mistakes and/or corruptions, the other manuscripts have been consulted. Significant variant readings featuring in these manuscripts have been noted in the critical apparatus. The Arabic text has been compared throughout with Galen's Greek text in the edition by García Novo.

[15]See A. Sidarus, "Un recueil de traités philosophiques et médicaux à Lisbonne," *Zeitschrift für Geschichte der Arabischen-Islamischen Wissenschaften* 6 (1990): 174–194, at 179; and García Novo, *Galen, On the Anomalous Dyskrasia*, 27. We are grateful to Cristina Alvarez Millán for providing us with photocopies of the manuscript.

[16]According to García Novo, *Galen, On the Anomalous Dyskrasia*, 27 n. 71, a thorough examination of the manuscript would have to be done in order to rule out the possibility that the missing folios of the text are scattered throughout the volumes.

[17]See Baron de Slane, *Catalogue de manuscrits arabes* (Paris, 1883–1895), 513; Ullmann, *Die Medizin im Islam*, 39, 138–139; and Sezgin, *Geschichte*, 109.

[18]See Sezgin, *Geschichte*, 109; E. Savage-Smith, "Galen's Lost Ophthalmology and the Summaria Alexandrinorum," in *The Unknown Galen*, ed. V. Nutton (London: Institute of Classical Studies, 2002), 121–138, at 130; and García Novo, *Galen, On the Anomalous Dyskrasia*, 27.

3. Ḥunayn's translation technique

From Ḥunayn's *Risāla*, we get a very good impression of his method of translation and edition.[19] It appears that he worked very much like scholars today in establishing a critical text: he corrected older Syriac or Arabic versions by means of the Greek original. He collected as many manuscripts as possible, to which end he traveled to Syria, Palestine, and even Egypt; he then collated the manuscripts available of one particular text, selected one as the basic text for the edition, and used the other manuscripts for emending corruptions, occasionally inserting significant variant readings from the Greek manuscripts at hand into the text itself. A good impression of his translation technique has been given by one of his later admirers, as-Safadī (d. 1363). Contrasting Ḥunayn's technique with that of those translators who painstakingly translated word for word from the Greek, as-Safadī remarks:

> This method is bad for two reasons. First, it is impossible to find Arabic expressions corresponding to all Greek words and, therefore, through this method many Greek words remain untranslated. Second, certain syntactical combinations in one language do not always necessarily correspond to similar combinations in the other; besides, the use of metaphors, which are frequent in every language, causes additional mistakes.

> The second method is that of Ḥunayn ibn Isḥāq, al-Jauharī [a famous tenth-century lexicographer], and others. Here the translator considers a whole sentence, ascertains its full meaning, and then expresses it in Arabic with a sentence identical in meaning without concern for the correspondence of individual words. This method is superior; and hence there is no need to improve the works of Ḥunayn ibn Isḥāq.[20]

Ḥunayn followed an ancient method of the Syriac translation tradition, represented by Sergius of Rēs'ainā: trying to render the sense more than the words. In order to clarify the sense of the Galenic text, he sometimes changed the word order within a clause, substituted a pronoun for a noun, used a paraphrase, or added short explanations. He also often used two synonyms for one Greek term.[21]

All these features of his technique recur in his *Fī sū' al-mizāğ al-muḫtalif*.
An example of a change in the order is the following:

1.2: وقد يكون من سوء المزاج المختلف صنف آخر من غير أن ينصبّ إلى الأعضاء فضل
لكن تتغيّر كيفيتها فقط (Gr.: ἄνευ δ' ὕλης ἐπιρρύτου, μόναις ταῖς ποιότησιν ἀλλοιουμένων τῶν μορίων, ἀνώμαλος γίγνεται δυσκρασία.)

---

[19]See Bergsträsser, *Ḥunain ibn Isḥāq.*
[20]Translation from Brock, "Syriac Background," 147.
[21]See Strohmaier, "Der syrische und arabische Galen," 101; García Novo, *Galen, On the Anomalous Dyskrasia*, 30. For a detailed survey of Ḥunayn's translation technique, see G. Bergsträsser, *Ḥunain ibn Isḥāq und seine Schule: Sprach- und literargeschichtliche Untersuchungen zu den arabischen Hippokrates- und Galen-Übersetzungen* (Leiden: Brill, 1913); M. Salama-Carr, *La traduction à l'époque Abbaside: L'École de Ḥunayn ibn Ishaq et son importance pour la traduction* (Paris: Didier Érudition, 1990), although she delivers less than the title promises; Brock, "Syriac Background"; Pormann, *Oriental Tradition*; O. Overwien, "The Art of the Translator, or: How did Ḥunain ibn Isḥāq and his School Translate?" in *"Epidemics" in Context: Greek Commentaries on Hippocrates in the Arabic Tradition*, ed. P. Pormann (Berlin-Boston: De Gruyter, 2012), 151–169.

Examples of explanations:[22]

1.1: وفي الحمّى التي يجد صاحبه فيها الحرّ والبرد في حال واحدة ويسمّيها اليونانيون انفيالس
(Gr.: τοῖς ἠπιάλοις καλουμένοις πυρετοῖς)

Ibid.: الترهّل وهو الورم البلغمي (Gr.: οἰδισκόμενον)

3.1: وأعني الأعضاء الأوّل في هذا الموضع العصب (Gr.: νεῦρα δ' ἐστὶ ταῦτα)

3.2: فلغموني وهي الورم الحارّ (Gr.: φλεγμονή)

Ibid.: إمّا أن يغلب الفضل الذي ينصبّ إلى العضلة
(Gr.: νικήσαντος μὲν τοῦ ῥεύματος)

5.3: اقطيقوس وهي الثابتة (Gr.: ἑκτικός)

6.1: قلّة التفاضل بينها في الحرّ والبرد (Gr.: τῷ μετρίῳ τῆς ὑπεροχῆς)

6.3: بالأشياء المشاكلة المشابهة للأبدان الصحيحة (Gr.: διὰ τῶν ὁμοίων)

7.1: عن الورم الحارّ المسمّى فلغموني (Gr.: ἐπὶ φλεγμονῇ)

8.1: المعى الذي يسمّى قولون (Gr.: τὸ κόλον)

8.2: وأمّا الحمّى التي يسمّيها اليونانيون انفياليس فالذي يناله من الحرّ
(Gr.: τοὺς ἠπιάλους πυρετούς)

8.4: من هذا سوء المزاج الذي تحدث عنه النافض التي لا تلحقها حمّى
(Gr.: ἐκ ταύτης τῆς δυσκρασίας)

Ibid.: الحمّى التي تسمّى انفياليس (Gr.: ὁ ἠπίαλος)

9.1: بمنزلة الورم الحارّ المعروف بفلغموني والورم الذي يعرف بالسرطان والورم الذي
يعرف بالحمرة والبثر الذي يعرف بالنملة والورم المعروف بالترهّل والورم المعروف
بالأكلة الذي يسمّيه اليونانيون عنقرانا وهو العارض مع سلوك العضو في طريق الموت
(Gr.: παραπλησίως τῇ φλεγμονῇ, καρκίνος, ἐρυσίπελας . . . ἕρπης,
οἴδημα . . . γάγγραινα)

9.2: الرطوبة التي تنصبّ إلى العضو (Gr.: τὸ ῥεῦμα)

Ibid.: الورم المسمّى فلغموني (Gr.: φλεγμονή)

Ibid.: فإن استحال كلّه عن آخره ظاهره وباطنه فصار كلّه بحال واحدة
(Gr.: ἐι δὲ πᾶν ὅλον δι' ὅλου μεταβάλλοι καὶ ἀλλοιωθείη)

Examples of paraphrase:

4.3: كان ذلك أعون على سرعة العفونة إليها (Gr.: τότε δὴ καὶ μάλιστα)

5.1: ذلك التجويف خاصّة من القلب (Gr.: ἐκείνην μάλιστα)

---

[22]Cf. García Novo, *Galen, On the Anomalous Dyskrasia*, 30.

5.2: حتّى لا تكون عند ذلك في حدّ ما هوذا ما يسخن لكن تكون في حدّ ما قدسخن وفرغ من سخونة خارجة عن الأمر الطبيعي

(Gr.: ὡς μηκέτι θερμαίνεσθαι μόνον, ἀλλ' ἤδη τεθερμάνθαι παρὰ φύσιν)

5.3: كلّ حمّى من هذا الجنس الذي نكرناه قبل المسمّى اقطيقوس

(Gr.: οἱ ἑκτικοὶ πυρετοὶ πάντες)

8.1: إن عمدت إلى إنسان فأقمته (Gr.: εἰ στήσας ἄνθρωπον)

8.2: في أجزاء صغار...ولا يكون بعدها في الصغر (Gr.: δι' ἐλαχίστου)

8.4: وأمّا الحمّى التي يسمّيها اليونانيون انفياليس هي مركّبة

(Gr.: σύνθετος δ' οὖν ἐστιν)

9.1: خلط من جنس المرار الأصفر (Gr.: χολώδους)

Ibid.: والذي يحدث منها عن الدم فبعضها يحدث عن دم حارّ رقيق يغلي وبعضها يحدث عن دم بارد غليظ وبعضها يحدث عن دم حاله حال حال أخرى

(Gr.: ἤτοι θερμοῦ καὶ λεπτοῦ καὶ ζέοντος ἢ ψυχροῦ καὶ παχέος, ἢ πως ἄλλως διακειμένου γίγνεσθαι)

Examples of the use of two synonyms for one Greek term:

1.2: بسيطة مفردة for Gr. ἁπλᾶ

3.1: ويزحمها ويضغطها for Gr. θλίβονται

4.2: ألطفها وأرقّها for Gr. λεπτομερέστατον

Ibid.: فبكّ وشدّة for Gr. δυσκόλως

Ibid.: لطيفا رقيقا for Gr. λεπτομερὲς

Ibid.: ثخينا غليظا for Gr. παχυμερὲς

5.2: تامّا مستكما for Gr. τελέως

5.3: التامّة المستحكمة for Gr. τελέως

Ibid.: وليس...ألم ولا وجع for Gr. ἀνώδυνος

Ibid.: مستوية على حال واحدة for Gr. ὁμοίως

Ibid.: الألم والوجع for Gr. ἡ ὀδύνη

Ibid.: ليس معها ألم ولا وجع for Gr. ἄπονοι

6.2: يبرز منه شيء فيخرج ويضغط ما يبقى منه ويفسخه for Gr. τὰ μὲν ἐκπιέζει τὰ δὲ θλᾷ

6.3: مفسدة قاتلة for Gr. φθαρτικούς

Ibid.: بمثله وشبهه for Gr. πρὸς τῶν ὁμοίων

Ibid.: بالأشياء المشاكلة المشابهة for Gr. διὰ τῶν ὁμοιων

Ibid.: والبرء والشفاء for Gr. ἀναιρεσις

7.2: سخن وغلى for Gr. ζέσαντος

8.1: يعرض الألم والوجع لمن for Gr. ἀλγοῦσιν

Ibid.: السبب في الألم والوجع for Gr. ὀδύνης αἰτίαν

9.2: أغلظ وأعسر for Gr. χαλεπωτέρα

We might add, finally, that García Novo was able to establish that Ḥunayn's Arabic text contained additions that reflected Galen's original text and needed to be inserted into her Greek edition:

1.2: تجاوزان مقدار القصد = Gr. <πάντως>

1.3: إنّما = Gr. <μόνον>

Ibid.: فغرضي = Gr. πρόκειται <μοι>

Ibid.: أذكرك = Gr. ἀναμνῆσαι <σε>

2.2: الفرج = Gr. χώρας <κενὰς>

6.1: على ما هو منها أبرد = Gr. ἢ ψυχρότερον

8.3: على حال = Gr. <κατὰ τὴν διάθεσιν>

One of her emendations raises a particularly interesting problem. In §8.1, where all the Greek manuscripts refer to pain without inflammation occurring in "the colon or the teeth [ὀδόντας]," she found that two copies of Ḥunayn's Arabic text (**AP**) speak of "the colon or the testicles [الأنثيين]" instead, and as a result, she emended ὀδόντας to ὄρχεις.[23] However, she did not consider that four other Arabic manuscripts (**BCLE**) do in fact read "teeth [الأسنان]" at this point, and since she acknowledges (p. 245) that there is independent evidence that Galen believed that pain in the colon and in the teeth had a common element (*De diff. sympt.* III.5), we have concluded that the actual reading of the Greek manuscripts here, ὀδόντας, is more likely to be correct. Our Arabic text consequently reads الأسنان with **BCLE**.[24]

---

[23]García Novo, *Galen, On the Anomalous Dyskrasia*, 30, 44, 245.

[24]How then might "testicles" as well as "teeth" have turned up in the Arabic textual tradition? Some (although not all) classicists believe that ὀδόντας was a Hellenistic euphemism for ὄρχεις, on the basis of a surviving fragment from Menander's *Epitrepontes*. In that case, we might speculate that the word *odontas*, used literally and intentionally by Galen, was glossed as *orcheis* by a later reader who thought he knew what Galen had meant to imply by that word, and that the two readings were associated in the manuscript from which Ḥunayn worked. If Ḥunayn had recorded both those readings, and later Arabic copyists had ended by following one or the other, we would have exactly the situation we find today in the manuscripts.

B. The Latin Translation from Arabic by Gerard of Cremona (d. 1187)

1. Introduction: Gerard of Cremona and his context

The Islamic invasion of Visigothic Spain began in 711, and within fifty years or so a new society, al-Andalus, had established itself in the peninsula. Its Umayyad rulers established themselves at Cordoba, and in the early tenth century assumed the title of caliph. Yet a hundred years later, the caliphate had collapsed and begun to break up into smaller kingdoms or *taifas*, and at the same time the Christian kings in the northwest of the peninsula were beginning to extend their power southward. For a time, the valley of the river Duero provided a kind of de facto boundary between the two worlds, but a permeable one. The king of León-Castile, Alfonso VI (1065–1109), began in the 1070s to repopulate the lands south of the Duero, with the tacit acquiescence of the Muslim ruler of the *taifa* of Toledo just beyond. When that ruler was assassinated, Alfonso decided to try to seize the territory for himself, which he did in 1085. With this act, he not only gave his kingdom its largest city, he brought back into Christian hands the most important archbishopric of the old Visigothic realm.

Alfonso looked south to extend his kingdom, but he looked north for support. He allied himself with the Cluniac movement that had begun in Burgundy and, gradually, a web of Cluniac monasteries began to cover Leon and Castile; the first archbishop of Toledo appointed after its recovery was, indeed, a Cluniac monk, Bernard de Sedirac (d. 1125). The king ensured papal support by decreeing (in 1080) that the old Visigothic liturgy maintained in Muslim Toledo by its tolerated Christian inhabitants, Mozarabs, should be replaced by the Roman rite. In turn, the popes encouraged in various ways the sending of money and men (knights and clerics both) across the Pyrenees into Christian Spain in order to consolidate and extend the reconquest—as it were, in a prelude to the First Crusade of the 1090s.

The cathedral was the natural center of intellectual activity in the newly Christian city of Toledo. It was governed by a chapter dominated by reforming churchmen who had come to León-Castile from elsewhere and who inevitably had relatively little in common with their Mozarab communicants, who in these first generations spoke Arabic as well as Romance.[1] But by the middle of the twelfth century, there are hints that the cathedral clergy were becoming interested in gaining access to Arabic-language texts that might be relevant to theological issues, in particular texts dealing with psychology and with the "spirits" of Galenic medicine. Toledo had been a great center of scientific learning under its *taifa* kings, and Arabic manuscripts of scientific works would not have been hard to come by. The earliest sign is the dedication by a certain John of Seville to the second postconquest archbishop of Toledo, Raymond de la Sauvetat (d. 1152; another Cluniac), of a translation of Qustā ibn Lūqā's work *De differentia spiritus et anime*. It was followed a little later, probably in the 1150s, by a translation of Avicenna's discussion of the soul in his encyclopedic *Shifā'*,

---

[1] On the following, see C. Burnett, "The Coherence of the Arabic-Latin Translation Program in Toledo in the Twelfth Century," *Science in Context* 14 (2001): 249–288, at 250–252.

prepared by a cathedral archdeacon, Dominicus Gundissalinus, in collaboration with "Avendauth," who was probably Abraham ibn Dāūd, a Jewish refugee from the intolerant Almohads who had taken control of al-Andalus. Avendauth read the Arabic words and translated them into the Romance vernacular, and Gundissalinus translated the vernacular into Latin. Thus at midcentury Toledo possessed both Arabic-language scientific texts and a community of scholars interested in encouraging their translation.

The twelfth century is famously an age of translation, when many translators, all over Europe, from Greek as well as from Arabic, sought to make Greco-Arabic learning available in Latin to the new schools of northern Europe.[2] But Toledo stands out because one individual who spent several decades working there in the second half of the century—Gerard of Cremona—has become iconic of the entire movement. His friends and associates (*socii*) were so impressed by his efforts that after his death they drew up a brief account of his achievement, and this little bio-bibliography has established him historically as a truly distinctive figure, in a way reminiscent of Ḥunayn three hundred years before. We can infer from this account that he was born in 1114, and that he left Italy for Toledo because he hoped to find Ptolemy's *Almagest* there. If the tale is true, it shows that Europe's contacts with Castile were already building Toledo up as a potential center of scientific knowledge. Exactly when he arrived we do not know, but by 1157 he had been made a canon of the cathedral, and his future there was thereafter secure. He died thirty years later, with (according to the list drawn up by his friends) more than seventy Arabic–Latin translations of philosophical, scientific, and medical works to his credit.

The translations named in the list are grouped under explicit headings: *dialectica, astrologia, phylosophia, fisica, alchimia,* and *geomantia.* Charles Burnett has proposed that they reveal a deliberate and conscious program, that they are meant in part to supply the needs of students of the liberal arts, and beyond that, for *phylosophia* at least, to make available to Latin readers the Aristotelian texts recommended by the philosopher al-Fārābī in his work *On the Classification of the Sciences,* which Gerard also translated.[3] Although Gerard's colleague Gundissalinus was simultaneously continuing his own translations of Arabic philosophical writings (including, curiously, al-Fārābī's treatise), he chose to stay away from Aristotle's writings, apparently leaving them to Gerard. *Fisica* in this list refers to medicine, and Gerard's medical translations were as influential as any he produced: twenty-five in total, including ten works by Galen as well as the enormous *Canon* of Avicenna, the *Chirurgia* of Albucasis, and two practical surveys by Rhazes, the *Liber ad Almansorem* and the *Liber divisionum.* Within a hundred years, European medical faculties would be grounding the training of students in these texts, as the *Canon* and what Luis García Ballester has called "the new Galen" began to dominate curricula there.[4]

Already in Gerard's lifetime, visitors from the north were coming to Toledo to see him at work or to obtain manuscripts of the new science and medicine to take away with them. The Englishman Daniel of Morley has left an often-quoted account of his experiences there: of how he had been disappointed by the content of studies at Paris and had left for Toledo, famous for its study of the natural sciences by the wisest philosophers in the world, and had

---

[2]M.-T. d'Alverny, "Translations and Translators," in *Renaissance and Renewal in the Twelfth Century,* ed. R. L. Benson and G. Constable with C. D. Lanham (Cambridge, MA: Harvard University Press, 1982; repr., Toronto: University of Toronto Press, 1999), 421–462.

[3]Burnett, "Coherence," 257–261.

[4]L. García-Ballester, "The *New Galen*: A Challenge to Latin Galenism in Thirteenth-Century Montpellier," in *Text and Tradition: Studies in Ancient Medicine and Its Transmission Presented to Jutta Kollesch,* ed. K.-D. Fischer, D. Nickel, and P. Potter (Leiden: Brill, 1998), 55–83.

subsequently returned to England with a priceless quantity of books. His language even suggests that Gerard's translation program might have been conducted as a kind of seminar—that as Gerard translated into Latin the Romance words that his Mozarab assistant Galippus was translating out of Arabic (the same procedure used by Gundissalinus and Abendauth), auditors were commenting on the language and debating the meaning of the results.[5]

2. Gerard's Latin text: *De malitia complexionis diverse*

Three Latin translations of Galen's work *Peri anomalou dyskrasias* are found in medieval manuscripts. One, beginning "Inequalis discrasia fit quidem," is attributed to Niccolò da Reggio (fourteenth century) in the colophon and is said to have been *capitulatus* by Francesco da Piemonte; like all Niccolò's translations, it was made from a Greek original.[6] A second, beginning "Inequalis distemperantia fit aliquando," has been identified by Elsa García Novo in three manuscripts; she attributes it to Pietro d'Abano, who also worked from a Greek text.[7] The third, beginning "Malitia complexionis diverse quandoque," is anonymous in the manuscripts, but the list of translations by Gerard of Cremona that his *socii* attached to his biography includes an item (no. 48) entitled "Liber Galieni de malitia complexionis diverse tractatus .i.," which must surely refer to this version.[8] We have edited it here under that title, which is also the title ordinarily given to it in manuscripts.

Even though the overall plan of *De malitia complexionis diverse* may not have been entirely clear to readers, the fact that it referred repeatedly to various fevers and their causes made it of great interest to medieval physicians and no doubt helped make the treatise an important part of the "new Galen" that emerged as the expanded basis for medical study at European universities circa 1300. Although only two formal commentaries on the work are known to have survived, by Arnau de Vilanova and Dino del Garbo, it was listed as one of the required books in the Montpellier curriculum of 1309, and it was one of the Galenic works summarized by Jean of Saint-Amand for students at Paris in the 1290s.[9]

Not surprisingly, there exist many manuscripts of Gerard's Latin translation: García Novo has identified eighty-five.[10] The text underwent a number of changes as it was copied and recopied, and a complete collation of all the sources has seemed to us not to be worthwhile. In preparing our edition, therefore, we made a preliminary collation of half a dozen manuscripts of the Latin version—chosen at random, but all, as it happened, of the

---

[5]K. Sudhoff, "Daniels von Morley Liber de naturis inferiorum et superiorum," *Archiv für die Geschichte der Naturwissenschaften und der Technik* 8 (1918): 1–40. Daniel mentions Galippus's role and the apparently public setting of the translation process at pp. 9, 39–40. A more recent edition is by G. Maurach, "Daniel von Morley, 'Philosophia,'" *Mittellateinisches Jahrbuch* 14 (1979): 204–255.

[6]R. J. Durling, "Corrigenda and Addenda to Diels' Galenica: I. Codices Vaticani," *Traditio* 23 (1967): 462–476, at 466. Durling identifies a copy of this translation in MS Vatican City, BAV Palat. lat 1211, fols. 53r–55r, and quotes its ending: "Explicit liber Galieni de inequali discrasia translatus a magistro Nicolao de Regio de Calabria capitulatus a magistro Francisco de Pedemonte." E. García Novo, *Galen, On the Anomalous Dyskrasia (De inaequali temperie)* (Madrid: Editorial Complutense, 2010), 80–92, identifies seven manuscripts containing this translation, gives the chapter divisions that survive in two of them, comments on some aspects of Niccolò's translation technique, and uses selected relationships between the manuscripts as a basis for a proposed stemma.

[7]E. García Novo, "Pietro d'Ábano y su traducción del tratado de Galeno *De inaequali intemperie*," in Φίλου σκιά: *Studia philologiae in honorem Rosae Aguilar*, ed. A. Bernabé and I. Rodríguez Alfageme (Madrid: Universidad Complutense, 2007), 223–234; idem, *On the Anomalous*, 73–80.

[8]Burnett, "Coherence," 279.

[9]Saint-Amand's summary has been quoted previously, p. vii.

[10]García Novo, *Galen, On the Anomalous Dyskrasia*, 52–64.

fourteenth century—and compared their readings with the text of the Arabic translation prepared by Ḥunayn ibn Isḥāq. This process brought to light a number of passages in the Latin seeming to show marked discrepancies from Ḥunayn's text, and we then focused on these passages in a partial collation of a much larger number of manuscripts. This led to our identification of three copies of the text, all of the first quarter of the thirteenth century, which consistently preserved readings clearly conforming to the Arabic:

> **A** = Paris, BN n.a.l. 343, fols. 37–39v; once Cluny 71, in a reasonably accomplished scribal hand, c. 1225.

> **H** = London, British Library Harl. 5425, fols. 53v–56v; in an informal scholar's cursive, probably French, c. 1200. The library's online catalogue dates it variously to "2nd half of the 13th century" and to "mid-13th cent." A digital version of the manuscript is accessible at http://www.bl.uk/manuscripts/Viewer.aspx?ref=harley_ms_5425_f053v

> **O** = Vatican City, BAV Ottob. 1158, fols. 86v–88v; a scholar's hand, perhaps Italian, first quarter of thirteenth century.[11]

A full collation of these three confirmed their general fidelity to the Arabic. The edition of the Latin translation that follows in part II of this study is based primarily on the Paris manuscript, but the readings of the other two have also been reported.

3. Gerard's translation technique

On the face of it, it is surprising that comparatively little close attention has been given to Gerard of Cremona's technique of translation; after all, his versions of Arabic philosophical, scientific, and medical writings were arguably the foundation of the European intellectual revival of the High Middle Ages. Of the very few relatively close-grained studies of Gerard's technique, ones that actually reflect on his vocabulary and his choice of words, most have focused on his translation of mathematical (including astronomical) texts, and scholars have been ambivalent about his skills.[12] Paul Kunitzsch, who has carefully studied Gerard's translation of Ptolemy's *Almagest*, has spoken somewhat disparagingly of his "sklavische Wörtlichkeit,"[13] yet he has conceded that that very literalness prevented Gerard from making major errors in translation, even though his misreading of individual words led him to produce "some of the most ridiculous absurdities."[14] Anthony Lo Bello's comments on individual features of Gerard's translation of al-Nayrīzī's commentary on Euclid's *Elements* are perhaps slightly more positive: he refers more tolerantly to Gerard's "Arabisms" (instances when, by his literalness, Gerard fails to reproduce exactly the implications of the Arabic terms), cites passages where he displays richness as well as poverty of expression, and identifies still other passages where he corrected or enlarged upon the original text.[15]

---

[11]We are grateful to the participants in the symposium on medical paleography held at the National Humanities Center in the fall of 2010, especially Rodney Thompson and Consuelo Dutschke, for looking at photocopies of these manuscripts and offering these tentative judgments.

[12]Despite its promising title, the study by I. Opelt, "Zur Übersetzungstechnik des Gerhard von Cremona," *Glotta* 38 (1959): 135–170, compares Gerard's Latin wording with its distant Greek original, not the Arabic from which it was immediately derived, and is of no use for our purposes.

[13]P. Kunitzsch, *Der Almagest: Die Syntaxis Mathematica des Claudius Ptolemaus in arabisch-lateinischer Überlieferung* (Wiesbaden: Harrassowitz, 1974), 104.

[14]Idem, "Gerard's Translations of Astronomical Texts, Especially the Almagest," in *Gerardo da Cremona*, ed. P. Pizzamiglio (Cremona: Biblioteca statale, 1992), 71–84, at 83.

[15]A. Lo Bello, *Gerard of Cremona's Translation of the Commentary of al-Nayrizi on Book I of Euclid's "Elements of Geometry"* (Boston-Leiden: Brill, 2003), 138–155.

Michael Weber, however, on the basis of his comparative study of two Latin translations (by Gerard and Dominicus Gundissalinus) of al-Fārābī's introduction to the philosophical sciences, offers a rather harsher assessment. For one thing, he declares, Gerard's "methodical, word-for-word translating . . . produced an inartistic Latin and a syntactical nightmare"[16]: Gerard insisted on providing Latin equivalents for Arabic particles that did not need to be translated, Weber says, and he repeatedly fell back on transliterations of the original wording. Moreover, he failed to understand even simple idiomatic usage, and above all (as Weber insists), he did not appreciate that the different forms of the Arabic verb have significantly different meanings and regularly simply adopted the meaning of the root form (form I). For Weber, Gerard's errors are so egregious that he must never have reread his translations, otherwise he would have caught his mistakes.

Although Gerard's mathematical and philosophical translations played a central role in the growth of thirteenth-century scholasticism, his contribution to the revival of European medical learning was even more critical: the translations ascribed to him include the works of Galen, Avicenna, Rhazes, Albucasis, and others, and they underpin the explosive growth of academic Latin medicine in the thirteenth century. Nevertheless, his medical translations have attracted relatively little interest. This lack of attention may be due in part to the inaccessibility of scholarly editions, not only of his translations, but of the Arabic texts that underlie them. Of the twenty-odd medical works he is supposed to have translated (more than a quarter of his total output), only three of the Latin products have so far been edited.

Yet even in the absence of such critical editions, Danielle Jacquart, the one scholar who has addressed Gerard's medical translations, has ventured to put forward something unique. She has looked closely at manuscripts and printed versions of Latin works attributed to him—most notably Avicenna's *Canon*, Rhazes' *Liber ad Almansorem*, and the *Breviarium* or *Practica* of Serapion—and she has compared them with Arabic manuscripts of the same works. On this basis, she has evolved what is in effect a systematization of the features that appear to define Gerard's translation technique, a systematization drawn from the medical translations but potentially applicable to those of other subjects as well.[17] We can summarize these features as follows:

a) First, the translations are extremely literal. They maintain the word order of the original Arabic, and consistently render Arabic nouns, verbs, and even conjunctions and particles, always with the same Latin word.
b) As a consequence of this literalism, they often misunderstand and fail to convey the sense of an Arabic idiom.
c) As a further consequence, their style is heavy and lumbering. Repetitive phrases in Arabic are repetitive in Latin, with no attempt at a variation in phraseology to give relief to the reader.
d) Gerard's evident concern for exactitude meant that, when faced with an unfamiliar Arabic word or one for which there was no obvious Latin equivalent, he tended to fall back on a transliteration of the Arabic.[18]

---

[16]M. C. Weber, "Gerard of Cremona: The Danger of Being Half-Acculturated," *Medieval Encounters* 8 (2002): 123–134, at 123–124.

[17]D. Jacquart, "Remarques préliminaires à une étude comparée des traductions médicales de Gérard de Crémone," in *Traduction et traducteurs au Moyen Age*, ed. G. Contamine (Paris: C.N.R.S., 1989), 109–118.

[18]Jacquart offers a suggestive typology of motives for such transliteration in D. Jacquart, "Note sur les *Synonyma Rasis*," in *Lexiques bilingues dans les domaines philosophique et scientifique: (Moyen âge - Renaissance)*, ed. J. Hamesse and D. Jacquart (Turnhout: Brepols, 2001), 113–121, at 113–115.

e) A number of the translations attributed to Gerard include explanatory glosses of varying extent evidently composed by a reader of Arabic, possibly the translator himself.
If so, this is a further feature of the Gerardian style.[19]

Jacquart recognizes that there may be a certain variability or range within each of
these characteristics, but she suggests that this variability might supply a key to understanding the way in which Gerard developed his translation skills over the course of his
career. As we have seen, most of these features have been commented on individually by
historians looking at Gerard's nonmedical translations, but by drawing them together in
this way she has provided an extremely useful framework for assessing any translation
ascribed to him, even if it carries with it a comparatively negative assessment of his work.
Let us see how well it might apply to his translations of the Galenic works (which were
not included among those Jacquart examined) by examining his version of Galen's *De
malitia complexionis diverse* and testing her model by looking for her proposed features
one by one.

Two of these features do not characterize *De malitia* to any degree. It is perhaps not
surprising that (e) is not an important element of this work: explanatory glosses might have
seemed unnecessary for such a brief and relatively nontechnical text. Even so, there are a
few passages where we might wonder whether we see a remark interpolated by the translator himself. In 4.3, the text speaks of the retention of putrefying humors, and the Latin
goes beyond the Arabic in a gloss, "in interioribus scilicet." In 8.2, where the fever known
as *epiala* is spoken of as attacking "someone" (*ei*), MS A preserves an early gloss "id est
patienti," which may have been widespread in early manuscripts, because it has become
largely incorporated into the manuscript tradition by the fourteenth century. (We will comment somewhat later on another possible addition by Gerard to the textual tradition.) Still,
there is certainly nothing in the *De malitia* like the obvious translatorial comments that
characterize many of his other works.

Moreover, (d) transliterations are also almost entirely lacking here. We have found
only two instances of a transcribed or transliterated Arabic word in *De malitia*. One occurs in 2.2, where Galen explained that the hand was composed of the wrist (*karpos*),
metacarpals (*metakarpia*), and fingers; Ḥunayn had rendered these respectively as رسغ
"wrist," مشط "comb" (coining by simile a new anatomical term to illustrate the separa-
tion of the individual metacarpals), and أصابع "fingers." Gerard had no trouble with
"fingers," not surprisingly, but he appears to have had difficulty in finding Latin anatomical equivalents for the other two. He could translate مشط literally as *pecten*, and did so,
but he could not do the same for رسغ and simply transcribed it as *rasceta*.[20] In this case,
he seems to have fallen back on a transcription only because he was forced to it. The
second transliterated word we have come upon in *De malitia* is *siphac* (صفاق), in 3.3,
used to refer to the peritoneum, but that is not a coinage original with Gerard. It goes

---

[19]To the examples of this feature given by Jacquart, "Remarques," 112, can be added the material attached to
Gerard's translation of Alkindi's *De gradibus*: see Arnau de Vilanova, *Aphorismi de gradibus*, ed. M. R. McVaugh,
Arnaldi de Villanova Opera Medica Omnia, II (Granada-Barcelona: University of Granada, 1975), 294–295,
299–301. See also Jacquart, "Note," 115–116.

[20]He used the exactly same terms, *pecten* and *rasceta*, when he translated Avicenna's *Canon*: cf. "De anatomia
rasete" and "De anatomia pectinis plante," *Canon* I.i.v.i.21–22 (Venice, 1507; repr. Hildesheim: Olms, 1964), fol.
12v. See also A. Fonahn, *Arabic and Latin Anatomical Terminology, Chiefly from the Middle Ages* (Kristiania:
Jacob Dybwad, 1922), 115, 126.

back to Constantine the African and the late eleventh century and was in wide currency by Gerard's day.[21]

Indeed, one might wonder whether Gerard had made something of an effort to search out meaningful Latin equivalents for Arabic terms rather than fall back on transliteration. In 1.2 and 9.1, he employed the word *estiomenus* to translate Ar. آكِل, meaning an eroding sore, a term that had been used by Ḥunayn to render Galen's word φαγέδαινα (a devouring ulcer) in *Peri anomalou dyskrasias*. The technical term *estiomenus* (or the phrase *herpes estiomenus*) was already being used by eleventh-century Latin medical writers and was evidently derived from Greek ἕρπης ἐσθιόμενος—that is, a "devouring" or corroding ulcer—as defined by Galen in *Ad Glauc.* II.1. It was perhaps via the old Greek-Latin translation of this text that it had entered Latin medical literature.[22] Gerard was thus using a contemporary Latin technical term to identify the Galenic condition hidden behind the Arabic word, and he seems to have made the identification consistently.[23] Evidently he either had a good knowledge of contemporary Latin medical literature or had access to someone who did.

Another possible example of his access to Latin medical terminology is his choice of the word *epiala* to render Ar. انفيالس. It seems less likely that this is Gerard's Latin transliteration of the Arabic *infiālis* than that the Greek word (ἠπίαλος) transliterated by Ḥunayn had independently made its way into medical Latin as *epiala* and that Gerard was applying it correctly. As more and more of his medical translations are studied, we may expect to learn more about the extent of his terminological sophistication.[24]

---

[21]Constantine entitled a chapter "De passionibus siphac" in his *Pantegni*, a translation of 'Alī ibn al-'Abbās's *Kitāb al-malakī: Pantegni*, Theorica 9.39, in *Opera Omnia Ysaac* (Lyon, 1515), II, fol. 49v. In his retranslation of the Arabic text (c. 1127), Stephen of Antioch continued to use Constantine's term: *Haly filius abbas, Liber totius medicine* (Lyon, 1523), Theorica 9.36, fol. 119. On these works, see *Constantine the African and 'Alī ibn al-'Abbās al-Maǧūsī: The Pantegni and Related Texts*, ed. C. Burnett and D. Jacquart (Leiden: Brill, 1994). The use of the term in Gerard's translation of the *Canon* is discussed by J. Hyrtl, *Das Arabische und Hebräische in der Anatomie* (Vienna, 1879; repr., Wiesbaden: M. Sandig, 1966), 221–223. Hyrtl does not comment on its presence in earlier Latin texts.

[22]The phrase is used and explained in the *Passionarius* of Gariopontus, at V. 38: "herpes estiomenus id est qui se comederit et in altum serpit et late pascitur," *Passionarius Galeni* (Lyons, 1526), fol. 74vb. Professor Eliza Glaze has kindly identified for us the corresponding passage in the old Latin translation of *Ad Glauconem* (corresp. *Galeni Opera*, ed. C. G. Kühn, vol. 11 [Leipzig, 1826], 74), which confirms Gariopontus's dependence on it for this term: "Nam erpes qui estyomenus dicitur, id est qui se commedet et in altum serpens late pascitur"; MS Vat. Barb. Lat. 160, fol. 69v. In that work, Galen explained that the term had already been used by Hippocrates, evidently referring to *Aphorisms* V.22, but the pre-Constantinian Greek–Latin translation of that aphorism was apparently not the source of the medieval neologism, for it renders Hippocrates' ἕρπησιν ἐσθιομένοισιν simply as "nervosis *consumentibus*" (MS Vat. Barb. Lat. 160, fol. 181v). It is also noteworthy that Constantine's Arabic–Latin translation of that aphorism did not use the phrase *herpes estiomenus* either, but instead used *herpes comedens*. Apparently Constantine was not acquainted with the former phrase.

[23]Thus, in *Canon* I.ii.i.iv (fol. 26va), Gerard translates آكِل with the expanded technical term as *herpes estiomenus* (I have confirmed the Arabic reading in the edition of Rome, 1593, at p. 38). By Gerard's day, to be sure, its use was not confined to the medical community. Thus, in about 1170, Peter of Blois can be found referring to someone who suffered from "herpes estiomenus, qui vulgo lupus dicitur" (J. P. Migne, *Patrologia Latina*, vol. 207, col. 293A), although the wording may perhaps suggest that Peter was not entirely sure what the condition really was.

[24]Paul Kunitzsch has already made the point that contemporary Arabic–Latin glossaries (like that published by C. F. Seybold, *Glossarium Latino-Arabicum* [Berlin, 1900]) simply did not include the technical terminology that Gerard often needed to be able to deploy: P. Kunitzsch, "Gerhard von Cremona als Uebersetzer des Almagest," in *Festgabe fuer Hans-Rudolf Singer: Zum 65. Geburtstag . . .*, ed. M. Forstner (Frankfurt am Main: P. Lang, 1991), 1.347–358, at 356.

These two features may be missing in *De malitia*, but the other three highlighted by Jacquart are certainly present. We will consider them in turn.

a) Gerard's generally word-for-word approach in this text is obvious, and helps us explain away at least one apparent confusion in his translation: Where, in 5.2, the Arabic text speaks of a "range" or "latitude," the Latin speaks instead of *intentum*, but it is at least possible that at this point Gerard saw غرض in his manuscript rather than عرض. It might be remarked that his maintenance of the structure of the Arabic sentences in the Latin version was often accomplished with little sense of awkwardness, despite what might appear to be a process of mechanical substitution. Thus, for example, his replacement of Arabic by Latin particles—connective, modal, and focal—was generally intelligent and effective. Interestingly, a number of the equivalences noted by Jacquart in the *Canon*—ولكن = *verum*, بل = *immo*, واذا = *cumque*—are not found in *De malitia*, for the words *verum* and *immo* are never employed there, and its one use of *cumque* corresponds to ومتى. Particularly distinctive in the latter work is إلّا = *verumtamen*. A number of Gerard's preferred terms as identified by Jacquart (*donec, semita*) do turn up frequently in *De malitia*, although *penitus* (occurring six times, always tr. Ar. أصلا) is a particular favorite there, but such frequencies obviously depend on the character of the Arabic text being translated. Still, one possible advantage to the historian of the word-for-word approach is that the choice of equivalences may prove to be a way of distinguishing among translators.

Charles Burnett has made it plain that word-for-word translation was a widespread ideal going back to late antiquity and was pursued by many twelfth- and indeed thirteenth-century figures, who argued that only in this way could the original text be conveyed faithfully, free of interference by the translator; although some critics wanted to see translations for sense, the *verbum e verbo* technique was the dominant one.[25] Thus we must be careful not to ridicule this feature of Gerard's work: it testifies neither to incapacity nor to unimaginativeness. We might wonder, in fact, whether his occasional addition of separate explanatory glosses might not have been his own deliberate attempt to keep the translation itself as pure and as accurate as possible.[26]

The word-for-word approach is so carefully maintained in *De malitia* that it is a little jarring when Gerard abandons it. This he does most often by making what we might call a "syntactical shift." Ordinarily, Gerard will translate a noun with a noun, a verb with a verb, a relative clause with a relative clause, and so forth, but not always. Occasionally, he will opt to replace one part of speech with another. Consider the end of 6.3, where the Arabic breaks off a digression by saying literally "speech [الكلام, a noun] about this is beyond what we are in." The Latin version reads "loqui de hoc est preter illud in quo sumus"; that is, it is as usual almost painfully literal, translating preposition by preposition, pronoun by pronoun, *except* that Gerard has chosen to use a verbal infinitive rather than a noun like *loquela* to translate الكلام. Another convenient example comes in 3.3, where the Arabic text reads adjectivally الخراجات الحادثة, "the exitures arising," and Gerard translates with a relative clause, *exiturarum que fiunt*, "the exitures which arise."[27]

---

[25]C. S. F. Burnett, "Translating from Arabic into Latin in the Middle Ages: Theory, Practice, and Criticism," in *Editer, traduire, interpreter: Essais de méthodologie philosophique*, ed. S. Lofts and P. Rosemann (Louvain-Paris: Peeters, 1997), 55–78.

[26]Cf. ibid., 69.

[27]Relative constructions were one of the stylistic devices being used by translators as far back as Cicero to make up for Latin's lack of a definite article, as Donna Shalev has pointed out to us; see Roland Poncelet, *Cicéron traducteur de Platon. L'expression de la pensée complexe en latin classique* (Paris, 1953), 139–157.

In a number of such cases he deviates from his normal custom of exact substitution and uses a different part of speech to render (almost always intelligently) the content; he may use a noun or a participle, for example, instead of a finite verb. It is a first sign of his readiness to transcend strict word-for-word translation, in favor, perhaps, of ease of Latin reading. We will come to others.

b) From the very outset of this project, we were struck by the general accuracy and general intelligibility of Gerard's translation of *De malitia*.[28] A few apparent mistranslations came to our attention at the beginning, but it soon dawned on us that most of these were accurate, word-for-word translations of variant readings to the Arabic text, and from one family of variants in particular. It is evident that Gerard was working from an Arabic text related closely to the Madrid and Escorial manuscripts (our **B** and **E**), because his translation often follows the exact wording of their variant readings. García Novo has independently offered evidence to show that Gerard's Arabic manuscript descended from an ancestor of **E** (she did not make use of **B**).[29] The following passages added to the ones she adduces in support of this conclusion do not exhaust the possible examples:

6.3 Ḥunayn, MS **A**, الأفعى ... ولا الأفعى ("nor a viper a viper"); Ḥunayn, MSS **BE**, مثلها ... ولا الأفعى ("nor a viper something similar"); Gerard, *neque vipera sibi similem*

8.1 Ḥunayn, MS **A**, الذي يشبهه فركساغورس بالزجاج ("which Praxagoras compares to glass"); Ḥunayn, MSS **BE**, الشبيها بالزجاج ("similar to glass"); Gerard, *similis vitro*

In one particularly interesting passage (3.4), the text reads يتغيّر, the **BE** variant reads يخرج, but the Latin text reads *alteratur et egreditur*; evidently Gerard's manuscript provided him with the variant reading from the other tradition, and he incorporated both into his translation. And although his manuscript may have been most closely related to **BE**, the Ayasofya manuscript (**A**) also presents at least one reading that helps explain an apparent oddity in his translation of *De malitia*: In 8.2, where **BE** follow the Greek manuscripts and read الأسنان "teeth," Gerard refers instead to the testicles! But, in fact, at this point **A** also reads الانثيين "testicles."[30] In the end, there seem to be relatively few serious problems with the translation, though 1.3 seems peculiar: البدن الذي يفسد مزاجه = *corporis cuius alteratur complexio*. Here perhaps يفسد was read as يغيّر.

There are a very few instances of the particular problem signaled by Jacquart, that literalness sometimes stands in the way of understanding an idiom, but they do appear. In his original text, Galen referred the reader twice to his work *On Anatomical Procedures*, and

---

[28]Some of the apparent errors in translation noticed by García Novo, *Galen, On the Anomalous Dyskrasia*, 65–66, seem to have arisen from her comparison of the Arabic text with a late version of the Latin text, as it had evolved and changed over time. (She reports only that she used "several manuscripts" of the late thirteenth century [p. 141].) For example, Ḥunayn's موجود في جميع الاشياء الخارجة ("and it is present in every external thing") does indeed appear in late manuscripts in the formulation she quotes, "in omnibus interioribus rebus et extrinsecis invenitur" (4.3), but in the earliest manuscripts it is simply translated "in omnibus rebus extrinsecis invenitur." See below, p. 89. Another error she discovers in this translation (E. García Novo, "Composition et style du traité de Galien *de inaequali intemperie*: Avantages et désavantages pour la transmission du texte," in *Storia et ecdotica dei testi medici greci*, ed. A. Garzya and J. Jouanna [Naples: M. D'Auria, 1996], 141–151, at 142–145) depends on the way in which the Latin translation is punctuated; in our version (below, p. 83) the "error" has disappeared.
[29]García Novo, *Galen, On the Anomalous Dyskrasia*, 66.
[30]See above, p. 8 n. 24.

Ḥunayn not surprisingly cited it by the title he had given it when he himself translated it into Arabic, كتاب في علاج التشريح, or "book on the treatment of anatomy."[31] "Treatment," علاج, can also mean a specifically medical treatment, and that is the sense (lacking a knowledge of the Arabic form of the Galenic titles) in which Gerard took it, calling it, somewhat curiously, a book "de medicatione anatomie."

c) One of the examples highlighted by Jacquart to illustrate the supposed stolid repetitiveness of Gerard's approach to translation is his systematic use of *oportet* in his rendition of the *Canon* to regularly represent Ar. ينبغي, in contrast, for example, to the supposedly Gerardian translation of Rhazes' *Liber ad Almansorem*, which alternated between the use of *oportet* and the use of the gerundive to indicate necessity. She has used the contrast to suggest that two different hands might have produced the two translations.[32] In *De malitia complexionis diverse*, as it happens, ينبغي is twice translated as *oportet*, but it is also translated once as *decens est* and once as *conveniens est*. Here is the first indication that Gerard (in this work, at least) was alert to the possibility of repetitiveness and sometimes tried to avoid it.

There are various other contexts that make it clear that Gerard did not automatically translate each Arabic word with one and only one Latin word. Ar. أيضا, for example, is rendered fourteen times as *etiam* in *De malitia* but also four times as *quoque*. Again, at the beginning of 6.4, in successive phrases, the Arabic reads صاحبها لا يحسها and then لا يحسه صاحبه; Gerard translates the noun (the same in both cases) as *qui ea laborat* the first time, but *patiens* the second. Or consider 2.1, where four parallel phrases contain the verb قسم; Gerard translates it as *dividere* twice, then uses *sequestrare*, and finally returns to *dividere*. It may be impossible to be sure of the reasons for his variation in wording, but at least it is obvious that he was consciously deciding not to use the same Latin word in all four phrases, and perhaps the simplest explanation is that here too he was alert to stylistic concerns and was trying to avoid repetitiveness.[33] Nothing is known about Gerard's early education in Cremona, but it is certainly not unlikely that he would have had some exposure there to rhetoric and to the Ciceronian conviction that *variatio delectat*.

On the basis of his version of Galen's *De malitia complexionis diverse*, Gerard of Cremona's abilities as a translator seem to us to deserve somewhat more than the merely grudging condescension that they are often accorded: He is by no means just a pedestrian, mechanical substituter of one word by another. His careful application of the *verbum e verbo* technique, sometimes complemented by independent explanatory glosses, marks him as a thoughtful follower of a contemporary ideal who was by no means rigid in his approach to texts. What is it that might explain why our judgment tends to be more positive than that offered by other scholars? There are a number of possible reasons why the translations ascribed to him by his students might vary in quality and might show differences of style, all of which indeed Jacquart has already sketched out. It might perhaps be that his style evolved; for example, he might have felt freer and less constrained in his work as his career developed. After all, his translations were produced in Toledo over a period of thirty

---

[31]G. Bergsträsser, *Ḥunain ibn Isḥāq über die syrischen und arabischen Galen-Übersetzungen*, Abhandlungen für die Kunde des Morgenlandes 17.2 (Leipzig: Brockhaus, 1925), 19 (Arabic text).

[32]Jacquart, "Remarques," 114–115; D. Jacquart, "Les traductions médicales de Gérard de Crémone," in Pizzamiglio, *Gerardo da Cremona*, 57–70, at 63. See also D. Jacquart, "Note sur la traduction Latine du *Kitāb al-Mansūrī* de Rhazès," *Revue d'Histoire des Textes* 24 (1994): 359–374.

[33]Lo Bello, *Gerard of Cremona's Translation*, 143, gives another example of such "richness of expression" (to use his phrase) in the commentary on al-Nayrīzī.

years or so. It would be remarkable if his approach (as well as his knowledge of Arabic) had not changed during that time, and a number of historians have explored this possibility.[34] Weber accepts a proposal by Burnett, that al-Fārābī's work served Gerard as an outline for his program of translations, and concludes that, therefore, he must have translated that work at the outset of his career, which would help explain its relative crudity.[35] And other stylistic features too might provide an index to the sequence of his writings. Jacquart has plausibly suggested that transliterations might have been more frequent in his earlier translations.[36] Or it might be that he had more difficulty with severely technical material, like the *Almagest*, than with Galen's more discursive texts. His biography tells us that he actually went to Toledo looking for the *Almagest*, and he may well have started to work on it at the very beginning of his career, before he had become a fully mature translator. Kunitzsch believes that he continued to struggle with it for most of his years in Toledo.[37]

Yet we are a long way from being able to identify a standard that will allow us to securely distinguish Gerard's early translations from his later ones. One of us has recently raised the possibility that his translations might be arranged chronologically by following the way in which he translated the common Arabic phrase وذلك أنْ ("and that is because"). In roughly half his known translations, Gerard rendered this phrase quite literally, *et illud ideo quoniam*, but in many others he gave it a much freer translation, *quod est quia*.[38] It would not seem implausible that he gradually moved from the more to the less literal version over the course of his career. As it happens, al-Fārābī's work is one of those translations in which Gerard consistently uses *et illud ideo quoniam*, which would reinforce Weber's notion that this latter work was an early one. Yet by this same token, Gerard's translation of *De malitia* would likewise have been produced in the first stages of his career, because the eight instances of وذلك أنْ in the Arabic text edited here are all rendered *et illud ideo quoniam*, and that would suggest that the competence that we think we observe generally in this translation was an early feature of Gerard's activity.

In any case, Jacquart's stylistic categories thus fit *De malitia* just as they do the *Canon*—or the translations of al-Fārābī or al-Nayrīzī, for that matter—but in each case perhaps to a different extent. In *De malitia*, Gerard's translation technique is very obviously grounded in dependence on a word-for-word equivalence, which in this case has served him quite well, yet he felt it possible and desirable to vary that technique within certain limits. For us to call it "sklavische Wörtlichkeit" would be too severe. What we have called syntactical shifts are one instance of this flexibility; if the frequency of such shifts should prove to vary from translation to translation, it might give a rough sense of chronological development. Moreover, he is more at ease with multiple meanings of Arabic words and idiomatic constructions in *De malitia* than Weber found him to have been in his translation of al-Fārābī. Weber commented somewhat dismissively that in the latter translation Gerard did not realize that, while the word نفس means "soul," it can also function as a reflexive

---

[34]Paul Kunitzsch, on the other hand, has argued that the Gerardian translations showing a more fluid style, like his translation of Euclid's *Elements*, must have been revised and polished by someone else; P. Kunitzsch, "Translations from Arabic (Astronomy/Astrology): The Formation of Terminology," *Bulletin DuCange* 63 (2005): 161–168, at 163–164.

[35]Weber, "Gerard of Cremona," 134.

[36]Jacquart, "Traductions médicales," 63.

[37]Kunitzsch, "Gerard's Translations," 82–83; idem, "Gerhard von Cremona," 351–354.

[38]M. McVaugh, "Towards a Stylistic Grouping of the Translations of Gerard of Cremona," *Mediaeval Studies* 71 (2009): 99–112.

pronoun, and for that reason he invariably rendered it simply as *anima*, with serious consequences for intelligibility.[39] Yet in the *De malitia* translation Gerard renders نفس as *anima* in 6.2 but as *sibi* in 4.3, in each case wholly appropriately. Still other comparable examples could be offered:

3.1: من نفس أبدان العروق = *ex ipso corpore venarum*[40]

Ibid.: نفس العروق الضوارب = *ipsas venas pulsatiles*

7.3: من نفس البدن = *ex ipso corpore*

8.3: في نفس أحشائه = *in ipsis suis visceribus*

Nor does he ever feel compelled in this work to fall back on creative transliterations of Arabic in order to represent words in the original. On all these grounds it seems to us necessary to acknowledge that in translating *De malitia complexionis diverse* Gerard was already demonstrating a certain sophistication and skill.

Finally, it may also be that, like a Rubens presiding over a translatorial workshop, Gerard worked with various assistants over those thirty years who inevitably made their own particular and distinctive contributions to the products of his evolving technique. We have already seen that the translators of the *Canon* and of *De malitia* agreed in their rendering of وذلك أنّ, employing a different locution from that used by the translator of Serapion. To this can be contrasted the fact that, as Jacquart has revealed, the Arabic word نوبة (meaning an attack of fever) is consistently translated as *paroxismus* in the *Canon* but as *accessio* in the *Liber ad Almansorem*, and in this instance the practice of the *De malitia* translator agrees with the *Liber ad Almansorem* against the *Canon*.[41] This would tend to reinforce the possibility that a number of persons may have been simultaneously active in a circle of translators centering on Gerard, and to indicate that distinguishing their individual contributions is likely to be an intricate puzzle.

Historians are obviously a long way from being able to explore these possibilities with any confidence. Indeed, there are still other questions to be pursued to which our edition of *De malitia* may have little or nothing to contribute: Did Gerard always work with a dragoman like Galippus, using the local vernacular orally as an intermediate stage between Arabic and Latin? Did he go back to translations a second time to polish or revise them?[42] What is needed is more work on the Gerardian translations and the Greco–Arabic works that they communicated to the Latin world, more editions of the Arabic and Latin texts themselves, so that more points of comparison can be accumulated for study. We hope that our study will encourage others to pursue this goal.

4. The Latin edition

In a very real sense there can be no one privileged Latin text of *De malitia complexionis diverse*, for the text was in continuous evolution from the moment of its translation, and the version that was an object of study in the medieval universities a hundred years

---

[39]Weber, "Gerard of Cremona," 128.

[40]Or, in our MSS **BE**, من نفس بدن العروق

[41]This particular contrast is paralleled by the fact that, as we pointed out previously, the Latin particles *immo* and *verum*, which are commonplace in the translation of the *Canon*, were never used by the translator of *De malitia*; see Jacquart, "Traductions médicales," 63.

[42]These questions are touched on by Jacquart, "Traductions médicales," 69–70, and (implicitly) in idem, "Note," esp. 373; and by Weber, "Gerard of Cremona," 127–128, 132–133.

later was already significantly different from that which came from Gerard of Cremona's pen. Our primary goal in editing a Latin version of Galen's treatise has therefore been to provide a text that is as close as reasonably possible to Gerard of Cremona's original. We have done this, as explained previously, by systematically comparing selections from many of the surviving Latin manuscripts to the Arabic version and identifying three early thirteenth-century manuscripts (**AHO**) whose particular readings are significantly closer to the Arabic, even though they are often less graceful in Latin. To give one example only: at one point (4.3) the Arabic refers to "a transformation that arises [literally, "an arising trans-formation"] in abscesses"; our manuscripts maintain the adjectival construction, *veniens apostematum resolutio*, whereas later manuscripts regularly change this to a noun, *eventus apostematum resolutio*. These manuscripts were then collated and their variants assessed against the Arabic text to construct the text given here. Of the three, **A**'s readings often prove to be the best, in the sense that they most consistently conform to the Arabic, and we have therefore followed the text of **A** when there was no reason to do otherwise. (We have examined both **A** and **H** directly, but have studied **O** only in a microfilm copy.) We have standardized the spelling of the text, however, and have not bothered to report spell-ing variants among the three manuscripts. All three have been corrected repeatedly by later scribes, and we have reported those corrections only when they seem to bear usefully upon the textual tradition.

At the end of the thirteenth century, *De malitia complexionis diverse* was the object of a scholastic commentary by Arnau de Vilanova at the medical faculty of Montpellier. The modern editors of that commentary have accompanied it with the Galenic text as found in MS Erfurt, Amplon. F. 249, fols. 234rb–236vb (**E**), a fourteenth-century copy whose language conforms closely to the Galenic passages embedded in Arnau's commentary.[43] A comparison of that text with ours makes clear that by 1300 the version of *De malitia* used in the schools had undergone a number of changes from Gerard's original text, some trivial, some less so. And it is only to be expected, therefore, that when *De malitia* was translated into Hebrew by David Caslari, at just about that moment, the translator would have been working with a manuscript that had acquired readings differing from those in Gerard's original version; not surprisingly, the Hebrew text edited in the last part of this study re-veals a number of such divergences. In order to make it possible partially to visualize the Latin that Caslari might have had before him, we have selected three other fourteenth-century manuscripts besides **E**, whose wording of certain passages in the Galenic text sometimes suggests the source of the Hebrew divergence:

F = Paris, BN lat. 6865, fols. 152–154v,

P = Cambridge, Peterhouse 33, fols. 23v–25, and

V = Vatican City, BAV Palat. Lat. 1095, fols. 51v–53v.

We have given the variant readings in **EFPV** for those passages—in boldface, for emphasis—together with the readings of **AOH**, the Hebrew, and the Arabic, to give the reader the opportunity to better understand why the Hebrew took the form that it did. Sometimes the Hebrew agrees, not with a variant shared by **EFPV**, but with one found in only one or two of these manuscripts. We have still called attention to the coincidence, even

---

[43]Arnau de Vilanova, *Commentum supra tractatum Galieni de malicia complexionis diverse*, ed. L. García Ballester and E. Sánchez Salor, in *Arnaldi de Villanova Opera Medica Omnia* XV (Barcelona: University of Barcelona, 1985). The editors explain their reasons for selecting **E** on p. 145.

though the agreement of the two might be due to independent decisions by a Latin and a Hebrew scribe. In a few cases, we have pointed to other divergences (between **AOH**, on the one hand, and **EFPV**, on the other), even when they are not obviously reflected in the Hebrew translation as well, for example in passages where Caslari did not offer a word-for-word translation of the Latin and might have been working from either tradition. Occasionally, these notes will reveal the evolution of the translation, as it were, in process, as in n. 168, where the original reading of *fit* (or perhaps *sit*) was revised to *deficit* by a later student of **A**, and where *deficit* has become the unquestioned reading in **V**. Likewise, in n. 101, we can see *ante* passing into *post*. But we should make it clear that we do not pretend by any means to provide a systematic or exhaustive list of all the passages in Gerard's translation that had undergone a change by the beginning of the fourteenth century.

Two such changes, however, are worth particular comment. At the end of 3.2, a long phrase, "and sometimes it is in the smallest of the spaces and furthest from the eruption, and it is the most dangerous" (*et quandoque est in minore foraminum et remotiore a loco exitus et est maioris periculi*), is included in **V** that is entirely absent in the Greek and Arabic manuscript traditions. The same phrase has also been added in the margin of **F**, but it is missing in **AHOEP** (indeed, **V** itself adds the marginal note "in alio loco vacat"), and it is probable that it was added by a later Latin scribe who wanted to round out Galen's enumeration at that spot of the possible sites in which pus can collect. This distinctive phrase is also incorporated into the Hebrew translation of the text and thus must have originated in the thirteenth century.

The other intriguing passage comes at the end of 8.2, where the Arabic text might be translated thus: "As everything that cools and heats is scattered through small parts, . . . it is impossible that there should be *one part among these small ones that has a single sensation of cold and heat without the other*." When MS **A** was copied, two competing translations of the italicized passage were already circulating: the text of **A** reads "aliqua harum minimarum partium sensus in aliquo frigido et calido absque alia" (version 1), but the scribe has added in the margin "in alio, pars ex istis parvis in qua sit sensus una caloris et frigoris absque alia" (version 2). **HOE** simply give version 1 and make no reference to the alternate possibility. In contrast, the Hebrew translation of David Caslari appears to be based on version 2 rather than on version 1. Surprisingly, the texts of MSS **FP** give *both* versions of this passage, first version 2 and then, immediately following, version 1.

Let us now look more closely at the Arabic itself of the words (italicized previously) from which the two versions derive:

$$[\ldots \text{لم يمكن أن يوجد}]$$

$$\ldots \text{جزء من هذه الأجزاء الصغار حسًّا فيه واحد من البرد والحرّ دون الآخر}$$

When we compare this with the two Latin versions, word by word, it is apparent that version 2 is written in Gerard's easily recognizable translational style of word-for-word substitution closely following the sequence of words in the Arabic, and that version 1 is much freer, especially for the first half of the passage. What presumably happened is that Gerard's original translation gave version 2 of these words, and that shortly thereafter, on a very early copy of the text, someone—conceivably even Gerard or an aide—entered a rewording of this passage (version 1) in the margin. Subsequent scribes either substituted the marginal version 1 for the original version 2 (as in **HOE**), or followed version 2 and ignored the marginal version 1 (the Hebrew translation was evidently based on such a text), or, in a failure of understanding, entered the marginal version 2 into the text proper immediately following version 1 (as in **FP**). In **V**, a further confusion has occurred. Originally, the text gave only version 1, as in **HOE**, but its scribe came upon a copy with version 2 in it as well and had placed it in the margin of **V**, thus reversing, if we are right, the relative positions in which versions 1 and 2 began. In the edition that follows, we follow version 2, which on this argument conveys Gerard's original language.

The several linguistic versions of our Galenic treatise have been differently broken up by their original editors. Galen's own Greek text was apparently not originally divided up into individual chapters.[44] The same is true of its Arabic translation by Ḥunayn. The early manuscripts **AHO** of the Latin version by Gerard show no subdivision either, nor indeed do the majority of the late ones (including **FPV**). But in at least four late manuscripts (and in the 1490 edition as well),[45] the text is broken up more or less consistently by rubrication into eight chapters that begin at the following words:

Chap. 1: *Malitia complexionis diverse* (1.1; the beginning of the treatise)
Chap. 2: *Mea igitur intentio* (beginning within our 1.3)
Chap. 3: *Nunc autem oportet* (2.3) or *Et nos iam in hiis* (within 2.3)
Chap. 4: *Inde est quod* (3.1)
Chap. 5: *Cumque calor sanguinis* (4.1)
Chap. 6: *Cum autem prima omnia* (5.3)
Chap. 7: *Redeamus autem ad species* (7.1)
Chap. 8: *Quis ergo cum sensibiliter* (within 8.1)

After that, the consistency disappears: One manuscript (**U**) marks off three additional chapters beginning *Ex hoc quidem sermone* (in 7.3), *Et preterea est febris* (in 8.2), and *Iam igitur manifestum* (in 8.4), respectively, whereas another (**S**) starts a separate unit only at the last of these passages.[46] Perhaps some later scribes decided that, as it stood, the final Chapter 8 was too long and required further subdivisions. In all these copies, these chapters carry titles, whether copied as part of the original text or filled in by a later hand, or in one case entered into a marginal gloss, although most of the titles show a certain variability from one copy to the next.

This attempt at chapterization and the imposition of titles apparently goes back at least to the end of the thirteenth century, the moment when the works of Galen were becoming central to academic medical training. In MS Vat. Urb. 209 (**U**), where the chapter titles are embedded in a regular marginal gloss, the glossator has written, opposite "Mea igitur intentio,"

cap^m ii^m in quo premittit in sua doctrina notitiam membrorum in quibus debet fieri secundum fit mala complexio diversa, vel ca^m ii^m cuius intentio est investigare diversa componentia membrorum secundum anathomiam. Prima tamen secundum magistrum Tadeum melior. . . .

As it happens, versions of these two competing chapter titles can be found, respectively, in **DGS** and **B**.[47] If, as appears likely, the glossator in **U** was referring to Taddeo

---

[44]"The treatise is *composed* of units . . . and not *divided* into chapters"; García Novo, *Galen, On the Anomalous Dyskrasia*, 139.

[45]We have examined the texts in MSS Basel D.1.5 (**B**), Cesena D.XXV.2 (**D**), Cesena S.V.4 (**S**), and Vat. Urb. 209 (**U**), as well as the 1490 Galen (**G**). García Novo, *Galen, On the Anomalous Dyskrasia*, p. 65, cites two other manuscripts where the text is broken into chapters (MSS Krakow BJ 800 and Klosterneuburg CCl 126), neither of which we have been able to consult.

[46]**G**, the 1490 text, includes only the first six of these chapter divisions (ii.21r).

[47]The chapter titles are as follows: *in quo investigat diversa continentia membrorum per hanotomiam* (**B**); *in quo premittit sue doctrine notitiam membrorum in quibus debet fieri mala complexio et diversa* (**D, G**); and *in quo premittit sue doctrine notitiam et membrorum in quibus debet fieri malitia complexionis diverse* (**S**).

Alderotti (d. 1295), who in the late thirteenth century profoundly shaped the form of medical teaching at Bologna,[48] his gloss seems to show us that at that moment some medical masters were beginning to try to impose an intellectual structure on *De malitia*, breaking it up into units titled so as to convey their understanding of the work's organization and meaning. Taddeo, incidentally, was the teacher of Dino del Garbo, one of the few medical academics known to have prepared a commentary on this Galenic text.[49] In any case, however, and for whatever reason, this chapterization never came to dominate the manuscript tradition of the work, and we have not followed it here.[50] (Indeed, the modern editors of Arnau de Vilanova's commentary concluded that by the fifteenth century a very different division of the text into twelve chapters of roughly equal length had become traditional in the medieval schools, and they found it useful to break up the text and Arnau's commentary accordingly.[51]) Instead, in order to provide a common system of reference for the three texts, we have maintained in the Latin version the chapter/section divisions introduced editorially into the Arabic edition (e.g., 3.3).

Niccolò da Reggio's translation of *De malitia* from Greek is not likely to have been prepared much earlier than 1310 (his earliest known translation was produced in 1308).[52] One copy of this version notes (above, n. 6) that it was divided into chapters by Francesco da Piemonte, who died in 1320, by which time of course the medieval chapterization of Gerard's translation had already taken place, and it is impossible not to wonder whether this might have determined some of Francesco's chapter divisions. A number of the earlier chapter breaks in the Gerardian version coincide with those in that of Niccolò/Francesco. The Gerardian Chapters 1 through 3 and 5 coincide exactly with Francesco's first four chapter breaks, there numbered Doctrine I Chapters 1 and 2, and Doctrine II Chapters 1 and 2. After that point, however, the two versions are divided up rather differently.[53]

---

[48]N. G. Siraisi, *Taddeo Alderotti and His Pupils* (Princeton: Princeton University Press, 1981).

[49]Ibid., 71–72.

[50]None of the later manuscripts that we collated for the Latin edition contain obvious chapter divisions or titles, but in two of them, **PV**, a later hand had written numbers in the margin to identify the beginnings of chapters 2–5 in the list given previously.

[51]Arnau de Vilanova, *Commentum supra . . . de malicia complexionis diverse*, ed. García Ballester and Sánchez Salor, 145–146.

[52]Lynn Thorndike, "Translations of Works of Galen from the Greek by Niccolo da Reggio (c. 1308–1345)," *Byzantina Metabyzantina* 1 (1946): 214.

[53] See García Novo, *Galen, On the Anomalous Dyskrasia*, 86–87.

C. The Hebrew Translation from Latin by David b. Abraham Caslari (d. c. 1315)

1. David Caslari, his *Sefer ro'a mezeg mithallef*, and its setting

MS Oxford, Bodl. Opp. Add. Fol. 18 (Neubauer 2083), contains at fols. 19v–27r a Hebrew version of Galen's *Peri anomalou dyskrasias* under the title *Sefer ro'a mezeg mithallef* (a literal rendering of *De malitia complexionis diverse*), which goes on to describe the text as "translated by the wise R. David Abraham ha-Kaslari from the Christian language into the holy tongue." The codex itself is a Hebrew medical miscellany comprising five treatises, of which our Galenic text is the second, preceded by a translation from the Arabic of Hippocrates' *Airs, Waters, Places* completed in 1299 by Solomon, son of the well-known translator Nathan ha-Me'ati.[1] Third in the manuscript comes an anonymous translation of the Avicennan work called "der kleine Kanon" by Moritz Steinschneider, then follows an equally anonymous translation from Latin of Rhazes' *De egritudinibus iuncturarum*.[2] The collection concludes with an original treatise on hemorrhoids composed by Solomon ibn Ayyub of Béziers (thirteenth century).[3] The copyist has dated the manuscript in a colophon immediately after the *Sefer ro'a mezeg mithallef* (fol. 28r): "Praise to the Living God. [This copy was done] by me, Yeḥi'el of Genzano, son of Mordechai the physician of blessed memory, of Grosseto. I have copied it in Genzano in the month of Sivan of the year 5235 [i.e., June 1475], may it be of blessing."[4]

There is still nothing to seriously challenge Steinschneider's presumption, set out more than a century ago, that this David b. Abraham Kaslari (or Castlari, Caylar, or Kaylar; today usually Caslari, which is the form we will use from here on out) is the man of that name who was an early member of a Jewish family prominent in fourteenth-century Languedoc and Catalunya,[5] at the moment when medieval Hebrew culture there was at its pinnacle,

---

[1]*Galen's Commentary on the Hippocratic Treatise Airs, Waters, Places in the Hebrew Translation of Solomon ha-Me'ati*, ed. A. Wasserstein, *Proceedings of the Israel Academy of Sciences and Humanities* 6.3 (Jerusalem: Israel Academy of Sciences and Humanities, 1982).

[2]M. Steinschneider, *Die Hebraeischen Übersetzungen des Mittlealters und die Juden als Dolmetscher* (rpt. Graz: Akademische Druck u. Verlagsanstalt, 1956), 696–697, 727.

[3]Solomon ben Joseph ibn Ayyub, "Ma'amar 'al ha-Ṭeḥorim," ed. L. M. Herbert, intro. A. Marx, *Harofé Haivri* 1 (1929), 62–111.

[4]*Catalogue of the Hebrew manuscripts in the Bodleian Library*, comp. A. Neubauer (rpt. Oxford: Clarendon Press, 1994), cols. 712–713; *Catalogue of the Hebrew manuscripts in the Bodleian Library*, supplement, comp. M. Beit-Arié (Oxford: Clarendon Press, 1994), col. 385.

[5]The discussion of the Caslari family by Ernest Renan (drawing on Adolf Neubauer's materials), "Les écrivains juifs français du XIVe siècle," *Histoire littéraire de la France* 31 (1893): 351–802, at 644–646, treats David after Abraham as if to imply that he was David's son. But Renan's only evidence for this would seem to be the fact that the introduction to the *Sefer ro'a* names the translator as "David the son of Abraham," which does not exclude the possibility that our David Caslari was the son as well as the father of an Abraham. He also quotes (p. 644) a text that apparently identifies Abraham's father David as the son of Yaḥse'el—"Abraham, fils de David, fils de Yahceel"—but in fact the Hebrew original actually reads "father" instead of "son"; that is, Abraham was the *father*

both economically and culturally[6]; his contemporaries were the frontrunners in the study of sciences in general and of medicine in particular. David (Davin) was part of this intellectual leadership. The Caslari family can be found in Perpignan from 1273 through 1286,[7] but David can be traced moving to Narbonne in the early 1280s, where he seems soon to have become an important figure in the Jewish community. He was a member of a group of notables that obtained a favorable charter from the city's archbishop in 1284.[8] A letter written to him there from his friend Abraham Bedersi survives, suggesting that he had both interest and skill in Hebrew letters.[9]

David Caslari was still living in Narbonne in 1305, as was his son Abraham,[10] but in the following year they, like all the Jews in France, were expelled from the royal domain. He and his family may have moved directly to Besalú, in Catalunya; at any rate, he was to be found living there in 1315. By March 1316, however, he had died.[11] David's son Abraham, also a physician, is more famous today.[12] In the year that his father died, Abraham contracted with the Catalan town of Castelló d'Empúries to act as its town physician, but by the 1320s he had returned to Besalú. Here, his prestige began to grow in both the Jewish and Christian worlds. When at some time during these years the identity of a certain Caslari living in Perpignan had to be established, Abraham's signature was sufficient to confirm the fact.[13] He composed the first of several original medical works in this period, and Kalonymos of Arles eulogized him after visiting him at Besalú at the end of 1322.[14] He also began to attend members of the Catalan royal family in their illnesses, and finally moved to Barcelona in 1334.[15] His last medical treatise was composed in 1349.[16] His son Yaḥse'el followed the profession of his grandfather and his father, but seems to have died before the latter.[17]

---

of Yaḥse'el, which is confirmed from other sources. J. Régné, *Étude sur la condition des juifs de Narbonne du V*e au XIV*e siécle* (Narbonne: Gaillard, 1912), 214, argues that the David who was Abraham's father is identified as a physician. M. Grau i Montserrat comes to the same conclusion: "Metges jueus a Besalú (s. XIV)," *Actes,* I Assemblea d'Estudis sobre el Comtat de Besalú, 1968 (Olot: Aubert, 1972), 29–33, at p. 30. So does R. W. Emery, *The Jews of Perpignan in the Thirteenth Century* (New York: Columbia University Press, 1959), 24 n. 2, who provides further detail about family relationships. Most recently, on the basis of an exhaustive examination of the Besalú archives, Grau i Montserrat has developed a full genealogical tree of the Caslari family in the fourteenth century: he depicts David the son of Abraham (d. 1315/16) as the father of Abraham (d. 1349), who was the father of Yaḥse'el (d. 1324/25), who was the father of David (d. bef. 1352), who was the father of Yaḥse'el (d. ca. 1423), who was the father of David (d. 1404); M. Grau i Montserrat, "La juderia de Besalú (Gerona)," 2 vols. (Ph.D. diss., Universidad de Barcelona, 1975), vol. 1, 366–367. If Grau is correct, and if our David b. Abraham is one of the Besalú Caslaris, he can only be the man who died in 1315/16.
[6]Steinschneider, *Hebraeischen Übersetzungen*, 653.
[7]Emery, *Jews of Perpignan*, 24 n. 2.
[8]Régné, *Étude*, 231–234 (doc. VIII).
[9]N. S. Doniach, "Abraham Bédersi's Purim Letter to David Kaslari," *Jewish Quarterly Review*, n.s., 23 (1932), 63–69. Cf. H. Gross, *Gallia Judaica* (Paris, 1897), 425.
[10]Régné, *Étude*, 214, 216. He infers this from a list of Jewish heads of families in Narbonne, recorded in 1305, which includes both a master Davin, physician, and an Abraham du Caylar (p. 123, n. 1).
[11]Girona, Arxiu Històric Provincial, fons de Castelló d'Empúries, manual 89: Abraham de Castlar, *judeus de Narbona phisicus filius quondam magistri Davidis de Castlar*, is contracted as town physician 3 non. Mar. 1315/16.
[12]Gross, *Gallia Judaica*, 619–621.
[13]*Teshuvot ha-RaN: Responsa of Rabbi Nissim Gerondi*, ed. Leon N. Feldman (Jerusalem: Mekhon Shalem,1984), no. 33, pp. 137, 141, 145.
[14]Renan, "Écrivains juifs," 451.
[15]Barcelona, Arxiu de la Corona de Aragó, Canc. reg. 487, fol. 266v.
[16]Renan, "Écrivains juifs," 645.
[17]Grau i Montserrat, "La juderia de Besalú," 1:367, fixes Yaḥse'el's death between April 1325 and January 1326.

Why might David Caslari, living in Languedoc/Catalunya around 1300, have singled out this relatively minor Galenic medical work for translation? As we have already pointed out, Gerard of Cremona's Latin version, *De malitia complexionis diverse*, was apparently "discovered" by Latin academic medicine in the 1290s through the agency of Arnau de Vilanova, who prepared a commentary on the work and helped see to it that it became a required element in the Montpellier curriculum formalized by Clement V in 1309. David Caslari might easily have heard of the interest being generated at Montpellier by the new work, for the Jewish medical community in the region was well acquainted with what was going on in the Christian faculty there, and it could have been brought to his attention (and a copy of the Latin text made available to him) in this way. Indeed, the prominence of fevers in the contents of *De malitia* might encourage pushing speculation a little further. In November 1325, David's physician son Abraham finished writing his work ʿAleh raʿanan ("Green leaf"), a treatise (in five books) on fevers[18]; it is intriguing to wonder whether the availability of his father's new Galenic translation might have been one of the factors leading him to compose the work, and when the ʿAleh raʿanan is eventually edited (at least five manuscripts of the work survive), we will be able to see whether it contains citations of *De malitia complexionis diverse*.

2. Caslari's translation technique

a. His encounter with his Latin source

Gerard of Cremona's translation of *De malitia complexionis diverse* was not the only one extant in David Caslari's lifetime. Two others had been completed in the early fourteenth century, both made from the original Greek version rather than from Ḥunayn's Arabic. One was prepared by Pietro d'Abano (d. 1315), the other by Niccolò da Reggio, apparently drawn up between 1308 and 1320.[19] However, we would naturally presume that Caslari worked from Gerard's Latin version, for this was the one that was already established in academic use at Montpellier and elsewhere. Moreover, the two Greek-based translations apparently had very little circulation in the later Middle Ages, for García Novo has identified a mere three surviving copies of Pietro's version and only seven of Niccolò's. Our presumption is confirmed when we compare virtually any passages across the various versions. Consider, for example, these two sentences towards the end of 8.3:

> And it seems that this symptom [ʿāriḍ] did not happen to anyone at all in the past [fī l-mutaqaddim], because no one followed this regimen of ease of life and the consumption of a large quantity of food. Therefore, we find ancient physicians judge [yaḥkamūna] it to be necessary that rigor is followed by fever. (The Arabic version, translated literally.)

> Et videtur quidem quod accidens hoc non accidit ante [ante **AHO**, post **FPV**] alicui penitus, quoniam non fuit aliquis hominum usus hoc regimine quietis et multitudinis cibi. Et propter hoc invenimus antiquos medicorum iudicantes quod necesse est ut tremorem consequatur febris. (The Latin version of Gerard.)

> It seems that this accident will not happen at all to those people who are not used to a regimen of rest and much food. And for this reason we find that the ancient doctors

---

[18]Renan, "Écrivains juifs," 645.
[19]E. García Novo, *Galen, On the Anomalous Dyskrasia* (Madrid: Editorial Complutense, 2010), 73–91.

decree that it is absolutely necessary that tremor will carry fever with it. (The Hebrew version, translated literally.)

In ancient days [*palai*], as it seems, nobody suffered this way, because no one happened to spend his life in such inactivity and satiety, and for that reason, it has been written [*gegraptai*] by the ancient doctors that fever necessarily accompanies rigor [*rhigos*]. (The Greek version, translated by García Novo, 169, 171.)

Olim autem ut videtur nullus ita passus est, quia nemo sit otiosis et impletive dietatus, et ideo scriptum est ab antiquis medicis ex necessitate rigorem sequi febrem. (Translation of Pietro d'Abano, MS Cesena S.V.4, fol. 136va.)

Antiquiter autem ut videtur nemo ita patiebatur, quoniam nullus tantum otiose et implete dietabatur, et propter hoc scriptum est ab antiquis medicis ex necessitate sequi rigorem febrem. (Translation of Niccolò da Reggio, MS London, Wellcome 286, fol. 133rb.)

Numerous features here indicate the dependence of the Hebrew on Gerard's Arabic-based translation rather than on either of those made from the Greek: the repetition of *'aridl/ac-cidens* in the Hebrew, a word not found in the Greek-based versions, as well as the echo of *yaḥkamuna* in Hebrew ("decree"), where the Greek-based translations instead follow Galen's language (*gegraptai*) in using *scriptum*; and, quite conclusively, Caslari's evident perpetuation in this passage of a scribal error found in some of the Latin manuscripts of the Gerardian text (which write *post* for *ante*) when he set the condition in the future rather than in the past. We can thus proceed to assess Caslari's Hebrew against Gerard's Latin in detail, with complete confidence. (Whether the two Greek translations are truly independent seems much less certain.)

How did David Caslari go about translating from a Latin manuscript? Scholarly studies of Latin–Hebrew translation practice are far rarer than those of Arabic–Latin translation. In the latter case, it is clear that one frequent approach was for an Arabic-reading assistant to translate the Arabic words out loud into a Romance vernacular, and for the translator to translate the Romance term into Latin,[20] but we have no reason to think that Caslari needed an intermediary to translate the Latin for him. To be sure, there are various signs in the translation as we have it that Caslari may have read the Latin text aloud in Hebrew, often word by word, sometimes phrase by phrase, and that an assistant copied down what he heard, but none of them is conclusive. In 6.1, for example, Latin *aer* should have been translated as *'avīr*, but instead was translated *'éver* (= *membrum*), suggesting the possibility of a word misheard in transmission, although the words are not sharply different orthographically—*aleph-bet-resh* versus *aleph-vav-yod-resh*—and the apparent mistranslation could have been the product of a later scribal error. Again, in the Middle Ages Jews typically pronounced (and often wrote) *dalet* occurring at the end of a word interchangeably with *tav*, and indeed, in 5.3 we find the plural of the word *ru(a)ḥ* (= "spirit") spelled as a scribe might have imagined he heard it, *ruḥod*, rather than the correct *ruḥot*. Similarly, some Jews pronounced the vowel "ah" as "oh," which could explain why in 7.2 "warm vapor" (properly *ha-ed ha-ḥam*) is spelled *ha-ed ha-ḥom*. Likewise, in 8.1, Latin *extremo* is translated as *keṣat* ("some") rather than the expected *keṣot*; the two words come from different Hebrew roots, but their second vowels can be easily confused in pronunciation (although here again a defective spelling may be involved instead).

---

[20]See above, 11.

The Hebrew version of *De malitia complexionis diverse* that Caslari produced in the early fourteenth century is here and there quite different from the Latin version that Gerard of Cremona had set down, two hundred and fifty years before. Many of these differences arose as a result of evolutionary changes over time in the intermediary Latin text from which the Hebrew was ultimately created, as scribes committed errors of various kinds, and they are easy to pick out because Caslari usually translated the Latin carefully and nearly word for word; even the postpositive words that are used in Latin to channel the flow of thought but do not necessarily deserve translation into English are routinely replaced by a Hebrew equivalent: for example, *vero* and *autem* are both normally rendered *'omnam*. A good example of this verbal evolution occurs in 5.2, where the word *dolor* that Gerard employed to translate وجع was in time mistakenly turned by Latin scribes into *calor* and therefore became *ha-ḥom* in Caslari's Hebrew version. Sometimes his faithfulness led him into error, as in 8.2, where Gerard's original text read *secundus*, which many late manuscripts converted into *sensus*; Caslari wrote here "sense of the second [body]," and it seems not improbable that he was following a Latin manuscript whose reading was something like *sensus al. secundus*. In a similar instance in 7.2, Gerard's *virtutem cause operantis* became *virtutem esse operantis* in later manuscripts, and we can infer that some of them preserved both readings, because Caslari wrote "the essence of the power of the cause's activity."

It is another mark of his faithfulness that passages omitted by eye-skip in the later Latin manuscripts also prove to be missing in Caslari's Hebrew text; in 8.1, for example, early manuscripts follow the Arabic in reading

> manifesta est quod accidit eis passio et dolor, *et passio et dolor etiam accidit* ei,

but the italicized words have dropped out in many later ones, and they are not to be found in the Hebrew. Such changes to Galen's original meaning are evidently not Caslari's mistakes but accurate translations of what he had before him. In other instances, however, this is less clear. In 8.3, the Latin manuscripts regularly read

> in hiis febribus etiam est diversa, *et est etiam diversa* in eo qui,

but nothing corresponding to the italicized phrase is present in the Hebrew. Was Caslari depending on a Latin copyist whose eye had slipped from one *diversa* to another? Was the Latin text correct, and was it Caslari's eye that slipped? Or did the eye of a Hebrew scribe slip in the century and a half intervening between Caslari's accurate original and Yeḥi'el's copy? At the moment we have no way of knowing.

The presence of chapter divisions (and sporadic chapter titles) in Caslari's translation is apparently a further indication of his dependence on a comparatively late Latin manuscript. We have shown previously (pp. 23–24) that chapter divisions and titles are present in a small number of the Latin manuscripts, and that their first introduction into the text seems to go back roughly to the last quarter of the thirteenth century. Caslari's Hebrew translation is marked off into eight chapters, which prove to coincide almost exactly with those in the few chapterized Latin manuscripts. Only Chapter 6 in the Hebrew is an exception, and it begins just one sentence before the start of the same chapter in the Latin version. Just three of its chapters carry titles, but they are evidently translations into Hebrew of the corresponding Latin ones:

> Chap. 1: "he will put in it the difference between illnesses of an unbalanced complexion" (cf. G = *Galieni Opera* [1490]: *in quo ponit divisionem et subdivisionem malitie complexionis diverse*).

Chap. 3: "he will teach in it all the essence of an illness of an unbalanced complexion and will put in it the difference between its kinds" (cf. G: *in quo determinat commune essentiam mal<iti>e complexionis diverse et docet communiter distinguere species eius*).

Chap. 4: "he will explain in it how a hot illness of an unbalanced complexion is generated" (cf. G: *in quo ponit qualiter generatur mala complexio diversa calida cum materia in musculo*).

Evidently the Latin manuscript from which Caslari worked was one of those relatively few copies into which chapter divisions had been inserted and at least some chapter titles incorporated.

Finally, the Hebrew presents a number of divergences from the Latin that are very likely to be the product of Caslari's difficulties in reading the manuscript from which he was translating and, in particular, his unfamiliarity with Latin handwriting. In 7.3, for example, where the Latin manuscripts read *qualitas*, Caslari seems to have thought he saw *equalitas*, for he translates *mi-shaveh*. He seems to have had particular problems with Latin abbreviations. In 3.4, *quoniam* (typically abbreviated *qm̃*) is translated *ke-she* (= *quando*, typically abbreviated *qñ*); in 7.1, *tantum* (*tm̃*) is translated *ve-'omnam* (= *tamen* or *tñ*); and so forth. In 4.1, Latin *quanto* seems to have been misread as *quando* (*ve-ka-'asher*).

In general, however, when Caslari read the Latin accurately, he translated it competently. In a few instances (e.g., 5.1, 5.3) he mistakes the subject of the sentence for the object; once (7.3), he seems to have interpreted the Latin *cum* as meaning "when" rather than "since." His most serious misunderstanding was corrected by a later editor. In 4.1, the Latin version began "Cumque calor sanguinis que est in membro apostemoso," but the Hebrew version had left out any word for *calor* and had translated the word *apostemoso* (meaning "of the nature of a tumor or abscess [in Hebrew, *mursah*]") as *mitmagel*, "of the nature of pus [*muglah*]." In the margin, however, *mitmagel* has been corrected to *mitmarsem*, "apostemelike," and below that correction a further note completely retranslates the original Latin phrase, now including the word *calor*, using the correct participle *mitmarsem*, and even glossing the participle as follows: "that is, possessing a *mursah*." In the next sentence of the Latin, the word *apostemoso* reappeared and was again rendered *mitmagel* in the Hebrew text, and again the word was corrected to *mursiy* in the margin, but this time the corrector went even further and added, in Hebrew characters, "*b. l.* [= *be la'az*, = 'in Latin'] *apos tomosa*." From this point on, however, although the mistranslation persists in the text, it is not corrected again; perhaps the editor felt he had called sufficient attention to it already. The original translation of *apostemosus* as *mitmagel* probably goes back to Caslari, but the correction with transliterated Latin attached shows that a later student of the Hebrew text with a better command of Latin medical terminology may have been reading it in conjunction with a Latin copy of Galen's work. (The text and the marginal corrections are both in the same hand, presumably Yeḥi'el of Genzano's, who appears to have copied automatically what he found before him.)

b. Caslari's Hebrew: The art of writing

At the end of the twelfth century, Maimonides set down his views on the proper approach to translation:

If someone plans to translate from one language to another, and tries to render word for word and to follow the order and presentation of the original, he will have a very hard time doing it and his translation will end up faulty and untrustworthy. Al-Baṭrīq [a famous Greek-to-Arabic translator, c. 800] dealt with the works of Aristotle and Galen in this manner, and as a result his translations are very confusing. It is wrong to translate like this; rather, a translator from one language to another first has to understand the subject-matter and then to express it in terms that will be best understood in the new language. He cannot achieve this without sometimes moving words back and forth [in a sentence], replacing a single word with several words (or several words with a single one), and even omitting some words and adding others, so that the subject will be dealt with clearly and understandably in the language in which he is expressing it. Ḥunayn ibn Isḥāq treated the Galenic books in this way, and his son Isḥāq did likewise with the Aristotelian ones. This is the reason why their translations are so remarkably understandable. . . .[21]

Maimonides might not have been entirely satisfied with David Caslari's translation of Galen. Caslari was certainly not as systematic a word-for-word translator as Gerard of Cremona, but as we have said, it was still, broadly speaking, the approach he tended to use in turning Latin into Hebrew. It was not that he ordinarily followed ploddingly the Latin word order in his Hebrew: he occasionally did that when the wording was simple and straightforward—

(2.2): ו-אלו הדברים ההכרח חייב זכרונם לפי שבעבורם יתאמת מה שנמשיך לזכור:
"And these things, necessity will oblige their remembrance because through them will be verified what we shall continue to narrate"; Lat., "Hec ergo sunt quorum necessario fuit rememorandum, ut per ipsa verificatur quod in sequentibus narrabo"

(4.2): אמנם מה שיתחמם ראשונה, כשיגבר החום, יתחמם הדם אשר בגידים הדופקים:
"But what will be heated first, when the heat becomes stronger, heated will be the blood which is in the pulsing veins"; Lat., "Primum vero quod ex sanguine calefit, cum in eo superfluit calefactio, est sanguis quod est in venis pulsatilibus"

—but he more often altered the sequence of words in the original sentence, changed singular nouns to plural, and the like.

In general, Caslari managed to replace each Latin word with a corresponding Hebrew word, but his replacements were by no means always identical, far less so than Gerard's Latin equivalents for Arabic words. In translating *De malitia* from Arabic into Latin, for example, Gerard had nine times replaced Ḥunayn's phrase *wa-dhalika anna* with the words *et illud ideo quoniam*, a curious verbal equivalence that can be traced as a kind of signature throughout many of Gerard's other Arabic–Latin translations.[22] There is no corresponding consistency in Caslari's translation of the Latin phrase *et illud ideo quoniam*, which most often becomes *ve-hayah zeh* (3.1, 6.2, 6.4, 8.2) or *ve-ha-sibbah* (5.3, 6.3, 9.2), but it also appears as *ve-la-zehu* (5.1), *ve-la-zeh* (6.2), and *ve-hayah ken* (5.3). Again, we have already mentioned Caslari's concern to supply a Hebrew equivalent when he came upon one of the particles or other short words like *vero* or *autem*, much more important to Latin than to Hebrew, that shape the relation of one clause to another. He did not, however, maintain a set of standard equivalences. *Vero* and *autem*, as we have said, both usually become *'omnam* in

---

[21]Translated from the text published in *Igrot ha-Rambam / Letters and Essays of Moses Maimonides*, ed. I. Shailat (Jerusalem: Ma'aleh Adumim, 5748/1987), vol. 2, 532. A slightly compressed translation of the entire letter from which this passage is taken is given in *Letters of Maimonides*, ed. L. D. Stitskin (New York: Yeshiva University Press, 5737/1977), 130–136. See also G. Bos, *Novel Medical and General Hebrew Terminology from the Thirteenth Century, Volume 2, Journal of Semitic Studies,* Supplement 30 (Oxford, 2013), 6–7.
[22]M. McVaugh, "Towards a Stylistic Grouping of the Translations of Gerard of Cremona," *Mediaeval Studies* 71 (2009): 99–112.

David's Hebrew, but *tamen* is rendered variously by *'omnam* (8.2, 8.4), *ve-hinneh* (1.2), and *ve-ulam* (6.4); *verumtamen* by *'omnam* but also by *'aval* (2.2; 8.4), *ve-hinneh* (6.1), *ve-ulam* (6.4), and *u-ve-'emet*; and *quidem* by *be-'emet* (2.2, 3.2), *hinneh* (8.3), and *'ella* (1.2).

Nor is it just with connectives, particles, and the like that Caslari permitted himself a considerable freedom of translation. Somewhat surprisingly, he would occasionally do the same thing when dealing with more denotative Latin nouns and verbs. Gerard of Cremona had always translated the Arabic word *shay'* as *res*, whenever he came upon it in *De malitia*. However, when in his turn David Caslari encountered Latin *res* in Gerard's translation, he rendered it in a variety of ways: as *'illah* ("cause"; 3.2), and sometimes (6.3) as *davar* or *'inyan*. Gerard used the verb *provenire* three times in two consecutive sentences in 8.3–4, each time to translate Ar. *ḥadatha*, but Caslari used a different Hebrew verb in each case to translate Gerard's word: first *yitḥaddesh* ("occur"), then *yavó* ("come"), and finally *tiqreh* ("happen"). To give one more example, Latin *resolutio* is rendered as both *killayon* and *hefsed* ("decay") by Caslari in 3.2, it is translated as both *hishtannut* and *mitpa'el* in one and the same sentence in 4.2, and shortly afterwards in 4.3 as *gevul*.

Indeed, at times his apparent search for an alternative translation could lead Caslari into patent absurdities. Ordinarily, he translated Latin *animal* quite normally as *ba'al ḥayyim* (6.3). But in 5.1, where what is in question is Galen's experiment of putting one's finger into the left side of a live animal's beating heart in order to feel its fiery hotness, Caslari instead translated *animal* as *ish* ("man")! Did he really intend the implication that he was making—or did he even recognize it—that Galen had practiced human vivisection, and that he, David, was endorsing it to his Hebrew readers?[23]

We have referred to this variability as "freedom," but it might equally well be called "inconsistency." Caslari evidently did not think it important to try to find a single Hebrew equivalent for each Latin word that would convey to the Hebrew reader the fact that the same Latin term was in question each time the Hebrew appeared. Nor, indeed, did he think that the reverse was important: he used the same Hebrew word to represent a variety of Latin ones, again often in close proximity to one another. In 5.2, Hebrew *taḵlit* is used to translate both *terminus* and *principium* (although the translation of *principium* as *taḵlit* might also be a copyist's error for *tehillah* or *hathalah*; as a matter of fact, in 3.4 Caslari does indeed use *hathalah* to translate *principium*). In 8.3, *miqreh* ("event") is used to render *accidens*—*miqreh* was the standard equivalent for *accidens* in philosophical literature—but shortly thereafter it is also used to translate both *eventus* and *proventus* in one and the same paragraph (9.2)! *Dereḵ* ("way") translates both *modus* and *dispositio* in 8.1 (elsewhere it also translates *via* and *semita*); *ṭeva'* is used for *natura*, for *complexio*, and for *dispositio*, all in a single sentence of 3.4. We have already seen that *'inyan* was one of five Hebrew words that Caslari used to translate *res* (1.2, 3.1, 3.2, 3.4), but he also used it to render five other Latin words: *modus* (1.2, 2.3), *sermo* (7.3), *aliquid* (6.2), *esse* (3.4), and *dispositio* (8.3)! On the face of it, such variability appears quite surprising. Maintaining consistency of terminology throughout a discursive treatise would seem to be essential to developing a train of thought and constructing a rational argument, and indeed Galen's Greek, Ḥunayn's Arabic, and Gerard's Latin all manage to do this across the sequence of translations. David Caslari's inconsistency (or freedom) of language would presumably have made it hard for the Hebrew reader even to understand that a sequential argument was being worked out.

---

[23] An excellent introduction to Galen's actual anatomical strategies, showing how he used animal dissections to make inferences about human anatomy, is J. Rocca, "The Brain beyond Kühn: Reflections on *Anatomical Procedures, Book IX*," in *The Unknown Galen*, ed. V. Nutton (London: Institute of Classical Studies, 2002), 87–100.

How might we explain this? At the outset we need to admit that Caslari's "freedom" was by no means unique to him. A century or so earlier, in translating Maimonides' *Guide to the Perplexed* from Arabic into Hebrew, Samuel ibn Tibbon, too, had used the word *'inyan* to translate six different Maimonidean terms.[24] One might imagine that early thirteenth-century Hebrew had not been yet rich enough to find a supple range of equivalents for the elements in a more developed Arabic vocabulary, yet at the end of the century, we find Zeraḥyah ben Isaac ben She'altiel Ḥen doing exactly the same thing, using *'inyan* to render six different Arabic terms in his translation of Maimonides' *Aphorisms*.

In David Caslari's case, at least, we can acknowledge that there were limits to his inconsistency, while agreeing that he was not as systematic a translator as Gerard of Cremona. We noted previously that Gerard seems to occasionally have searched for Latin synonyms for an Arabic word, perhaps to avoid repetitiveness, but this practice is by no means obtrusive, and it never prevents the Latin reader from following the course of an argument. With technical terms Gerard usually followed an invariable translation: for example, he always (eight times) rendered Ar. *ḥāl*, into Latin as *dispositio*. We have already commented on Caslari's inconstancy in translating *dispositio* as *'inyan*, as *dere<u>k</u>*, and as *ṭeva'*, but we should also recognize that these were unique occurrences and that, in most passages, he rendered Gerard's technical term with the word *te<u>k</u>unah* and thus made it possible to follow the chain of Galen's reasoning in Hebrew. Yet there remain the occasional passages—for instance, the sentence in 3.4 just commented on, in which he translated three different Latin terms as *ṭeva'*—where his decisions as a translator were bound to stand in the way of the meaning of the text.

Perhaps we might wonder whether David Caslari could have been self-consciously attentive to features of literary quality and not always primarily concerned with scientific exactitude. His possible literary pretensions are implied by the reactions of his friend Abraham Bedersi, who once named him to a jury to judge a poetry competition,[25] and who wrote to him in the 1290s to ask for his views on a new poem. The letter takes for granted that Caslari shares Abraham's distaste for Spanish neologisms and Arabic literature, an old controversy in Jewish letters. Already in the tenth century Menaḥem ben Saruq and Dunash ben Labrat were famously debating the same issue. The letter also obviously takes for granted that Caslari will understand and appreciate Abraham's recondite allusions to the Bible and the Talmud. Here it is worth remarking on the very rare name given to David Caslari's grandson, Yaḥse'el b. Abraham Caslari, named for a son of Naftali mentioned obscurely once in Genesis and once in Numbers. Was it perhaps Yaḥse'el's grandfather rather than his father whose unusual familiarity with the Bible is suggested here?[26] Hence we might guess that David Caslari, not being a professional translator, sometimes chose his terminology in order to make his translation, in his view, more attractive as literature, without appreciating its cost to the meaning of Galen's argument. Yet this is not an entirely satisfactory answer, because it remains utterly perplexing why, on the other hand, he should sometimes have abandoned preexisting variety in favor of misleading uniformity, which would have worked against its quality as literature. In the end, all we can say is that it is by no means clear what "translation" meant to him and why he made the decisions that he did.

---

[24]I. Efros, *Philosophical Terms in the Moreh Nebukim* (New York: Columbia University Press, 1924), 95–96.

[25]J. Schirman, "Studies on the Poems and Letters of Abraham Bedresi," in *Yitzhak F. Baer Jubilee Volume on the Occasion of His Seventieth Birthday,* ed. S. W. Baron et al. (Jerusalem: Historical Society of Israel, 1960), 154–173, at 173.

[26]Later Caslaris continued to give the name Yaḥse'el to their sons; Gross, *Gallia Judaica*, 620–621.

c. Matters of vocabulary

In translating Galen, Caslari also had to deal with a problem that confronted every medieval translator of scientific texts into Hebrew: the need to find verbal equivalents for the technical or philosophical terms in the target language, whether Arabic or Latin. In the twelfth century, Hebrew was still primarily a religious language whose vocabulary was almost entirely biblical, talmudic, or rabbinic, although a corpus of Hebrew scientific and philosophical literature was already beginning to take shape. With a few exceptions, however, a specifically medical Hebrew terminology really only began to develop in the thirteenth century.[27]

Considerable attention has been given by historians to the many medieval translations from Arabic into Hebrew in this period, but comparatively little to the *Latin*–Hebrew translations that were made with increasing frequency during the fourteenth century in southern France and Catalunya, as Jewish scholars lost their familiarity with Arabic at the same time that they were coming to appreciate the growing sophistication of Latin academic medicine.[28] Lola Ferre was the first person who tried seriously to consider broad issues of technique, style, and competence in these translations from the Latin, and she herself has commented that, for the moment, the principal obstacle to such studies is the limited number of works for which both Latin and Hebrew editions currently exist. She had to base her pioneering study of 1991 on three brief translations of the fourteenth century with only a restricted medical range: one a set of medical aphorisms, and the other two treatises on medicines and their properties. Here she usefully called attention to a number of ways in which Jewish translators dealt with the problem of converting Latin medical terminology into Hebrew equivalents: (a) by giving existing biblical or rabbinic words a new medical significance; (b) by offering a semantic calque on a Greek or Latin original; (c) by using a periphrastic construction, that is, unpacking the meaning of a single Latin term into a longer explanatory Hebrew phrase; and (d) by transliterating the Latin term (or, as commonly in the case of medicines, the Romance equivalent for that term) into Hebrew characters.[29]

More recently, Gerrit Bos has studied Hillel ben Samuel's Hebrew translation (1254) of Bruno Longoburgo's *Chirurgia*, identifying very similar kinds of new coinages or extensions of meaning, well over a hundred in all, in a new medical field, surgery. Such new coinages included semantic borrowings from the original Latin, broadening of meaning of biblical and rabbinic terms, and Hebrew transcriptions of Latin words.[30] Whether these words were commonplaces of a newly emerging Hebrew technical vocabulary or were unique to Hillel remains an open question, for Bos also considers contemporary Hebrew

---

[27]For the translation movement of philosophical and scientific texts from Latin and Arabic into Hebrew, see A. S. Halkin and A. Sáenz Badillos, "Translation and Translators," in *Encyclopaedia Judaica, 2nd ed.* (Detroit: Macmillan, 2007), vol. 20, 94–102; D. Romano, "La transmission des sciences arabes par les Juifs en Languedoc," in *Juifs et judaïsme de Languedoc*, ed. M.-H. Vicaire and B. Blumenkranz (Toulouse: Privat, 1977), 363–386; G. Freudenthal, "Les sciences dans les communautés juives médiévales de Provence: Leur appropriation, leur rôle," *Revue des Etudes Juives* 152 (1993): 29–136; idem, "Arabic and Latin Cultures as Resources for the Hebrew Translation Movement," in *Science in Medieval Jewish Cultures*, ed. G. Freudenthal (Cambridge: Cambridge University Press, 2011), 74–105; M. Zonta, "Medieval Hebrew Translations of Philosophical and Scientific Texts: A Chronological Table," ibid., 17–73.

[28]L. García Ballester, L. Ferre, and E. Feliu, "Jewish Appreciation of Fourteenth-Century Scholastic Medicine," *Osiris*, 2d ser., 6 (1990): 85–117.

[29]L. Ferre, "La terminologia médica en las versiones hebreas de textos latinos," *Miscelánea de estudios árabes y hebraicos* 40 (1991): 87–107.

[30]G. Bos, "Novel Medical and General Hebrew Terminology from the Thirteenth Century," *Journal of Semitic Studies* Supplement 27 (Oxford, 2011): 9–46.

translations of medical works from Arabic and shows that, for example, anatomical entities such as wrist, diaphragm, and armpit were expressed differently by different Hebrew translators, as though a unified anatomical terminology had not yet emerged. David Caslari was translating Galen fifty years or so after Hillel was active. How does his terminology compare?[31]

Galen's *Peri anomalou dyskrasias* was a work at the intersection of a number of medical fields that we might anachronistically call physiology, anatomy, and pathology, and it required the specialized vocabularies of all three in order to express its conclusions. This was, of course, just as true of the Hebrew version as of the Greek original. For all these vocabularies, Caslari could draw on a wide variety of Hebrew translations that had been produced since the second half of the twelfth century and were distributed to a lesser or greater extent in Jewish circles. For example, he could have found much broadly physiological language newly coined in the early thirteenth-century translations of Maimonides' *Guide to the Perplexed* from Arabic into Hebrew by Samuel b. Judah ibn Tibbon (d. 1232) and Judah al-Ḥarīzī (d. c. 1230). Both men composed glossaries to their translations of the *Guide* that contained a number of philosophical terms relevant to Caslari. They included words like *eykut* ("quality"), *havayah* ("being"), *mezeg* ("compound"), *miqreh* ("accident"), *ṭeva'* ("nature"), *tekunah* ("essence"), and *taklit* ("terminus"), all of which (with many others) thus became available for Caslari to deploy in his Galen translation two generations later.

The anatomical terminology used by Caslari in his translation overlaps with that used by thirteenth-century translators, and he employed it knowledgeably and intelligently, but it is still not clear how far this terminology had become standardized by Caslari's day and how far his uses arose out of his own specific intellectual formation. Of course, the names for many anatomical features were established in biblical language, and he normally used them, although at least once he used a nonbiblical term where a biblical one would have served him perfectly well. Latin *viscera*, for example, he translated as *'avarim pnimiyim* ("interior members," an instance of Ferre's periphrastic constructions), even though *qravayim* ("entrails," as in, e.g., Exodus 29.13) would certainly have been familiar to him and had been employed by major translators like Nathan ha-Me'ati (fl. 1280) and Zeraḥyah ben Isaac ben She'altiel Ḥen (fl. 1290) for the Arabic equivalent *aḥṣā'*.[32]

But many human structures are never mentioned in the Bible, and terms for them had to be created. Consider the Hebrew word *qerum*, for example, which was being used by Nathan ha-Me'ati and Zeraḥyah Ḥen to translate Arabic *ġašā'* ("membrane"). Hillel of Verona used a different word, *beged*, to translate the Latin equivalent *panniculum* in Bruno's statement that "Sunt enim velamina cerebri duo panniculi, quorum unus dicitur dura mater et alius pia mater." In Caslari's translation of Gerard's Latin Galen, he renders *panniculum* as *qerum* and later translates the Latin phrase "duabus matribus [i.e., the pia and dura mater] cerebri" simply as *ha-shnei qerumim*, "the two membranes [of the brain]." In the same passage, he expands the Latin word *siphac* as "the *qerum* which is called *sifac*"; medieval anatomical Latin had adopted the word *siphac* as a transliteration of Arabic *ṣifāq*, denoting the peritoneum (above, pp. 14–15). Nathan and Zeraḥyah, translating from Arabic, sometimes rendered *ṣifāq* as *qerum* and sometimes simply transliterated it as Caslari would do; once, indeed, Nathan equated the two terms just as Caslari did: הקרום הנקרא צפאק.

---

[31]For an account of Caslari's terminology more detailed than the general considerations that follow, see Bos, *Novel Terminology, Volume 2*, 165–170.

[32]Cf. ibid., 165–166.

This particular example, taken in conjunction with others, suggests that Caslari was well acquainted with existing translation terminology, even if Hebrew anatomical language was not yet fully standardized at the beginning of the fourteenth century.[33]

As for Caslari's language for pathology, we have as yet relatively little comparable material by which to assess it. Yet, pathology and nosology were at the heart of *Peri anomalou dyskrasias*—the classification of fevers above all. The names of the continued fevers that are so important a feature in Galen's work were often passed on in Greek forms through the Arabic and Latin translations, and these continued to be transliterated by Caslari (e.g., *efiala, etika, shinoqa*), but to some extent he seems to have coined his own terminology in this area, above all in his efforts to create different equivalents for Gerard of Cremona's recurrent phrase *febris fixa* (translating Ar. الحمى الثابتة, "hectic fever").[34] When he refers to the four humors (*leḥah*) whose imbalance is a cause of illness, his language is distinctive, although not necessarily original. *Colera rubea* (choler, red bile) is simply rendered as *adumah* "the red," and melancholia as *sheḥorah* "the black"[35]; the adjective "flegmatica" is translated *leḥiyit*, as one might say "humor-ish."[36] For most other Latin disease names, he was able to find Hebrew equivalents in the Bible (*lepra* = צרעת) or earlier Hebrew medical literature (*ydropisis* = שיקוי, *formica* = נמלה),[37] and occasionally he would fall back on transliteration (*qaqrene* ["gangrene"], *herpes estiomenos*). Curiously, when Caslari first came upon Latin *cancer* in 1.1, he chose to transliterate it, but when the word came up again at the end of the work, in 9.1, he rendered it instead with the commonly used term *ṣarṭan*, "crab." When his son's *Green Leaf* is edited, we may have a better idea as to whether Caslari's pathological terminology was to any extent idiosyncratic.

---

[33]Cf. ibid., 169.
[34]Ibid., 168–169.
[35]Ibid., 170.
[36]Ibid., 167.
[37]Cf. Bos, *Novel Terminology* (n. 32), 32, 170.

II. THE TEXTS

A. The Arabic Text

بسم اللّه الرحمن الرحيم[1]

مقالة[2] في سوء المزاج المختلف لجالينوس

ترجمة[3] حنين بن اسحق[4]

(Ch. 1)

١. قال جالينوس إنّ سوء المزاج المختلف ربّما كان في البدن كلّه من الحيوان كالذي يعرض له من ذلك في النوع المعروف بالاستسقاء باللحمي وفي الحمّى التى يجد صاحبه فيها الحرّ والبرد في حال واحدة ويسمّيها اليونانيون انفياليس[5] وفي جلّ الحمّيات الآخر خلاّ الحمّى المعروفة بالثابتة[6] المسمّاة باليونانية اقطيقوس.

٢. وقد يكون سوء المزاج المختلف في عضو واحد من الأعضاء أيّ عضو كان عند ما يعرض فيه الترهّل وهو الورم البلغمي أو يحدث فيه الورم[7] الدموي الحارّ[8] وهو المعروف بفلغموني أو[9] يصير في حدّ ما قد أخذ في طريق الفساد والموت وهو الورم الذي يعرفه

---

1. الرحيم: اللهم صلّى على محمد وآله add. B عونك اللهم ‹...› add. E صلّى اللّه على أنبياه وعلى آله(؟) add. C ربّ يسّر خيرا برحمتك يا أرحم الراحمين add. P

2. مقالة في سوء المزاج المختلف لجالينوس: كتاب جالينوس في سوء المزاج المختلف BE كتاب جالينوس في سوء المزاج C

3. ترجمة حنين بن اسحق: نقل أبي زيد حنين بن اسحق A

4. اسحق: المتطبّب add. E

5. انفياليس: انثياليس A without punctuation بغياليس A¹ without punctuation انثيالس B بغيالس ἠπίαλος g P

6. بالثابتة المسمّاة باليونانية اقطيقوس: بلاقطيقوس وهي الحمّى الثابتة P

7. الورم: الآخر add. B

8. الحارّ وهو المعروف بفلغموني: om. BEP

9. أو: وهو أن B إلى أن C أو يصير في حدّ ما قد أخذ في طريق الفساد والموت وهو الورم الذي يعرفه

اليونانيون بغنغرينا [10] ويحدث [11] فيه الورم الآخر المعروف بالحمرة [12] والورم [13] الآخر
المعروف بالسرطان والجذام أيضا من هذا الجنس وكذلك الأكلة والنملة إلاّ [14] أنّ هذه
العلل كلّها لا تخلو من أن يكون معها فضل ينصبّ [15] إلى العضو الذي تحدث فيه. وقد
يكون من سوء المزاج المختلف صنف آخر من غير أن ينصبّ إلى الأعضاء فضل لكن
تتغيّر كيفيتها [16] فقط عندما يغلب عليها [17] الحرّ أو البرد من الشمس أو [18] عند رياضة
تتجاوز المقدار الذي [19] ينبغي أو [20] عند خفض ودعة تجاوزان [21] مقدار القصد أو غير
ذلك ممّا أشبهه. وقد يحدث [22] سوء المزاج المختلف [23] في أبداننا أيضا من الأشياء التي
تلقاها من خارج بأن تسخن من [24] تلك الأشياء أو تبرد أو تجفّ أو ترطب. وهذه

اليونانيون بعبغرايا: ἢ γαγγραινούμενον g

10. بغنغرينا: emendation eds. بعنقر <...> B بعنقرايا C بنعنقرايا(؟) E
بعبقريثا يعني قرحة الأكلة A[1] بعبعرايا P without punctuation

11. ويحدث فيه الورم الآخر المعروف بالحمرة: om. BE

12. بالحمرة والورم الآخر المعروف: om. C

13. والورم الآخر المعروف: أو يحدث فيه الورم الآخر المعروف B أو يحدث فيه الأورام الآخر المعروفة E

14. إلاّ أنّ هذه: وهذه BC

15. ينصبّ إلى العضو الذي تحدث فيه: om. g

16. كيفيتها: كيفيته B كلها B add.

17. عليها: om. A

18. أو عند رياضة تتجاوز المقدار: أو رياضة مجاوزة للقدر BE

19. لذي ينبغي: om. BCE

20. أو عند خفض ودعة تجاوزان مقدار القصد: om. E أو يغلب عليها البرد من مقاربة شيء بارد مثل الجمد أو
الجليد أو هواء شديد البرد BC

21. تجاوزان مقدار القصد: πάντως< >g

22. يحدث: B[2] يختلّف B

23. المختلف: B[1]

24. من: om. BE

الأربعة[25] الأصناف من سوء المزاج بسيطة مفردة كما قد بيّنت في كتابي في المزاج.

٣. ومنه أيضا أربعة أصناف أخر مركّبة تكون إذا سخن البدن ورطب معا أو[26] سخن وجفّ معا أو برد ورطب معا أو برد وجفّ معا. ومن البيّن أنّ هذه الأصناف من سوء المزاج إنّما[27] تخالف أصناف سوء[28] المزاج المستوي لأنّها ليست في جميع أجزاء البدن[29] الذي يفسد مزاجه موجودة. فغرضي في هذا الكتاب أن أخبر[30] كيف يكون تولّد جميع[31] أصناف سوء المزاج المختلف. وكيما يكون قولي في ذلك واضحا فقد ينبغي أن أذكرك[32] بحال[33] الأعضاء كلّها وأبتدئ بذكر أكبرها التي[34] يعرفها من ليس عنده معرفة بالطبّ فإنّ اليدين والرجلين والبطن والصدر والرأس ليس ممّا يذهب أمرها على أحد.

(Ch. 2)

١ فلنعمد إلى واحد منها فنقسمه إلى أقرب الأجزاء التي هو منها مركّب حتّى نقسم الرجل في المثل إلى الفخذ والساق والقدم ونقسم[35] اليد إلى العضد والساعد والكفّ

---

25. الأربعة .om. AE

26. أو سخن وجفّ معا :om. BE

27. إنّما: g <μόνον>

28. سوء :om. P

29. البدن الذي يفسد مزاجه موجودة: g τοῦ δυσκράτως διακειμένου σώματος

30. أخبر: أذكر B

31. جميع :om. BCE

32. أذكرك: أذكر BP

33. بحال :om. P

34. التي يعرفها: الذي يعرفه B الذي يعرفها EP

35. ونقسم اليد إلى العضد والساعد والكفّ :om. B

ونقسم أيضا [36] الكفّ إلى الأعضاء التي تخصّها وهي الرسغ والمشط والأصابع ونقسم الأصابع أيضا إلى الأجزاء التي [37] تخصّها وهي مؤلّفة منها وهي العظام والغضاريف والرباطات والعصب والعروق الضوارب وغير الضوارب والأغشية واللحم والوترات والأظفار والجلد والشحم.

٢. وأما هذه الأعضاء التي ذكرناها بآخرة فليس يمكن قسمتها إلى نوع [38] آخر بعد [39] لكنها أعضاء متشابهة الأجزاء أوّليّة خلا [40] العروق الضوارب وغير الضوارب فإنّ هذين مركّبان [41] من الليف والأغشية كما قلت في كتابي في علاج التشريح. وقد وصفت أيضا في ذلك الكتاب أنّ بين الأعضاء الأوّل المتشابهة الأجزاء فرجا كثيرة وأكثر منها وأعظم في ما بين الأعضاء المركّبة الآلية وربّما وجدنا مثل تلك الفرج في [42] الواحد من الأعضاء المتشابهة الأجزاء كما قد نجد ذلك في العظم وفي [43] الجلد. [44] إلّا أنّ ما كان من الأعضاء ليّنا فإنّ بعض أجزائه ينطبق [45] على بعض فتخفى عن الحسّ الفرج التي في ما بينها. وأمّا ما كان من الأعضاء صلبا يابسا [46] فإنّك تدرك ما فيه من الفرج والخلل

---

36. أيضا (αὖ): BCE .om

37. التي تخصّها وهي: التي هي BCE

38. نوع: أنواع CP

39. بعد: بعدها BCEP

40. خلا...مـركّـبـان: <...> אן אלערוק אלצ'ואַרב <ו>גיר אלצ'ואַרב מרכבין ליסת מן אל עאצא אלמתשאבהה' אלאג'זא B[1]

41. مركّبان: مركّبين BEP

42. في الواحد: g καθ’ ἓν ὁτιοῦν

43. وفي الجلد: A[1]

44. الجلد: καὶ περὶ τούτων ἁπάντων ἐν ταῖς ἀνατομικαῖς ἐγχειρήσεσιν εἴρηται add. g

45. ينطبق على بعض: g ἀλλήλοις ἐπιπίπτοντα

46. يابسا: جافًا؟ B

بالحسّ كما قد نجد في المشاش [47] من العظام. وفي خلل [48] تلك [49] المشاش [50] من العظام رطوبة بالطبع غليظة بيضاء أعدّت للعظام لتغتذي بها. وأمّا المسامّ التي في الجلد فقد بيّنت في كتابي في المزاج كيف تحدث. فهذا ما كان يحتاج إلى الإذكار به ضرورة ليضح به ما أنا واصفه في ما بعد.

٣. وقد ينبغي الآن أن نقصد قصد سوء المزاج المختلف فنصف ما طبيعته وعلى كم ضرب يحدث. وقد قلنا في ما تقدّم إنّه ليس يكون في أجزاء الجرم الذي يعرض فيه سوء المزاج المختلف مزاج واحد لأنّ [51] هذا أمر عامّ مشترك لكلّ سوء [52] مزاج مختلف. وأمّا أصنافه فتابعة لطبائع الأجرام التي تحدث فيها. فإنّ حدوث سوء المزاج المختلف في اللحم المجرّد [53] غير حدوثه في العضلة كما هي وكلّ [54] واحد منهما يكون على غير الجهة التي يكون عليها الآخر.

(Ch. 3)

١. من ذلك إنّه إذا انصبّ إلى عضلة فضلة [55] حارّ فإنّ ما [56] فيها من العروق التي هي

---

47. المشاش: المسامّ B[2]

48. خلل: .om E

49. تلك: ذلك A

50. المشاش: المسامّ B[2]

51. لأنّ: إلاّ أنّ LP

52. سوء: .om BCE

53. المجرّد: المفرد .add P

54. وكلّ واحد منها يكون على غير الجهة التي يكون عليها الآخر: .om g

55. فضل g ῥεῦμα

56. ما فيها من: .om g

أعظم عروقها الضوارب منها [57] وغير الضوارب تمتلئ أوّلا وتتمدّد ثمّ من بعد ذلك العروق التي هي أصغر [58] ولا يزال كذلك [59] يسري حتّى يبلغ إلى أصغر العروق. فإذا [60] غاص [61] ذلك الفضل في تلك العروق فلم تضبطه ندر [62] منه شيء من أفواه تلك العروق ورشح منه شيء فخرج من [63] نفس أبدان العروق. فإذا كان ذلك امتلأت الفرج التي في ما بين الأعضاء الأوّل من [64] ذلك الفضل حتّى يعرض لها أن تسخن وتبتلّ من جميع جهاتها من تلك الرطوبة المحيطة بها. وأعني بالأعضاء [65] الأوّل في هذا الموضع العصب والرباطات والأغشية واللحم وقبل هذه نفس العروق الضوارب وغير الضوارب التي قد يعرض فيها خاصّة أوّلا الوجع على أنحاء شتّى. وذلك أنّ الفضل من داخلها يسخنها ويمدّدها ويصدعها والفضل من خارجها يسخنها ويزحمها [66] ويضغطها ويثقلها. وأمّا سائر الأعضاء فبعضها إنّما تؤلمه السخونة فقط وبعضها [67] إنّما يؤلمه الضغط [68] وبعضها يؤلمه الأمران جميعا.

٢. ويقال لهذه العلّة عند اليونانيين فلغموني وهي الورم الحارّ وهو سوء مزاج مختلف

---

57. منها: om. BCE

58. أصغر: العروق add. L

59. كذلك: ذلك LP

60. فإذا فاض: ὅταν ἰσχυρῶς σφηνωθῇ g

61. غاص: فاض A'BCE غاض A

62. ندر: AP without punctuation ندر بمعنى سقط من جوف شيء A¹ برز 'BEC بدر CL διηθεῖται g

63. من نفس أبدان العروق: من نفس بدن العروق BCE من نفس تلك العروق L
διὰ τῶν χιτώνων g(K) διὰ τῶν κινούντων αὐτὸ χιτώνων g

64. من ذلك الفضل: om. A

65. بالأعضاء: ذكر الأعضاء الأوّل ‹...› A¹

66. ويزحمها ويضغطها: θλίβονται g

67. وبعضها إنّما يؤلمه الضغظ: om. L

68. الضغط: الرطوبة B² فقط add. BC

يعرض في العضلة. وذلك أنّ الدم[69] الذي[70] فيها يكون قد سخن وحدث له شبيه بالغليان ثمّ تسخن بسخونته أوّلا خاصّة أبدان[71] العروق الضوارب وغير الضوارب ثمّ جميع ما هو خارج عنها ممّا[72] تفيض عليه حتّى يستغرقه. ولا بدّ من أن يؤول الأمر في ذلك إلى إحدى خلّتين:[73] إمّا أن يغلب الفضل الذي ينصبّ إلى العضلة فيفسد الأجسام التي يغلب عليها وإمّا أن يغلب ذلك الفضل فتعود[74] العضلة إلى حالها الطبيعية. فأنزل°[75] أوّلا أنّ الفضل غُلِبَ إذ كان الابتداء بما[76] هو أحمد[77] وأولى[78] فأقول[79] إنّ البرء يكون[80] عند ذلك على أحد ضربين إمّا بأن[81] تتحلّل جميع تلك الرطوبة التي انصبّت إلى العضلة وإمّا بأن تنضج. وأحمد البرئين ما كان بالتحلّل. وأمّا النضج فيلحقه[82] أمران ضرورة: أحدهما تولّد المدّة والآخر الجمع[83] والجمع ربّما كان إلى أعظم الفرج[84] القريبة من

---

69. الدم: الورم C

70. الذي: التي A

71. أبدان: τοὺς χιτῶνας g

72. ممّا: بما E

73. خلّتين: حالتين g LP om.

74. فتعود: فيعيد E

75. فأنزل°: καὶ δὴ καὶ g

76. بما: إنّما ALP

77. أحمد: جيد BCE

78. وأولى: وأحمد add. BC

79. فأقول: أن أقول A أقول BCE

80. يكون: A¹

81. بأن: أن L

82. فيلحقه: فيحدث منه L

83. الجمع: ἀπόστασις g

84. الفرج: القروح L

43

الموضـع وأقلّها[85] خطـرا وهـذا أحمد ما يكون مـن الجمـع. وربّما كان إلى أعظم الفرج[86] القريبة لكـن تلك الفرجة[87] لا تكون بقليلة الخطر أو يكون في فرجة[88] قليلة الخطر لكنها لا[89] تكون أعظم الفرج[90] ولا[91] قريبة.

٣. فإن كان ذلك في نواحي المعدة فأحمد الجمع ما كان في[92] الفضاء الذي في داخلها وإليه[93] في أكثر الأمر تنفجر المدّة.[94] وأمّا الجمع[95] إلى ما دون الصفاق فردئ. وإذا كان ذلك في نواحي الدماغ والجمع في التجويفين المقدّمين منه محمود والجمع[96] تحت أمّي الدماغ وفي التجويف الذي في مؤخّر الدماغ مذموم ردئ. وأمّا في الخراجات[97] التي تكون في نواحي الأضلاع فانفجارها يكون إلى فضاء الصدر والخراجات التي تكون في العضل فانفجارها يكون نحو[98] الجلد. وأمّا الخراجات الحادثة في[99] الأحشاء

---

85. وأقلّها خطرا: ἀκυροτάτην g

86. الفرج: القروح L

87. الفرجة: القرحة L

88. الفرجة: القرحة LP

89. لا تكون أعظم الفرج ولا قريبة: οὐ μεγίστην δέ g οὐ

90. الفرج: القرح L

91. ولا قريبة: om. g

92. في: إلى A'LP

93. وإليه في أكثر الأمر تنفجر المدّة: εἰς ἣν καὶ συρρήγνυται τὰ πολλὰ ‹τῶν ἀποστάσεων› g

94. المدّة: om. g

95. الجمع: ما ينفجر AP الذي add. C

96. والجمع: om. A

97. الخراجات: ἀποστάσεις g

98. نحو: ὑπὸ g

99. في: نحو BE

فانفجارها يكون إمّا[100] إلى العروق التي[101] فيها الضوارب منها[102] وغير الضوارب وإمّا نحو الغشاء الذي يحيط بها وهو لها بمنزلة الجلد.

٤. فإن غلب الفضل على[103] الأعضاء فيبين[104] أنّه يبلغ[105] من غلبة سوء المزاج المختلف[106] عليها أن يبطل فعلها ويفسد[107] على طول المدّة. وأوّل سكون الألم عنها يكون إذا تشبّهت بالشيء الذي يحيلها ويغيّرها وذلك أنّ الأعضاء ليس[108] إنّما يعرض لها الألم[109] عندما يكون مزاجها قد استحال وفرغ لكن في حال الاستحالة كما وصف من أمرها العجيب أبقراط حين قال إنّ الأوجاع إنّما تكون في الأعضاء في حال[110] تغيّرها وفسادها وخروجها عن طبائعها. وإنّما يتغيّر[111] كلّ واحد من الأعضاء عن

---

100. إمّا: B¹

101. التي فيها: فمنها E

102. منها: om. BCE

103. على: om. ABE في P

104. فيبين: فيقن(؟) L

105. يبلغ: ينبغي ABCE

106. المختلف: om. AP

107. ويفسد: ويعسر BCE

108. ليس: om. LP

109. الألم: لا add. P

110. في حال تغيّرها وفسادها وخروجها عن طبائعها: τοῖσι γὰρ τὴν φύσιν διαλλασσομένοισι καὶ διαφθειρομένοισιν g

111. يتغيّر: يخرج BCE

طبيعته ويفسد [112] إمّا بأن يسخن وإمّا [113] بأن يبرد وإمّا [114] بأن يجفّ وإمّا [115] بأن يرطب وإمّا [116] بأن يتفرّق اتّصاله [117] . وأمّا في سوء المزاج المختلف فمن قبل أنّ العضو يسخن أو يبرد خاصّة وذلك أنّ هاتين الكيفيتين أقوى الكيفيات فعلا وقد [118] يكون ذلك من [119] قبل أنّ العضو يجفّ أو يرطب وأمّا في الجوع والعطش فيعرض [120] الألم لفقد الجوهر اليابس في حال الجوع ولفقد الجوهر [121] الرطب في حال العطش وأمّا [122] عند تأثير [123] ما يؤثّر في العضو ممّا [124] ينخسه [125] أو يأكله أو يمدّده أو يضغطه أو [126] يفسخه فحدوث [127] الألم يكون بسبب تفرّق الاتّصال.

---

112.   ويفسد: ويعسر BCE

113.   وإمّا بأن: أو BCEL

114.   وإمّا بأن: أو BCE

115.   وإمّا بأن: أو BCE

116.   وإمّا بأن: أو BCE

117.   اتّصاله: أيضا له L

118.   وقد يكون ذلك من قبل: ἤδη δὲ καὶ διὰ g

119.   من قبل أنّ العضو يجفّ أو يرطب: διὰ τὸ ξηραίνεσθαι τε καὶ ὑγραίνεσθαι g

120.   فيعرض الألم: om. g

121.   الجوهر الرطب: الرطوبة BCE

122.   وأمّا عند تأثير ما يؤثّر في العضو ما ينخسه: ἐν δὲ τῷ τιτρώσκεσθαι g

123.   تأثير: om. BCE

124.   ممّا: ما ABCE

125.   ينخسه: يسحقه(؟) C

126.   أو يفسخه: om. B

127.   فحدوث الألم يكون: om. g

(Ch. 4)

١. ومتى كانت حرارة الدم الذي [128] في العضو الوارم حرارة هـادئة [129] وكان الدم الذي [130] يحويه البدن كلّه معتدل المزاج لم يكد [131] يعرض له أن يسخن بسخونة العضو العليل. ومتى [132] كانت الحرارة من الدم الذي في العضو الوارم حرارة قوية أسخن [133] البدن بقوة غليانه إن [134] كان الدم الذي [135] يحويه البدن كلّه قد غلب عليه المرار فإنّه لا يلبث أن يسخن كلّه [136] سخونة مفرطة وأحرى أن يكون ذلك [137] متى ما [138] اجتمع الأمران [139] حتّى [140] يكون الدم الذي في العضو الوارم قوي الحرارة والدم الذي في البدن قد غلب عليه المرار.

٢. وأوّل [141] ما يسخن من الدم حتّى تفرط عليه السخونة الدم الذي في العروق الضوارب من قبل أنّه في طبيعته أسخن وأقرب إلى طبيعة الروح ثمّ من بعده الدم الذي في العروق غير الضوارب. فإن كان العضو الوارم مجاورا لبعض الأحشاء الغزيرة الدم كانت

---

128. الذي: التي BC²E

129. هـادئة g ἐπιεικὴς

130. الذي: التي A

131. يكد AL أن add. EL

132. ومتى كان الحرارة من الدم الذي في العضو الوارم حرارة قوية أسخن البدن بقوة غليانه [τοι] εἰ δὴ ζέοι σφοδρότερον g

133. أسخن البدن: om. LP

134. وإن: أو إن A إن L

135. الذي: التي A

136. كلّه سخونة مفرطة: سخونة مفرطة كلّه BCE

137. ذلك: كذلك C ذلك كذلك BE

138. ما: om. BCELP

139. الأمران: جميعا add. C

140. حتّى: καὶ g

141. وأوّل ما يسخن من الدم حتّى تفرط عليه السخونة: ἐκθερμαίνεται g

الحرارة منه تلجأ إلى الدم الذي يحويه البدن كلّه أسرع. وبالجملة فإنّ أوّل ما يسخن من قبل كلّ شيء ما كان سريعا إلى الاستحالة أو كان في طبيعته حارًّا. وكذلك أوّل ما يبرد من قبل أنّ [142] الشيء الذي يبرد [143] إنّما [144] هو ما كان سريعا إلى الاستحالة أو كان في طبيعته باردا. وأسرع ما في البدن إلى الاستحالة الروح من قبل أنّه ألطفها [145] وأرقّها. وأسخن ما في [146] البدن المرّة الصفراء وأبرد ما فيه [147] البلغم. وأمّا سائر الأخلاط فالدم منها حارّ بعد المرّة [148] الصفراء والمرّة السوداء باردة بعد البلغم. والمرّة [149] الصفراء تستحيل بسهولة وسرعة [150] من كلّ ما يعمل فيها. وأمّا السوداء فبكدّ [151] وشدّة ما تستحيل. وبالجملة كلّ ما كان [152] لطيفا رقيقا فهو سريع الاستحالة وكلّ [153] ما كان ثخينا غليظا فبطيء [154] الاستحالة.

٣. فيجب من ذلك أن تكون الاستحالة الحادثة من الأورام مختلفة كثيرة الاختلاف لاختلاف حال الأجسام. أمّا أوّل الأمر فإنّ الخلط الذي يحدث عنه الورم إمّا أن يكون

---

142. أنّ الشيء الذي: كلّ ما L

143. يبرد: أيضا add. and deleted A add. BCE

144. إنّما om. BCE: إنّما هو om. L

145. ألطفها وأرقّها: λεπτομερέστατον g

146. في البدن: φύσει g

147. فيه: في البدن LP

148. المرّة: om. BCE

149. المرّة: om. BCE

150. وسرعة: om. g

151. فبكدّ وشدّة: δυσκόλως g

152. كان لطيفا رقيقا: λεπτομερὲς g

153. وكلّ...الاستحالة: om. P: وكلّ ما كان ثخينا غليظا: παχυμερές g

154. فبطيء: فهو بطيء E فإنّه بطيء L

أزيد حرارة وإمّا [155] أن يكون أنقص حرارة. ثمّ من بعد ذلك فإنّ عفونته إنّما يكون
بحسب طبيعته وبحسب [156] فضل لحوجه أو قلّة لحوجه. فإنّ ما لا تنفّس له تكون العفونة
إليه أسرع وذلك موجود في جميع الأشياء الخارجة. فإذا اتّفق مع ذلك أن يكون مزاجها
حارًا رطبا كان [157] ذلك أعون على سرعة العفونة إليها. والعضو [158] الذي يحدث فيه
الورم أيضا إمّا أن يكون بالقرب من الأحشاء الغزيرة الدم وإمّا بالبعد منها. [159] فإنّ
الدم كلّه [160] إنّما تغلب عليه الصفراء [161] والسوداء أو البلغم أو الريح وجميع [162] هذه
الأحوال تختلف في [163] القلّة والكثرة. فيجب ضرورة أن تكون الاستحالة مختلفة كثيرة
الاختلاف إذا قيس الواحد [164] إلى غيره وإذا قيس بنفسه.

(Ch. 5)

١. وهذه [165] كلّها تكون [166] أسبابا لسوء المزاج المختلف وذلك أنّ أغلب ما تكون

---

155.   وإمّا أن يكون أنقص حرارة: وإمّا أنقص BE وإمّا أن يكون أنقص C

156.   وبحسب: οὐχ ἥκιστα δὲ καὶ g

157.   كان ذلك أعون على سرعة العفونة إليها: τότε δὴ καὶ μάλιστα g

158.   والعضو: وان كان add. A وان كان العضو A¹P وان العضو L

159.   منها: عنها BCE

160.   كلّه إنّما: كلّه أيضا BE أيضا كلّه C

161.   الصفراء والسوداء: المرار الأصفر والمرار الأسود LP المرّة الصفراء والسوداء C

162.   وجميع هذه الأحوال تختلف بالقلّة والكثرة g: καὶ ταῦτα σύμπαντα μᾶλλόν τε καὶ ἧττον g

163.   في: ب - LP

164.   الواحد: ‹σωματος› g add

165.   وهذه كلّها: وكلّها BCE

166.   تكون أسبابا: γίγνονται g

الحرارة على الدم الذي هـو في العضو [167] الوارم ثمّ من بعده على الدم الذي في الأحشاء [168] وخاصّة [169] على الدم الذي في القلب ومن هذا خاصّة ما في تجويفه الأيسر فإنّك إن عمدت إلى هذا التجويف من [170] القلب والحيوان بعد حيّ ولم تعرض له بعد [171] حمّى فأدخلت فيه إصبعك كما وصفت في كتابي في علاج التشريح أحسست منه [172] بأقوى ما يكون من الحرارة. فليس بالبعيد متى ما كان البدن كلّه قد سخن سخونة خارجة عن الطبع أن يبلغ ذلك [173] التجويف خاصّة من القلب غاية الحرارة. وممّا [174] يعين على ذلك أنّ فيه من الدم أرقّه وأقربه من طبيعة الروح ويتحرّك أيضا حركة دائمة.

٢. إلاّ أنّه يوجد في أمثال هذه من الحمّيات الدم كلّه قد [175] استحوذت عليه السخونة وقبل تلك الحرارة الخارجة عن المجرى الطبيعي المتولّدة عن عفونة الأخلاط قبولا [176] مستحكما. وأمّا [177] أبدان العروق الضوارب وغيرها من الأجسام التي تجاورها وتحيط

167.	العضو الوارم: g φλεγμονὴν	
168.	الأحشاء: g τἄλλα σπλάγχνα	
169.	وخاصّة: g καὶ	
170.	من القلب: om. BCE C¹	
171.	بعد: om. A	
172.	منه: om. g	
173.	ذلك التجويف خاصّة من القلب g ἐκείνην μάλιστα	
174.	وممّا يعين على ذلك: g καὶ γὰρ	
175.	قد استحوذت عليه السخونة: g ἐκθερμαίνεται	
176.	قبولا مستحكما: om. g	
177.	أبدان: g χιτῶνες	

بها فليس يوجد قد [178] تغيّر مزاجها [179] وفرغ تغيّرا تامّا [180] مستحكما [181] لكنها تكون بعد هوذا [182] تستحيل وتتغيّر إلى [183] السخونة. وإن دام ذلك بها مدّة طويلة صارت إلى حدّ تكون فيه قد غلبت واستحالت أصلا حتّى [184] لا تكون عند ذلك في حدّ ما هوذا يسخن فيه لكن تكون في حدّ ما قد سخن وفرغ من [185] سخونة خارجة عن الأمر الطبيعي. وحدّ الاستحالة في كلّ واحد من الأعضاء هو ضرر الفعل. [186] وأمّا العرض كلّه الذي [187] منذ أوّل الأمر إلى أن ينتهي إلى هذا الحدّ فإنّما هو طريق الخروج إلى الحال الخارجة عن الأمر الطبيعي ممزوج [188] مشترك متوسّط في ما بين الضدّين أعني بين الحال التي هي بالحقيقة طبيعية وبين الحال التي هي خارجة عن الطبيعة أصلا. ففي هذه المدّة كلّها من الزمان يكون بالجسم الذي يسخن من الوجع بمقدار [189] ما يناله من الاستحالة.

---

178. قد: فيه L

179. مزاجها: مزاجه AL

180. تامّا محكما g τελέως

181. مستحكما: A¹ محكما ABCE

182. هوذا: مدّة BCE

183. إلى السخونة: g θερμαινόμενα

184. حتّى لا تكون عند ذلك في حدّ ما هوذا يسخن فيه لكن تكون في حدّ ما قد سخن وفرغ من سخونة خارجة عن الأمر الطبيعي: g ὡς μηκέτι θερμαίνεσθαι μόνον, ἀλλ᾽ ἤδη τεθερμάνται παρὰ φύσιν

185. من: om. BEP

186. الفعل: فعله BCEP

187. الذي om. A

188. ممزوج: وأمر ممزوج C أمر ممزوج g L οἷον ἐπίμικτον

189. بمقدار ما يناله من الاستحالة: g ποσῷ τῆς ἀλλοιώσεως ἀνάλογον

٣. فإذا سخن جميع الأعضاء الأصلية [190] من البدن السخونة التامّة [191] المستحكمة قيل لتلك الحمّى اقطيقوس [192] وهي [193] الثابتة وذلك أنّ قوامها عند ذلك ليس يكون بالرطوبات [194] والروح فقط لكنه [195] يكون مع ذلك في الأجسام التي لها ثبات وليس [196] مع هذه الحمّى ألم ولا وجع ويظنّ صاحبها أنّه لا حمّى به أصلا وذلك [197] أنّ صاحبها لا يحسّ بحرارتها لأنّ أعضاءه كلّها تكون قد سخنت سخونة مستوية [198] على حال واحدة. وقد اتّفق على هذا أصحاب النظر في أمر الطبائع عند نظرهم في أمر الحواس من أنّ الحسّ ليس يكون بغير [199] استحالة ولا يكون الألم [200] والوجع في ما قد استحال وفرغ. ولذلك صارت كلّ حمّى [201] من هذا الجنس الذي ذكرناه قبل المسمّى اقطيقوس ليس [202] معها ألم ولا وجع ولا يحسّ بها صاحبها أصلا وذلك إنّه ليست حال الأعضاء منه حال ما يكون بعضها يفعل وبعضها ينفعل إذ كانت كلّها [203] قد صارت بحال واحدة وصار

---

190. الأصلية: στεριὰ g

191. التامّة المستحكمة: τελέως g

192. اقطيقوس: ايطيقوس A without punctuation

193. وهي الثابتة: om. g

194. بالرطوبات: في الرطوبات LP

195. لكنه: لكن BCE

196. وليس مع هذه الحمّى ألم ولا وجع: ἀνώδυνος g

197. وذلك أنّ صاحبها: لأنّه BCE

198. مستوية على حال واحدة: ὁμοίως g

199. بغير استحالة: إلّا بالاستحالة BCE

200. الألم والوجع: ἡ ὀδύνη g

201. كلّ حمّى من هذا الجنس الذي ذكرناه قبل المسمّى اقطيقوس: oἱ ἑκτικοὶ πυρετοὶ πάντες g

202. ليس معها ألم ولا وجع: ἄπονοι g

203. كلّها: A¹

مزاجها مزاجا[204] واحدا متّفقا.

(Ch. 6)

١. وإن كان أيضا بعضها أزيد سخونة وبعضها أزيد بردا[205] فإنّ ليس يبلغ من فضل سخونة ما هو منها أسخن على ما هو منها أبرد أن يؤذي ما يجاوره بسخونته. ولو كان الأمر كذلك لقد كانت الأعضاء سيؤذي بعضها بعضا وهي بالحال الطبيعية فإنّ الأعضاء في[206] تلك الحال أيضا مختلفة في مزاجها. وذلك أنّ اللحم عضو حارّ والعظم عضو بارد إلاّ أنّ اختلاف[207] هذه وغيرها[208] ممّا[209] أشبهها ليس معه وجع ولا ألم من قبل قلّة[210] التفاضل بينها في الحرّ والبرد. من ذلك أنّ الهواء المحيط بالأبدان ليس يؤذيها دون أن يستحيل حتّى يفرط عليه الحرّ أو البرد. وأمّا أصناف اختلافه في ما بين إفراط الحرّ وإفراط البرد على كثرتها وبيان التفاضل[211] بينها فإنّ الأبدان[212] تحسّها بلا أذى بها.

٢. فتكاد[213] النفس[214] على هذا القياس أن[215] تسكن إلى ذلك[216] القول الذي قيل كما

---

٢٠٤. مزاجا: om. BCEL

٢٠٥. بردا: برودة E

٢٠٦. في تلك الحال: om. g

٢٠٧. اختلاف g: ἀνωμαλία

٢٠٨. وغيرها: om. BCE

٢٠٩. ممّا أشبهها: وما شاكلها B وما شابلها CE g ἀπάντων

٢١٠. قلّة التفاضل بينها في الحرّ والبرد: g τῷ μετρίῳ τῆς ὑπεροχῆς

٢١١. التفاضل g: ὑπεροχὴν

٢١٢. الأبدان تحسّها: g αἰσθανόμεθα

٢١٣. فتكاد النفس على هذا القياس أن تسكن إلى القول الذي قيل: κινδυνεύει τοι γὰρ οὖν ἐκ τῶνδε κἀκεῖνος ὁ λόγος ἔχειν ἐπιείκειαν g

٢١٤. النفس: <...> A

٢١٥. أن: om. A

٢١٦. ذلك: om. A

قال أبقراط في [217] بعض كتبه إنّ جميع الأمراض إنّما هي قروح. وذلك أنّ القرحة إنّما هي تفرّق الاتّصال والحرارة المفرطة والبرد المفرط يكاد أن يفرّقان الاتّصال. أمّا الحرارة الشديدة [218] فمن قبل أنّها تفرّق وتقطع اتّصال الجوهر الذي [219] تغلب عليه وأمّا البرد المفرط فمن قبل أنّه يجمع ويعصر [220] الجوهر الذي [221] يغلب عليه إلى داخل حتّى يندر [222] منه شيء فيخرج ويضغط [223] ما يبقى منه ويفسخه. وإن جعل جاعل هذا هو الحدّ في إفراط الحرّ والبرد فخليق [224] أن يكون غير بعيد من أن يتوهّم عليه أنّه قد أصاب. إلّا أنّه إن كان هذا [225] هو الحدّ في [226] الإفراط وإن كان الحدّ في [227] ذلك غيره فالأمر على حال بيّن أنّ كلّ إفراط [228] إنّما يفهم على طريق الإضافة إلى شيء. وذلك أنّه ليس الذي ينال كلّ بدن من الأشياء التي [229] هي بحال واحدة من الحرّ والبرد شيء [230] واحد.

---

217. في بعض كتبه: om. g

218. الشديدة: المفرطة A الشديدة المفرطة P

219. الذي تغلب عليه: om. g

220. ويعصر: ويقبض BCE

221. الذي تغلب عليه: om. g

222. يندر: برز B يبرز C يتبدد A¹ يبدر L يندر منه شيء فيخرج: τὰ μὲν ἐκπιέζει g

223. ويضغط ما يبقى منه ويفسخه: τὰ δὲ θλᾷ g

224. فخليق أن يكون غير بعيد من أن يتوهّم عليه أنّه قد أصاب: τάχ᾽ ἂν οὐκ ἄπο τρόπου γιγνώσκειν δόξειεν g

225. هذا: ليس add. BL

226. في الإفراط: τῆς ἀμετρίας g

227. في ذلك غيره: A¹ في غير ذلك A

228. إفراط: ἀμετρίαν g

229. التي هي بحال واحدة: om. g

230. شيء واحد: أمرا واحدا BC أمر واحد E

٣. ولذلك صار بعض الحيوان [231] ما فيه من الأخلاط بعضه بعضا وبعضه [232] ليست تلك الأخلاط بموافقة من البعض منه للبعض لكنها مع ذلك مفسدة [233] قاتلة مثل الإنسان والأفعى فإنّ لعاب كلّ واحد منهما للآخر قاتل. ومن هذا الطريق صار الإنسان إذا بزق [234] على العقرب وهو على الريق قتلها وأمّا الإنسان فليس يقتل إنسانا مثله إذا عضّه ولا الأفعى تقتل الأفعى [235] ولا [236] الثعبان [237] الثعبان. وذلك أنّ المثل موافق محبوب والضدّ عدو مؤذ. وممّا يدلّ على ذلك أنّ جميع ما ينمي ويغتذي إنّما ينمي ويغتذي بمثله [238] وشبهه وكلّ ما يعطب وينقض [239] فإنّما يعطب وينقض [240] من ضدّه. ولذلك حفظ الصحّة إنّما يكون بالأشياء [241] المشاكلة المشابهة للأبدان الصحيحة والبرء [242] والشفاء من الأمراض إنّما يكون بالأشياء المضادّة لها إلّا أنّ الكلام في هذا غير ما نحن فيه.

---

231.   يوافق ما: موافقا بما BCE

232.   وبعضه ليست تلك الأخلاط بموافقة من البعض منه للبعض: وبعضه ‹...› الأخلاط ليس يوافق من البعض منه للبعض B وبعضه ليست الأخلاط يوافق البعض منه للبعض C وبعضه ليست الأخلاط موافقة من البعض منه البعض E وليست الأخلاط بموافقة من البعض منه للبعض P

233.   مفسدة قاتلة: φθαρτικούς g

234.   بزق: بصق BCE

235.   الأفعى: مثلها BCE

236.   ولا الثعبان الثعبان: om. BCE

237.   الثعبان: ἀσπίς g

238.   بمثله وشبهه: πρὸς τῶν ὁμοίων g

239.   وينقض : وينتقض BCE

240.   وينقض: om. BCE

241.   بالأشياء المشاكلة المشابهة للأبدان الصحيحة: διὰ τῶν ὁμοίων g

242.   والبرء والشفاء: ἀναίρεσις g

٤. وأمّا تلك الحمّى الثابتة التي[243] تشبّثت بالجوهر الثابت[244] من جوهر الحيوان[245] فإنّ صاحبها لا يحسّها وأمّا سائر الحمّيات فليس منها شيء لا[246] يحسّه صاحبه إلّا أنّ بعضها[247] ما[248] يحسّه صاحبه وتأنّى به أكثر وبعضها ما[249] يحسّه أقلّ. ومن[250] الحمّيات حميات يكون معها نافض وهذا العارض أيضا نافض أعني النافض مثل كثير من غيره من الأعراض إنّما يكون عن سوء المزاج المختلف. وليس يمكن أن أصف كيف يتولّد هذا العارض في هذا القول الذي أنا فيه دون أن أبيّن القوى الطبيعية كم هي وأيّ القوى هي وما[251] الذي من شأن كلّ واحدة منها أن تفعل. لكني سأصف[252] أمر[253] جميع الأعراض في كتابي في العلل والأعراض.

(Ch. 7)

١. وأنا راجع إلى أصناف سوء المزاج المختلف. وقد قلت في ما تقدّم كيف تتولّد

---

243. التي تشبّثت بالجوهر الثابت من جوهر الحيوان: ὁ τὴν ἕξιν ἤδη τοῦ ζῴου κατειληφώς g

244. الثابت: om. g

245. الحيوان: البدن B

246. لا: ليس ALP

247. بعضها ما يحسّه صاحبه وتأنّى به أكثر وبعضها ما يحسّه أقلّ: ὃι μὲν μᾶλλον, ὃι δ' ἧττον ἀνιαροὶ τοῖς νοσοῦσιν g

248. ما: om. BCE

249. ما يحسّه: om. BCE

250. ومن الحمّيات حميات: ومنها ما BCE

251. وما الذي من شأن كلّ واحدة منها أن تفعل: καὶ ὅ τι δρᾶν ἑκάστη πέφυκεν g

252. سأصف: أصف BCE

253. أمر جميع الأعراض: ὑπὲρ ἁπάντων g

الحمّى [254] عن [255] الورم الحارّ المسمّى فلغموني وأنّ كلّ ورم من هذا الجنس وكلّ حمّى خلا الحمّى التي [256] تعرف بالثابتة هي من الأمر أخر التي يكون فيها المزاج مختلفا. وقد تكون حمّيات من عفونة الأخلاط فقط من [257] غير ورم وذلك أنّه ليس الذي يعفن [258] هو ما قد لحج وعدم التنفّس فقط لكن ما أسرع ما تكون العفونة إلى هذا وأقوى ما تكون عليه وقد [259] تعفن أشياء أخر كثيرة ممّا هي متهيّئة لأن تعفن. وسنصف الأمر في تهيّؤ ما هو متهيّئ للعفونة في كتاب غير هذا.

٢. وقد يكون سوء المزاج المختلف على جهة أخرى في البدن كلّه وربّما كان ذلك عند احتقان بخار حارّ فيه وربّما كان تتزيّد الحرارة بسبب رياضة [260] أكثر من المقدار الذي ينبغي وربّما كان من قبل أنّ الدم سخن [261] وغلى غليانا مفرطا بسبب غضب أو سخن سخونة مفرطة [262] بسبب [263] لبث في شمس حارّة. ومن البيّن عندي أنّ جميع هذه الحمّيات الحادثة [264] عن الأورام بحسب قوة السبب الفاعل في الأبدان [265] وبحسب حال كلّ واحد من الأبدان قد تكون الحمّى في بعض الأبدان أقوى وفي بعضها أضعف

---

254. الحمّى g πυρετὸς ἅπας

255. عن الورم الحارّ المسمّى فلغموني: g ἐπὶ φλεγμονῇ

256. التي تعرف: BCE المعروفة

257. من غير ورم: g χωρὶς φλεγμονῆς

258. يعفن: add. A إنّما add. L دائما

259. وقد: AB وقت

260. رياضة: ἢ πόνων add. g

261. سخن وغلى: g ζέσαντος

262. مفرطة: ἔξωθεν add. g

263. بسبب لبث في شمس حارّة: g δι' ἔκκαυσίν τινα

264. الحادثة عن الأورام: g ὥσπερ κἀπὶ τῆς φλεγμονῆς ἔμπροσθεν ἐλέγετο

265. الأبدان: للأبدان(؟) P² للحيوان P

وبعضها لا تحمّ أصلا.

٣. ومن البيّن أنّ سوء المزاج ربّما [266] حدث في الروح فقط وربّما تجاوزها إلى الأخلاط أيضا. وممّا ليس بدون ذلك في البيان أيضا أنّ جميع الحمّيات إذا تطاولت قد تلحقها الحمّى الثابتة وكأنّه [267] قد تبيّن من هذا القول أنّ سوء المزاج المختلف ربّما حدث عن رطوبة حارّة أو باردة تسيل إلى عضو من الأعضاء كما وصفت من [268] أمر الأعضاء التي يحدث فيها الورم. وربّما [269] لم يكن الأمر كذلك لكنه يكون عند تغيّر مزاج البدن في كيفيته. وإنّ بعض الأسباب التي تغيّره تهيج من نفس البدن وبعضها تأتيه من خارج. إمّا عند حدوث الحمّى عن عفونة وحدها وإمّا عن بعض الأورام [270] فمن [271] نفس البدن. أمّا عند [272] حدوث الحمّى عن سخونة الشمس أو عن إفراط الرياضة فمن خارج. وسأصف ذلك بأكثر من هذا القول [273] في كتابنا [274] في [275] أسباب الأعراض. وكما قد تحدث الحمّى عن حرارة الشمس إذا استحال مزاج البدن كذلك قد يعرض لبعض الناس من [276] برد الهواء كثيرا أن يغلب عليهم البرد غلبة قوية في البدن كلّه حتّى يموت بعضهم. والأمر

---

266. ربّما حدث في الروح فقط وربّما تجاوزها إلى الأخلاط: ποτὲ μὲν ταύτης τῆς πνευματώδους οὐσίας μόνης, ἐνίοτε δ' ἅπτεται καὶ τῶν χυμῶν g

267. وكأنّه: καί g

268. من أمر الأعضاء التي يحدث فيها الورم: ἐπὶ τῶν φλεγμαινόντων g

269. وربّما: πολλάκις g

270. الأورام: φλεγμοναῖς g

271. فمن: فذلك لا محالة من P

272. عند: om. BE

273. القول: الوصف LP

274. كتابنا: كتاب BCEL كتابي P

275. في: om. BCEL

276. من برد الهواء: om. BE

في هؤلاء ²⁷⁷ أيضا كلّهم بيّن أنّهم يعرض لهم الألم والوجع.

(Ch. 8)

١. وقد يعرض ²⁷⁸ الألم والوجع أيضا لمن غلب عليه البرد غلبة قوية من قرّ ²⁷⁹ شديد ثمّ رام أن يسخن بدنه إسخانا سريعا بالاصطلاء. ²⁸⁰ وكثير ²⁸¹ ممّن أصابه ذلك لمّا أدنا بدنه ²⁸² من النار بغتة أحسّ بوجع شديد جدًّا في أصول الأظفار. فمن يقدم ²⁸³ وهو يرى عيانا في هذه الحال أنّ السبب ²⁸⁴ في الألم والوجع إنّما هو سوء المزاج ²⁸⁵ المختلف أن يدفع ذلك في الأوجاع التي تعرض من داخل أو ²⁸⁶ يتعجّب كيف يعرض الوجع كثيرا من الناس من غير ورم ²⁸⁷ إمّا في المعى ²⁸⁸ الذي يسمّى قولون وإمّا في الأنثيين ²⁸⁹ وإمّا في غيرها ²⁹⁰ من سائر الأعضاء وذلك أنّه ليس شيء من هذا بعجب. ولا كيف تعرض الحمّى والنافض لبعض الناس في حال واحدة من قبل أنّه إذا كثر في البدن الخلط البارد

---

277. في هؤلاء أيضا: أيضا في هؤلاء BE

278. يعرض الألم والوجع لمن g ἀλγοῦσιν

279. قرّ: فرط P برد BCE

280. بالاصطلاء: om. g

281. وكثير ممّن أصابه ذلك: πολλοί γε αὐτῶν g

282. بدنه: τὰς χεῖρας g

283. يقدم: يقدر A²LP يقدم...أن يدفع ذلك g ἔτ' ἀπιστεῖ

284. السبب في الألم والوجع: g ὀδύνης αἰτίαν

285. المزاج المختلف: مزاج مختلف BCE

286. أو يتعجّب: أو يعجب A¹P أو تعجب L

287. ورم: g φλεγμονῆς

288. المعى الذي يسمّى قولون: το κόλον g

289. الأنثيين: ὀδόντας g BCEL الأسنان τοὺς ὄρχεις corr. g (following Ḥunayn)

290. غيرها: غيرهما LP

البلغمي الذي [291] يشبهه [292] فركساغورس بالزجاج والخلط [293] الحارّ الذي من جنس الصفراء [294] حتّى يغلبا [295] معا على البدن ويتحركا [296] فيه [297] وخاصّة [298] في الأعضاء [299] الحسّاسة فليس بعجب أن يحسّ من تلك حاله بالأمرين جميعا. فإنّك إن [300] عمدت إلى إنسان فأقمته في شمس حارّة ثمّ رششت عليه ماء باردا فليس [301] من المحال أن يحسّ معا [302] بحرارة الشمس وبرد الماء إلاّ أنّ هذين جميعا في [303] صاحب هذه الحال إنّما تناله [304] من خارج ويناله أيضا كلّ واحد منهما في أجزاء من بدنه عظيمة.

٢. وأمّا الحمّى التي يسمّيها اليونانيون انفياليس [305] فالذي [306] يناله من الحرّ والبرد إنّما

---

291. الذي يشبهه فركساغورس بالزجاج: الشبيه بالزجاج BCE الذي يشبه الزجاج L

292. يشبهه: καλεῖ g

293. والخلط الحارّ الذي من جنس المرار: καὶ ὁ πικρόχολος καὶ θερμὸς g

294. الصفراء: المرار BCE

295. يغلبا معا على البدن: يغلبا عليه معا πλεονάζοιεν ἐν αὐτοῖς g BCE

296. ويتحركا فيه: ويتحركا في البدن BL ويتحركان في البدن E

297. فيه: om. g

298. وخاصّة: om. gP

299. الأعضاء الحسّاسة... لا تلحقها حمّى (٤): om. B

300. إن عمدت إلى إنسان فأقمته: εἰ στήσας ἄνθρωπον g

301. فليس من المحال أن يحسّ: ἀδύνατον αὐτῷ τὸ μὴ οὐχ...αἰσθάνεσται g

302. يحسّ: A¹ om. CE

303. في صاحب هذه الحال: om. g

304. تناله: ينالانه LP

305. انفياليس: A without punctuation امفياليس C انفياليس E انتياليس L انفيالوس P ἠπιάλους g

306. فالذي يناله من الحرّ والبرد إنّما يناله: om. g

يناله من داخل[307] ويناله أيضا كلّ واحد منهما في أجزاء بدنه الصغار حتّى[308] يكون الأوّل ليس[309] من بدنه أجزاء عظيمة ينالها البرد إلّا[310] إلى جانب كلّ واحد منها جزء عظيم يناله الحرّ ويكون الثاني ليس من بدنه جزء صغير يناله البرد إلّا وإلى جانبه جزء آخر صغير يناله الحرّ ولذلك صار[311] هذا الثاني يظنّ أنّه يحسّ في بدنه كلّه بالأمرين جميعا وذلك لمّا كان كلّ واحد من المبرد والمسخن مبثوثا في[312] أجزاء صغار جزء[313] بعد جزء ولا يكون بعدها في الصغر غاية لم يمكن أن يوجد جزء من هذه الأجزاء الصغار حسًّا فيه[314] واحد من البرد والحرّ دون الآخر.

٣. وبعض من يحمّ فقد[315] يعرض له في[316] أوّل أخذ الحمّى له في[317] كلّ نوبة من نوائبها أنّ[318] يحسّ معا بالبرد المفرط والحرّ المفرط لكنه ليس يحسّ كلّ واحد منهما

---

307. داخل: ويناله من خارج add. L

308. حتّى يكون الأوّل ليس من بدنه أجزاء عظيمة ينالها البرد إلّا إلى جانب كلّ واحد منها جزء عظيم يناله الحرّ ويكون الثاني ليس من بدنه جزء صغير يناله البرد إلّا وإلى جانبه جزء آخر صغير يناله الحرّ om. g

309. ليس: om. ALP

310. إلّا: om. ALP

311. صار هذا الثاني: om. g

312. في أجزاء صغار...ولا يكون بعدها في الصغر: g δι᾽ ἐλαχίστου

313. جزء بعد جزء: om. g

314. فيه واحد: A¹ في واحد A واحدا L

315. فقد يعرض له: om. g

316. في أوّل أخذ الحمّى له في كلّ نوبة من نوائبها: κατὰ μέντοι τὴν εἰσβολὴν τῶν παραξυσμῶν g

317. في كلّ نوبة من نوائبها: om. g

318. أن يحسّ معا بالبرد المفرط والحرّ المفرط: أن يحسّ معها بالبرد والنافض وبالعطش لا بل يحسّ بالبرد المفرط والحرّ المفرط L أن يحسّ معها بالبرد والنافض المفرط والحرّ المفرط P καὶ ῥιγῶσι καὶ πυρέττουσιν καὶ ἅμα ἀμφοτέρων αἰσθάνονται, ψύξεως ἀμέτρου καὶ θέρμης ὁμοῦ g

61

في الموضع الذي يحسّ فيه الآخر. لكن الذي يصيبه ذلك[319] يقدر أن يفرّق تفرقة بيّنة بين ما يسخن من أعضائه وبين ما يبرد منها وذلك أنّه يحسّ بالحرّ من داخل في نفس أحشائه ويحسّ بالبرد في جميع ما في ظاهر بدنه من الأعضاء. ومن الحمّى حمّى يسمّيها اليونانيون ليفورياس[320] لا[321] تزال دائما على هذه الحال وكذلك أيضا جنس من الحمّيات المحرقة قتّال. فالذي[322] يعرض في هذه الحمّيات في الأجزاء الكبار هو الذي يعرض في الحمّى التي يسمّيها اليونانيون انفياليس[323] في الأجزاء الصغار فإنّ سوء المزاج في[324] هذه الحمّيات أيضا مختلف. وهو أيضا مختلف في من يصيبه النافض من غير أن يلحقه الحمّى. وقليل ما يعرض هذا العارض إلاّ أنّه على[325] حال قد يعرض لبعض النساء وبعض الرجال. إلاّ أنّه لا محالة يجب أن يكون قد تقدّمه تدبير خفض أو يكون صاحبه قد أدمن مدّة طويلة الإكثار من الطعام المولّد خلطا[326] باردا نيئا[327] بلغميا بمنزلة[328] الخلط الشبيه بالزجاج ويشبه أن يكون هذا العارض لم يكن يعرض

---

319. ذلك: A¹

320. ليفورياس P انوري‍اس emendation eds.: ليثورياس B(؟) A without punctuation
<...وماس> سرب E(؟) سرب دباس C ليغورياس g λειπυρίαι P

321. لا تزال...انفيالس: om. L

322. فالذي...انفيالس: P¹

323. انفياليس: A without punctuation امفياليس(؟) C امفياروس(؟) E افيالس P g ἠπιάλοις

324. في هذه الحمّيات: τῶν συνθέτων πυρετῶν g

325. على حال: <κατα την διαθεσιν> add. g (following Ḥunayn)

326. خلطا: ἀργὸς add. g

327. نيئا: om. EL

328. بمنزلة الخلط الشبيه بالزجاج: بمنزلة الذي يشبهه بعض اليونانيون بالزجاج L بمنزلة الخلط الذي يشبهه فركساعورس بالزجاج P g ὁποῖόν τινα καὶ Πραξαγόρας ἡγήσατο τὸν ὑαλῶδη

لأحد³²⁹ في المتقدّم أصلا³³⁰ لأنّه لم يكن أحد من الناس يتدبّر بهذا التدبير من الخفض والإكثار من الطعام. ولذلك نجد القدماء³³¹ من الأطبّاء يحكمون بأنّه لا بدّ من أن يلحق النافض حمّى. إلّا أنّا نحن قد رأينا كثيرا ورأى غيرنا من الحدث من الأطبّاء نافضا قد حدثت لم يلحقها حمّى.

٤. وأمّا³³² الحمّى التي يسمّيها اليونانيون انفياليس³³³ فهي مركّبة من هذا سوء المزاج الذي³³⁴ تحدث عنه النافض التي لا تلحقها حمّى ومن³³⁵ سوء المزاج الذي يكون في³³⁶ الحمّى. ومتى³³⁷ قلت انفياليس³³⁸ فإنّما³³⁹ أعني بهذا الاسم الحمّى التي يعرض فيها الأمران جميعا دائما. وأمّا الحمّى التي يتقدّمها النافض ثمّ يلحقها الصالب كالذي يعرض في الغبّ³⁴⁰ والربع فلست أسمّيها انفياليس.³⁴¹ فقد³⁴² بان أنّ

---

329. لأحد: om. AL

330. أصلا: οὕτως g

331. القدماء من الأطبّاء: الحكماء BCE

332. وأمّا الحمّى التي يسمّيها اليونانيون انفياليس هي مركّبة: σύνθετος δ' οὖν ἐστιν g

333. انفياليس: A without punctuation انثيالس B امفياليس C انفياليس E انتياليس L افيالوس P

334. الذي تحدث عنه النافض التي لا تلحقها حمّى: om. g

335. ومن سوء المزاج الذي يكون في الحمّى: καὶ προσέτι τῆς τῶν πυρεττόντων g

336. في: عنه BC?E

337. ومتى: οὕτω g

338. انفياليس: انثيالس B انقياليس L انفيالوس P

339. فإنّما أعني بهذا الاسم: om. g

340. الغبّ: الحمّى الغبّ P

341. انفياليس: A without punctuation امفياليس C انفياليس E انثيالس B انتبالس L انبيالوس P
τὸν πυρετὸν ἐκεῖνον g

342. فقد بان: ὥστε g

الحمّى [343] التي تسمّى انفياليس [344] مركّبة من ضربين من سوء المزاج مختلفين وكذلك الحال في سائر الحمّيات خلا الحمّيات [345] الثابتة.

(Ch. 9)

١. وكذلك أيضا [346] الأمراض التي تخصّ واحدا من الأعضاء مع ورم فكلّها [347] يكون عن سوء مزاج مختلف بمنزلة الورم [348] الحارّ [349] المعروف بفلغموني والورم [350] الذي يعرف بالسرطان والورم [351] الذي يعرف بالحمرة [352] والبثر [353] الذي يعرف بالنملة والورم [354] المعروف بالترهّل [355] والورم [356] المعروف بالأكلة الذي يسمّيه اليونانيون

---

343. الحمّى التي تسمّى انفياليس g: ὁ ἤπιαλος

344. انفياليس: A without punctuation انفياليس E انثياليس B امفياليس C انتياليس L انبيالوس P

345. الحمّيات الثابتة وكذلك أيضا الأمراض التي تخصّ واحدا: خلا الحمّيات L

346. أيضا: om. BE

347. فكلّها: om P فكلّها يكون عن سوء مزاج مختلف: om. BCE

348. بمنزلة الورم الحارّ المعروف بفلغموني: παραπλησίως τῇ φλεγμονῇ g

349. الحارّ: A¹ الحادث A

350. والورم الذي يعرف بالسرطان: والمعروف بالسرطان καρκίνος g BCEP

351. والورم الذي يعرف بالحمرة: ἐρυσίπελας g والورم الذي يعرف بالحمرة والبثر الذي يعرف بالنملة: والبثر المعروف بالنملة والورم الذي يعرف بالحمرة B والمعروف بالنملة والبثر الذي يعرف بالحمرة CE والمعروف بالنملة والبثر الذي يعرف بالخمر الصيفي P

352. بالحمرة: ἄνθραξ add. g

353. والبثر الذي يعرف بالنملة: ἕρπης g

354. والورم المعروف بالترهّل: οἴδημα g

355. بالترهّل: φαγέδαινα add. g

356. والورم المعروف: والمعروف BEP والورم المعروف بالأكلة الذي يسمّيه اليونانيون عنقرانا: γάγγραινα g

غنغرينا 357 وهو 358 العارض مع سلوك العضو في طريق الموت. فإنّه يعمّ جميع هذه الأمراض أنّها 359 إنّما تحدث عن رطوبة تنصبّ إلى 360 بعض الأعضاء وتختلف فإنّ بعضها يحدث عن خلط بلغمي وبعضها يحدث عن خلط 361 من 362 جنس المرار الأصفر وبعضها 363 يحدث 364 عن خلط سوداوي وبعضها يحدث 365 عن الدم. 366 والذي يحدث منها عن الدم فبعضها يحدث عن دم حارّ رقيق يغلي وبعضها 367 يحدث عن دم بارد غليظ وبعضها 369 يحدث عن دم حاله حال أخرى. فإنّي سأستقصي تلخيص أصناف هذه العلل في كتاب غير هذا.

٢. وأمّا في هذا الكتاب فأكتفي بأن أقول 370 كيف كانت الحال 371 في الرطوبة التي 372 تنصبّ إلى العضو وأحداثها ما تحدث من كلّ واحد من العلل التي ذكرنا أنّها تكون على

---

357. غنغرينا emendation eds. : عنعرابا AP without punctuation L عنفرايا BE

358. وهو العارض مع سلوك العضو في طريق الموت: om. g

359. أنّها: A¹

360. إلى بعض الأعضاء: om. g

361. خلط من P om

362. من جنس المرار الأصفر: g χολώδους

363. وبعضها يحدث عن خلط سوداوي: om P

364. يحدث عن خلط سوداوي: عن الأسود BCE

365. يحدث: om. BCEg

366. الدم. والذي يحدث منها عن الدم فبعضها يحدث عن: om P

367. والذي يحدث منها عن الدم فبعضها يحدث عن دم: g ἤτοι

368. وبعضها يحدث عن دم: g ἤ

369. وبعضها يحدث عن دم حاله حال أخرى: g ἤ πως ἄλλως διακειμένου γίγνεσθαι

370. أقول: بأن أقتصر أن أقول L

371. الحال في: om. g

372. التي تنصبّ إلى العضو: om. g

قياس ما [373] وصفنا في ما تقدّم من حدوث الورم [374] المسمّى فلغموني عن الخلط الحارّ الدموي وأنّ كلّ واحد من الأعضاء المتشابهة الأجزاء البسيطة [375] الأوّل إذا [376] غلبت تلك الرطوبة عليه أدّته [377] إلى سوء المزاج [378] المختلف وذلك أنّه من [379] ظاهره إمّا أن يسخن وإمّا أن يبرد وإمّا أن يجفّ وإمّا أن يرطب بحسب ما عليه حال [380] تلك الرطوبة التي [381] تجاوره وباطنه [382] لم يصر [383] بعد إلى مثل تلك حال بعينها. فإن استحال كلّه عن آخره ظاهره [384] وباطنه فصار كلّه بحال واحدة سكن عنه على المكان الوجع أصلا إلّا أنّ علّته عند ذلك تكون أغلظ [385] وأعسر. ومن تقدّم فعلم ما وصفت من هذا فهو

---

373. ما وصفنا في ما تقدّم: فيما ذكرنا أنّها تكون P

374. الورم المسمّى فلغموني: g φλεγμονήν

375. البسيطة الأوّل: الأوّلي البسيطة P

376. إذا غلبت تلك الرطوبة عليه: g ὑπὸ τοῦ ῥεύματος τοῦδε διατιθέμενον

377. أدّته: آل أمره أيضا L آل أمره P دال (= آل) أمر ‹...› إلى سوء من A[1]

378. المزاج المختلف: مزاج مختلف AP

379. من ظاهره: بيّن ظاهر AB

380. حال: om. BCE

381. التي تجاوزه: om. g

382. وباطنه: وتباطنه A وباطنه لم يصر بعد إلى مثل تلك حال بعينها: μέχρι δὲ τοῦ βάθους μήπω διακείμενον ὁμοίως g

383. يصر: P[2] يصل P

384. ظاهره وباطنه فصار كلّه بحال واحدة: om. g

385. أغلظ: وأيبس add. BE أغلظ وأعسر: om. E وأيبس C وأيبس g χαλεπωτέρα

عندي[386] كاف[387] حتّى[388] يفهم به كتابي في الأدوية[389] ثمّ من بعده كتابي في حيلة البرء.

تمّ[390] كتاب[391] جالينوس في سوء المزاج المختلف والحمد[392] للّه على عونه وأحسانه وصلّى اللّه على محمد خاتم أنبياه وسلّم

---

386. عندي: om. BCE

387. كاف: له add P

388. حتّى يفهم به: τοῖς μέλλουσι...ἀκολουθήσειν g

389. الأدوية: المفردة add. A

390. تمّ...وسلّم: تمّت المقالة الرابعة من كتاب جالينوس في المزاج التي يذكر فيها سوء المزاج المختلف نقل حنين بن اسحق تفصيل أحمد بن محمّد المعروف بابن الأشعث وللّه الحمد P

391. كتاب: مقالة C كتاب جالينوس في سوء المزاج المختلف: om. L

392. والحمد للّه على عونه وأحسانه وصلّى اللّه على محمّد خاتم أنبياه وسلّم: والحمد للّه كثيرا صلّى اللّه على محمّد وعلى آله B نقل حنين بن اسحاق بحمد اللّه وعونه وصلّي اللّه على <...> E والحمد للّه وحده والصلوة والصلوة على محمّد وأله L

67

B. The Arabic–English Translation

We provide here a literal English translation of Ḥunayn's text that tries to maintain the structure and order of the original as far as reasonably possible, in order to help the modern reader move more easily between the Arabic text and the Latin translation made from it in the twelfth century. Words and phrases in angle brackets have been supplied editorially to bring out the meaning of the text; those in square brackets provide alternative wording or phraseology.

In the name of God, the Merciful, the Compassionate.

Treatise on the anomalous dyscrasia by Galen. Translated by Ḥunayn ibn Isḥaq.

(Chap. 1).

1. Says Galen: An[1] anomalous dyscrasia may occur in the entire body of the animal, like the one that occurs to it in the kind of dropsy known as "<dropsy> of the flesh," or in the fever during which the patient suffers from heat and cold at the same time which is called "'NPY'LYS" [= *epialos*][2] by the Greeks, and in most other fevers except for the fever known as "hectic fever" which is called "'QṬYQWS" [= *hektikos*][3] in Greek.

2. An anomalous dyscrasia may also occur in any part of the body, whatever part it is, when it is affected by a swelling, that[4] is a phlegmatic swelling, or[5] is affected by a hot sanguine swelling which is known as "PLĠMWNY" [= *phlegmonē*],[6] or <the affection> reaches a degree where <the part of the body> starts to decay and die off. This is the swelling which the Greeks know as "ĠNĠRYN'" [= *gangraina*].[7] It may also be affected by another swelling known as "erysipelas" and <yet> another swelling known as "cancer." Elephantiasis also belongs to these kinds <of swellings>, likewise canker[8] and

---

[1]"An anomalous dyscrasia . . . or is affected by a hot sanguine swelling"; cf. Maimonides, *Medical Aphorisms*, Treatises 1–5, parallel Arabic–English edition ed., transl., and annot. G. Bos (Provo: Brigham Young University Press, 2004), 3.27, 39–40: "A varying bad temperament can occur in the whole body, as [in the case of] dropsy and in the case of all the fevers except for hectic fever. It can also occur in one part of the body, as [in the case of] a swelling of the flesh—that is, a phlegmatic swelling. 2. An anomalous dyscrasy may also occur in any part of the body, whatever part it is, when it is affected by a swelling, that is a phlegmatic swelling, or is affected by a hot sanguine swelling. Any swelling of this type contains a varying bad temperament."

[2]That is, ἠπίαλος; see Galen, K7:733, l.3; GN 142, l.4. Note that the Arabic term is actually a transcription of the dat. plur. ἠπιάλοις. This and a number of other Arabic terms for pathological conditions have been transcribed in capital letters, without vocalization; since we no longer have any idea how these words were pronounced, we have thought it misleading to offer vocalized forms for them.

[3]That is, ἑκτικός; see Galen, K7:733, l.4; GN 142, l.5.

[4]"That is a phlegmatic swelling": om. Galen.

[5]"Or is affected by a hot sanguine swelling which is known as 'PLĠMWNY' [= *phlegmonē*]": "or is affected by a sanguine swelling" MSS **BE.**

[6]That is, φλεγμονή (hot swelling); cf. Galen, K7:733, l.6; GN 142, l.5: φλεγμαῖνον.

[7]That is, γάγγραινα (gangrene); cf. Galen, K7:733, l.6: γαγγραινόμενον; GN 142, l.5: γαγγραινουμενον.

[8]That is, φαγέδαινα (cancerous sore, canker); Galen, K7:733, l.7; GN 142, l.8.

shingles.[9] However, all these afflictions come with a residue streaming[10] to the affected part. There is another kind of anomalous dyscrasia whereby no residue streams to the <affected> part but merely the quality <of that part> changes, <namely> when it is overcome by the heat of the sun or by cold or by immoderate exercise or by[11] immoderate idleness and restfulness or by other similar <afflictions>. An anomalous dyscrasia may also occur in our body because of that which affects it from the outside, when these things heat or cool or dry or moisten. These are the four kinds of <anomalous> dyscrasia that are simple, noncompound, as I explained in my book *On Temperaments*.

3. There are also four other compound kinds <of anomalous dyscrasia>, which occur when the body is both hot and moist, or hot and dry, or cold and moist, or cold and dry. It is clear that these kinds of anomalous dyscrasia differ from the uniform kinds of anomalous dyscrasia, because <these kinds> do not exist <in like manner>[12] in all the parts of the body that has a corrupt temperament. My intention in this treatise is to inform <you> how all the different kinds of anomalous dyscrasia originate. In order that my words in this matter will be clear I must mention to you the disposition of all the parts of the body. I will begin with the largest <parts>, which are known <even> to those who do not have medical knowledge, for there is no one who forgets [does not know] what the arms and legs and belly and chest and head are.

(Chap. 2)

1. Let us take one part of the body and divide it into the most immediate parts it is composed of: for instance, the leg we divide into thigh, lower leg, and foot, and the arm into upper arm, forearm, and hand, and the hand again into the parts that are peculiar to it, namely wrist, metacarpus, and fingers, and the fingers again into the specific parts they are composed of, namely bones, cartilages, ligaments, nerves, pulsating and nonpulsating vessels, membranes, flesh, tendons, nails, skin, and fat.

2. These last-mentioned parts cannot be divided further into other <parts>, but they are homoiomerous, primary parts, except for the pulsating and nonpulsating vessels, since these are composed from fibers and membranes, as I said in my book *On Anatomical Procedures*. I also mentioned in that book that there are many spaces between the primary, homoiomerous parts, and that most and the largest of them are between the composite, instrumental parts. Sometimes we find such spaces in one <particular> homoiomerous part, as can be found in bones and in the skin.[13] However, the soft parts of the body cover[14] each other so that the spaces between them are hidden from the eye. But in the case of the hard and dry parts of the body one can discern the spaces and gaps with the senses, as we may find <them> in the marrow of the bones. The cavities of the bone marrow have by nature a thick and white fluid to feed them, prepared by the bones. As for the pores in the skin, I have explained how they come to be in my book

---

[9]"Shingles" (i.e., ἕρπης); see Galen, K7:733, l.8; GN 142, l.8 (trans. GN: *"herpes"*).

[10]Om. Galen.

[11]"By immoderate idleness and restfulness"; cf. Galen, trans. GN 143: "having been completely inactive." The term "completely" (Gr. πάντως) is an emendation by GN following Ḥunayn's تجاوزان مقدار القصد (immoderate).

[12]"In like manner": cf. Galen, K7:734, l. 12; GN 144, l.7: ὡσαύτως.

[13]Galen adds: "about all this has been told in *On Anatomical Procedures*" (trans. editors); "And of all of them, in the Anatomical Procedures, have been told" (trans. GN 147).

[14]Cf. Galen, trans. GN 147: "colliding into each other."

On Temperaments. It was necessary to mention these things so that my following words will be clear.

3. Now I have to address <the matter of> the anomalous dyscrasia, and to describe its nature and in how many ways it occurs. I have said above that the parts of the body that are affected by an anomalous dyscrasia do not have <just> one humoral composition. For that is something that is common to and shared by every anomalous dyscrasia. Its different kinds follow the nature of the affected <parts>[15], for the occurrence of an anomalous dyscrasia in the mere [simple] flesh is different from that in the muscle, on the whole. Every[16] single <anomalous dyscrasia> is different from the others.

(Chap. 3)

1. For instance, when a hot residue[17] streams to a muscle, then the vessels there,[18] that is the largest pulsating and nonpulsating ones, are first of all filled and stretch, then the vessels which are smaller, and this continues until <the residue> reaches the smallest vessels. And when[19] that residue enters into those vessels and they can no longer contain it, part of it emerges from the openings of those vessels, and part of it exudes and streams forth from[20] the very body of those vessels. When this is the case, the spaces between the first parts are filled with that residue to such a degree that it happens to them that from every side they become hot and moist through the surrounding moisture. With "first parts" in this place I mean the nerves, ligaments, tunics, and flesh, and prior to these the pulsating and nonpulsating vessels themselves, which are first of all and above all affected by pain in various ways. This happens because the residue which is inside them heats them, stretches them, and causes them to split, while the residue that is outside them heats them, pushes[21] against them, puts pressure on them, and bears them down. As for the other parts, some of them are merely hurt by the heat, others are hurt by the pressure, and yet others are hurt by both.

2. This illness is called "PLĠMWNY" [= *phlegmonē*] by the Greeks; it is an inflamed swelling, and it is an anomalous dyscrasia occurring in a muscle. For the blood in <the muscle> will have become hot and been affected by something similar to cooking; then through its heat the bodies[22] of the pulsating and nonpulsating vessels become hot first of all and above all, and then <it will heat> everything over which it flows until it immerses them. And this must necessarily lead to one of two <things>[23]: either the residue which streams to a muscle overpowers it and corrupts <the part> it overpowers, or the residue is overpowered and the muscle returns to its natural condition. Let it first

---

[15]Lit. "bodies"; see Galen, K7:736, l. 12. Cf. GN 149, l.1: σώματα; ibid., n. 4: "Galen sometimes uses the Greek word for body (σῶμα) for referring to parts and even to humours."

[16]"Every single <anomalous dyscrasia> is different from the others": om. Galen.

[17]Cf. Galen, trans. GN 149: "flux," adding in n. 8: "That is, the blood."

[18]"There": om. Galen.

[19]"And when that residue enters into those vessels"; cf. MSS BCE: "when that residue abounds in those vessels"; cf. Galen, trans. GN 149: "when the flow gets violently constricted."

[20]"From the very body": Galen (K7:737, l. 2) reads "through the tunics"; and Galen (GN trans. 149): "through the coats that move it."

[21]"Pushes against them, puts pressure on them": cf. Galen, trans. GN 149: "[they get] compressed."

[22]Cf. Galen, trans. GN 151: "coats."

[23]Arab. *ḥallatayn*; cf. G.W.F. Freytag, *Lexicon Arabico-Latinum*, 2 vols. (Halle, 1830–1837), 1: 510, s.v. *ḥalla*: "necessitas, res necessaria"; cf. MSS LP: "*ḥālatayn*" (conditions).

be posited that the residue is overpowered, since it is more appropriate to begin with what is better. I say that the healing should take place in one of two ways: either that the whole moisture [residue] that streamed to the muscle is dissolved, or that it is concocted. The best healing is the one through dissolution. Coction is necessarily followed by two things: one is the generation of pus, and the other is its concentration [collection].[24] A concentration sometimes occurs in the largest hollow space that is nearest to the <affected> spot and is the most unimportant [least dangerous], and this is the best <kind of> concentration; and sometimes <the concentration> occurs in the largest nearest hollow space, but that hollow space is quite important; or it occurs in a hollow space that is of little significance and is not the largest and not near.

3. If the [concentration] happens in the region of the stomach, the most laudable concentration is that which occurs in the empty space inside [the stomach]; in[25] most cases, pus is discharged therein [as well]. But the concentration into that which is below the peritoneum is bad. If it happens in the region of the brain, and the concentration occurs in its anterior ventricles, it is laudable; [but] the concentration in the meninges and the posterior ventricle of the brain is reprehensible and bad. As to the abscesses[26] forming in the region of the ribs, their eruption is in the hollow space of the chest, and abscesses in the muscles erupt [beneath] the skin. Abscesses occurring in the viscera erupt either in the vessels there, <that is,> the pulsating and nonpulsating <vessels>, or <in> the membrane that surrounds them and is to them like a skin.

4. If the residue overpowers the parts of the body, the domination of the anomalous dyscrasia over them will clearly have the effect that their activity is abolished and corrupted in the course of time. The pain will begin to ease in them when they become similar to that which transforms and transmutes them. For parts of the body are not affected by pain when the change of their temperament has been completed, but during the transmutation, as the marvelous Hippocrates explained when he said that pains only occur in parts of the body during[27] their transmutation and corruption and departure from their natures.[28] Every single part of the body transmutes from its nature and is corrupted because it is heated or cooled or dried or moistened or its continuity is dissolved. And in an anomalous dyscrasia <this is especially the case>, because the <affected> part of the body is extremely heated or cooled, and this is because these two qualities have the strongest effect. And then it may also happen because[29] the part of the body is dried or moistened. And[30] pain occurs because of the lack of a dry substance during hunger and because of a lack of moist substance during thirst. And[31] when the part of the body is affected by something that stings or corrodes or stretches or squeezes or tears, pain[32] occurs because the continuity is dissolved.

---

[24]"Concentration" (*ğam'*); cf. Galen, trans. GN 151: "deposit."

[25]Cf. ibid.: "towards which most of them" (i.e., of the deposits) "break away together."

[26]"Abscesses" (*khurāğāt*): cf. ibid.: "deposits."

[27]"During . . . natures"; cf. Galen, trans. GN 153: "in those (parts) being changed and destroyed in their nature."

[28]Cf. Hippocrates, *Places in Man* 42, ed. and trans. P. Potter (Cambridge, MA: Loeb Classical Library, 1995), 84–85: "For in each thing that is altered with respect to its nature and destroyed, pains arise."

[29]"Because the part of the body is dried or moistened": cf. Galen, trans. GN 153: "because of getting dry and humid."

[30]"And pain occurs": om. Galen.

[31]"And . . . stings"; cf. Galen, trans. GN 153: "when getting wounded."

[32]"Pain occurs": om. Galen.

(Chap. 4)

1. And when the heat of the blood in the swollen member is quiet,[33] and the blood contained in the whole body is of a balanced temperament, it hardly ever happens that it [i.e., the blood] will be heated through the heat of the affected part. But[34] when the heat of the blood that is in the swollen part is a strong heat that heats the body through the strength of its boiling, or when the blood contained in the entire body is dominated by bile, it will not take long before all of it will be exceedingly hot, and this will be all the more likely when the two things come together, <namely> that the blood in the swollen part is very hot, and that the bile dominates the blood that is in the body.

2. The first blood to be heated until it becomes exceedingly hot is that in the pulsating vessels, because it is by nature hotter and closer to the nature of spirit; then after that, the blood that is in the nonpulsating vessels. If the swollen part is close to one of the intestines abounding in blood, the heat will flee rapidly to the blood contained in the entire body. In short, that which is heated first with regard to everything is that which changes fast or is hot by nature. The same holds good for that which gets cold first, because that which gets cold is that which is quick to change or which is cold by nature. And spirit is the fastest of all things in the body to change, because it is the[35] finest and thinnest. The hottest <thing> in[36] the body is the yellow bile and the coldest the phlegm. Of the other humors, blood is hot<test> after yellow bile, and black bile is cold<est> after phlegm. Yellow bile is changed easily and[37] quickly by everything that acts on it. Black bile is changed <only> by[38] exertion and strain. In short, everything that is fine[39] and thin is quick to be changed, and[40] everything that is thick and gross is slow to be changed.

3. Hence the change in swellings necessarily varies greatly according to the diversity of the disposition of the bodies.[41] In the first place, because the humor from which the swelling arises is either hotter or less hot. After that, because its putrefaction is according to its nature, and[42] according to the excess or paucity of its tightness [constrictedness]. For something that does not have perspiration[43] putrefies more quickly, and this can be found in all external things. And if it happens with this that its temperament is hot and moist, this[44] will contribute greatly to the rapidity of its putrefaction. Moreover, the part of the body in which the swelling occurs will either be close to the intestines which abound in blood or far from them, for yellow bile, black bile, phlegm, or ventosity are dominant over all the blood, and[45] all these dispositions vary to a smaller or larger extent. Hence, the alteration<s> necessarily vary very much, when one <humor> is compared to another or when it is compared to itself.

---

[33]"Quiet"; cf. Galen, trans. GN 153: "adequate."

[34]"But . . . boiling"; cf. ibid.: "However, if it boiled harder."

[35]"Is the finest and thinnest"; cf. Galen, trans. GN 155: "is also thinnest."

[36]"In the body"; cf. ibid.: "by nature."

[37]"And quickly": om. Galen.

[38]"By exertion and strain"; cf. Galen, trans. GN 155: "with difficulty."

[39]"Fine and thin"; cf. ibid.: "formed by thin parts."

[40]"And everything that is thick and gross"; cf. ibid.: "whereas everything formed by thick parts."

[41]"Bodies"; cf. ibid.: "humours"; ibid., n. 16: "In Greek, 'bodies.'"

[42]"And according to": cf. ibid.: "not the least insignificant."

[43]"Perspiration" (Arab. *tanaffus*); lit. "breath." In the sense of perspiration, Arab. *tanaffus* is a semantic borrowing from Greek διαπνοή.

[44]"This will contribute greatly to the rapidity of its putrefaction"; cf. Galen, trans. GN 155: "then even much more so."

[45]"And. . .extent"; cf. ibid.: "and all of that to a more or lesser extent."

(Chap. 5)

1. And[46] all these things are the cause of an anomalous dyscrasia. This is because the heat is most dominating over the blood which is in the[47] swollen part of the body, then, after that, over the blood which is in the[48] intestines, and especially[49] over the blood which is in the heart, and, of that, especially that which is in its left ventricle. For if you approach this ventricle of the heart, while the animal is still alive and is not yet affected by fever, and you put your finger into it, as I have described in my book *On Anatomical Procedures*, you will feel the strongest heat there is. Therefore, it is not farfetched, when the whole body has been heated by an unnatural heat, that that ventricle of the heart especially should reach the highest degree of heat. Among[50] those things that contribute to this is that the blood therein is the thinnest and closest to the nature of spirit, and that it moves with a constant motion.

2. Moreover, in these types of fever one finds that the heat has overwhelmed all the blood, and that it [i.e., the blood] has firmly[51] accepted the unnatural heat that originated from the putrefaction of the humors. The temperament of the bodies [membranes][52] of the pulsating vessels and other bodies that are nearby and surround them is not found to be altered completely, but it is still changing and altering towards[53] heat. And if this were to continue for a long time in them, they would come to the point that they would be fundamentally dominated and changed <by the heat>, so that then they do not fall under the definition of that which is being heated but under the definition of that which has fully attained an unnatural heat. The limit of change in any of the parts of the body is the harm to its functioning. The total range [latitude] from the beginning of the matter [i.e., the heating of a part] until it finally reaches this limit [i.e., when the functioning of a part is harmed] is the way [process] that leads to the unnatural disposition—mixed,[54] combined, <and> in the middle between two opposites, that is, between the disposition that is truly natural and the disposition that is fundamentally unnatural. During this entire period of time, there will be in the body that is heated a measure of pain <analogous> to the alteration which it undergoes.

3. When all the main[55] parts of the body are fully[56] and perfectly heated, that fever is called "'QṬYQWS" [= *hektikos*], which means fixed, and this because it does not only exist in moistures and in spirit but also in bodies that have firmness. And[57] there is neither suffering nor pain with this fever, and the patient thinks that there is no fever in him at all because he does not feel its heat, since all the parts of his body have become hot equally,[58] in like manner. Concerning this matter natural philosophers agree, in their study of the matter of sensation, that there is no sensation except through alteration, and

---

[46]"And ... dyscrasia": cf. Galen, trans. GN 157: "All these anomalous *dyskrasias* of the body happen."
[47]"The swollen part of the body"; cf. ibid.: "inflammation."
[48]"The intestines"; cf. ibid.: "the rest of the viscera."
[49]"Especially": om. Galen.
[50]"Among those things that contribute to this"; cf. Galen, trans. GN 157: "for in fact."
[51]"Firmly": om. Galen.
[52]"Membranes"; cf. Galen, trans. GN 157: "coats."
[53]"Towards heat"; cf. ibid.: "as they are becoming heated."
[54]"Mixed"; cf. ibid.: "like something mixed."
[55]"Main": cf. Galen, trans. GN 159: "solid."
[56]"Fully and perfectly"; cf. ibid.: "completely."
[57]"And there is neither suffering nor pain with this fever"; cf. ibid.: "It is painless."
[58]"Equally, in like manner"; cf. ibid.: "in a similar way."

that there is no suffering[59] or pain in that in which the alteration has already been completed. For this reason there is no suffering or pain with any[60] fever of this kind—which we called hectic shortly before—and the patient does not feel it at all, and this is because the disposition of the parts of his body is not one in which some of them act and others are acted upon, since all of them are of a single disposition and their temperament has become one and the same.

(Chap. 6)

1. And even though one of them is hotter and the other colder, the excess heat of the hotter part over the colder part is not such that it will harm the adjacent part with its heat. For if this were the case, the parts of the body would harm each other even though they are of a natural disposition, for in that disposition also[61] the parts of the body differ in their temperament. For although the flesh is a hot part and the bone a cold one, their dissimilarity[62] and that of the other[63] similar parts does not bring pain or suffering, because of the[64] small measure of disparity between them in heat and cold. In the same way also the air which surrounds the bodies does not harm them as long as it is not altered by extreme heat or cold. But the kinds of diversity <of the air> in that which lies between excessive heat and excessive cold, in spite of their frequent occurrence and their obvious disparity,[65] are[66] being felt by the bodies without any harm.

2. According[67] to this argument the mind would almost incline to rely upon the statement that has been made, just as Hippocrates did in[68] one of his books, that all illnesses are simply wounds.[69] And this is so because a wound is simply a dissolution of continuity, and excessive heat and cold nearly dissolve the continuity. Severe heat does so because it dissolves and cuts the continuity of the substance over[70] which it dominates, and excessive cold because it contracts and compresses the substance over[71] which it dominates inwards until[72] something protrudes and emerges, and[73] what remains in it is squeezed and torn apart by it. And if someone should make this the limit regarding the excess of heat and cold, it[74] is proper <to say> that the suggestion that he is right is not farfetched. However, whether this is the limit in excess[75] or whether the limit is different, it is clear

---

[59]"Suffering or pain"; cf. ibid.: "pain."

[60]"Any fever of this kind—which we called hectic shortly before"; cf. ibid.: "the *hektikoi* fevers, all of them."

[61]"In that disposition also the parts of the body differ": cf. ibid.: "for they are in fact different in their *krasis*."

[62]"Dissimilarity"; cf. ibid.: "anomaly."

[63]"Other similar parts"; cf. ibid.: "all the others."

[64]"The small measure of disparity between them in heat and cold"; cf. Galen, trans. GN 159–161: "because of the moderation of the excess."

[65]"Disparity"; cf. Galen, trans. GN 161: "excess."

[66]"Are being felt by the bodies": cf. ibid.: "we perceive (them)."

[67]"According . . . made": cf. ibid.: "In fact, on those grounds, that reasoning is probably appropriate."

[68]"In one of his books": om. Galen.

[69]Cf. Hippocrates, On *Fractures* 31, trans. E. T. Withington, (Cambridge, MA: Loeb Classical Library, 1928), III, 171: "Unless one calls all maladies wounds, for this doctrine also has reasonableness, since they have affinity one to another in many ways."

[70]"Over which it dominates": om. Galen.

[71]"Over which it dominates": om. Galen.

[72]"Until something protrudes and emerges"; cf. Galen, trans. GN 161: "so that they squeeze out some matter."

[73]"And what remains in it is squeezed and torn apart by it"; cf. ibid.: "and crush some other."

[74]"It is proper <to say> that the suggestion that he is right is not farfetched"; cf. ibid.: "would seem not to err in his knowledge."

[75]"Excess"; cf. ibid.: "disproportion."

in <any> case that every excess[76] must be understood as in relation to something. This is so because not every body is affected in the same way by things which[77] have the same disposition of heat and cold.

3. For this reason, the humors that are in some animals are mutually fitting, while in other animals they are not [just] mutually incompatible, but also corrupting[78] and destroying <each other>, like man and viper, of which the saliva of each of them is fatal for the other. And thus when a man who has an empty stomach spits upon a scorpion, he kills it; but a man does not kill a man like himself when he bites him, nor a viper a viper, nor a serpent[79] a serpent, for the similar is fitting and beloved, but the opposite is hostile and harmful. Among the things which indicate this is that everything that grows and is nourished, only grows and is nourished by something that is similar to it and resembles it, while everything that is destroyed and annihilated, is only destroyed and annihilated by its opposite. For this reason, the preservation of health is achieved only by[80] things that are similar to and resemble healthy bodies; the[81] healing and the cure of illness are only achieved by contrary things. But to discuss this is beyond our current subject.

4. But someone who suffers from the hectic fever that[82] is inherent in the fixed substance of an animal will not feel it, while of all the other fevers, there is none that he will not feel; some[83] he will feel more and will suffer more harm from, others he will feel less. Some fevers are accompanied by rigor, and this symptom—that is, rigor—like many other symptoms, only arises from an anomalous dyscrasia. But I cannot explain in the current treatise how this symptom originates, unless I explain regarding the natural faculties how many there are, what sort of faculties they are, and[84] what it is of the property of each of them to effect. However, I will explain the matter of all the symptoms in my book *On the Causes and Symptoms <of Diseases>*.

(Chap. 7)

1. But let us return to the <different> kinds of an anomalous dyscrasia. I have already said in what preceded how fever arises from a[85] hot swelling, which is called "PLĠMWNY" [= *phlegmonē*], and that every swelling[86] of this kind and every fever, except the fever known as hectic, arises from illnesses in which the temperament is anomalous. And some fevers arise only from the putrefaction of humors, without a swelling,[87] for what putrefies is not only that which is obstructed and does not breathe [exhale]—and its putrefaction is very fast and very strong—but also many other things disposed to putrefaction. I will explain the matter of the disposition of what is disposed to putrefaction in another book.

---

[76]"Excess"; cf. ibid.: "disproportion."

[77]"Which have the same disposition": om. Galen.

[78]"Corrupting and destroying <each other>."; cf. Galen, trans. GN 161: "destructive."

[79]"A serpent": cf. ibid.: "asps"; ibid., n. 22: "Egyptian cobra."

[80]"By things that are similar to and resemble healthy bodies"; cf. Galen, trans. GN 163: "by means of similars."

[81]"The healing and the cure"; cf. ibid.: "the destruction."

[82]"That is inherent to the fixed substance of an animal"; cf. ibid.: "which has already seized the permanent condition of the animal."

[83]"Some . . . less"; cf. ibid.: "some are more, some are less painful to the patients."

[84]"And what it is of the property of each of them to effect"; cf. ibid.: "and what each of them does according to nature."

[85]"A hot swelling which is called 'phlegmonē': cf. ibid.: "inflammation."

[86]"Swelling of this kind": cf. ibid.: "inflammation."

[87]"Swelling"; cf. ibid.: "inflammation."

2. An anomalous dyscrasia may also occur in another way in the entire body; sometimes this happens when a hot vapor is congested in it, and sometimes when the heat increases because of immoderate exercise,[88] and sometimes because the blood is[89] hot and boils excessively due to anger, or it is heated excessively[90] because[91] it was for a long time in the hot sun. It is clear, in my opinion, that all these fevers that[92] arise from swellings, are, according to the strength of the efficient cause in the body and according to the disposition of every singular body, stronger in some bodies and weaker in other [bodies], while some bodies will not be feverish at all.

3. It is clear that a dyscrasia sometimes occurs[93] in the spirit alone and sometimes also passes beyond it to the humors; it is not less clear that all fevers, when they are prolonged, are joined by hectic fever. And from this statement it is <somehow>[94] evident that an anomalous dyscrasia sometimes originates from hot or cold moisture which flows to some part of the body, just as I have explained in[95] the case of bodily parts in which a swelling occurs. And sometimes[96] it does not happen like this, but <it happens> when the temperament of the body changes in quality. Some of the causes which alter <the temperament> arise from the body itself, and some affect <the body> from the outside. When the fever arises from putrefaction alone or from some swelling,[97] <in both cases> it hails from the body itself. But when the fever arises from the heat of the sun or from excessive exercise, then it comes from the outside. I shall speak about this more elaborately in my book *On the Causes of Symptoms*. And just as fever sometimes arises from the heat of the sun when the temperament of the body is altered, so it sometimes happens to some men from the severe cold of the air that the cold dominates so strongly over their entire body that some of them die. It is clear regarding all these men that suffering and pain befall them.

(Chap. 8)

1. Suffering and pain may also happen to someone when he is totally overcome by an intense cold <resulting> from a severe chill and then tries to warm his body quickly by[98] bringing it close to the fire. And[99] many of those to whom this happens feel a very strong pain in the roots of their nails when they suddenly bring their body[100] close to the fire. Who, therefore, since in this case he sees with his own eyes that the cause of the suffering and pain is nothing else but the anomalous dyscrasia, would[101] dare to reject such a thing in the case of pains that occur inside <the body>? Or would wonder how pain

---

[88]"Exercise"; Galen, trans. GN 165: "gymnastic exercises or bodily exertion."
[89]"Is hot and boils"; cf. ibid.: "boils."
[90]"Excessively"; Galen, trans. GN 165, adds: "from the exterior."
[91]"Because it was for a long time in the hot sun"; cf. ibid.: "by heat-stroke."
[92]"That arise from swellings"; cf. ibid.: "as upon inflammation it was told before."
[93]"Occurs in the spirit alone and sometimes also passes beyond it to the humors"; cf. ibid.: "sometimes just attacks that pneumatic substance, at times the humours as well."
[94]"Somehow"; ibid., for Greek πῶς.
[95]"In the case of bodily parts in which a swelling occurs"; cf. ibid.: "in the case of a part getting inflamed."
[96]"Sometimes"; cf. ibid.: "Many times."
[97]"Swelling"; cf. ibid.: "inflammations."
[98]"By bringing it close to the fire": om. Galen.
[99]"And many of those to whom this happens"; cf. Galen, trans. GN 167: "and many of them."
[100]"Body"; cf. ibid.: "hands."
[101]"Would dare to reject such a thing"; cf. ibid.: "is still incredulous."

often affects men without any swelling,[102] either in the[103] intestine called "colon," or in the testicles,[104] or in another part of the body? For nothing of this is amazing. Nor <is it amazing> how fever and rigor occur to some men at the same time, for if the cold phlegmatic humor which Praxagoras compares[105] to glass and the[106] hot humor which belongs to the same kind as yellow bile increase in the body until together they dominate[107] it and move[108] in it, especially in the sensitive organs, it is not amazing that someone who has this disposition senses both at once. For if you approach a man and let him stand in the hot sun, and then sprinkle cold water over him, it[109] is not impossible that he should feel the heat of the sun and the cold of the water together. But these two affect that[110] man in that situation only from the outside, and each of them affects him <only> in the large parts of his body.

2. But in the fever which the Greeks call "'NPY'LYS" [= *epialos*], heat and cold affect <the patient> from the inside, and each one of them may affect <the patient> <not only in the large parts> but also in the small parts of his body, to a degree[111] that in the first case [i.e., the patient affected in the large parts] there is no large part of his body affected by cold, unless next to it there is <another> large part affected by heat, and in the second case [i.e., the patient affected in the small parts] there is no small part affected by cold, unless next to it there is another small part affected by heat. Therefore, it happens in[112] the second case that <the patient> seems to sense both things together in his body. And this is because, as everything that cools and heats is scattered through small parts, one[113] after the other (and there is no limit to their smallness), it is impossible that there can be one part among these small ones that has a single sensation of cold and heat without the other <half of the hot/cold pair.>

3. And[114] sometimes it happens to some fever patients in the beginning of a fever attack, in every paroxysm, that they feel excessive cold and heat, but <they> do not feel each of them in the place where <they> feel the other. However, he to whom this occurs, can clearly distinguish between the parts which are heated and those which are cooled, for he feels the heat inside in his intestines themselves and feels the cold in every part that is at the outside of his body. And among the fevers, the fever which the Greeks call "LYPWRY'S" [= *leipurias*][115] is always of this disposition, and, likewise, a kind of ardent fever [that is] mortifying. And that which happens in these fevers in the larger

---

[102]"Swelling"; cf. ibid.: "inflammation."

[103]"The intestine called 'colon'"; cf. ibid.: "the colon."

[104]"Testicles"; cf. ibid. The Greek text actually has "teeth" (cf. MSS **BE**), but was emended by GN following Ḥunayn. See above, p. 8, where we discuss the emendation in more detail.

[105]"Compares to"; cf. ibid.: "calls."

[106]"The hot humor which belongs to the same kind as yellow bile"; cf. ibid.: "and the bitter, bilious and hot" (i.e., humor).

[107]"Dominate it"; cf. ibid.: "would . . . abound in them."

[108]"Move in it, especially in the sensitive organs"; cf. ibid.: "move through the sensitive bodies."

[109]"It is not impossible that he feels"; cf. ibid.: "(it is) impossible for him not to perceive."

[110]"That man in that situation": om. Galen.

[111]"To a degree . . . another small part affected by heat": om. Galen.

[112]"In the second case": om. Galen.

[113]"One after the other": om. Galen.

[114]"And . . . heat": cf. Galen, trans. GN 169: "Nevertheless, in the attack of paroxysms, some of the feverish patients suffer *rhîgos* and fever, and they perceive both of them: disproportionate cold and heat at the same time."

[115]That is, λειπυρίαι (malignant intermittent fevers); cf. Galen, K7:750, l.7; GN 168, l.7; trans.GN 169: "lipyriai."

parts is what happens in the smaller parts in the fever that the Greeks call "'NPY'LYS" [= *epialos*], for the dyscrasia that occurs in these[116] fevers is also anomalous; it is also anomalous in someone affected by rigor, without being followed by fever, but this symptom occurs rarely, although it can happen to some women and men in[117] <certain> conditions. But it is doubtless necessary that a regimen of ease of life preceded it, or that the patient applied himself for a long time to the consumption of a large quantity of food which produces a cold, crude, phlegmatic humor, like[118] the humor similar to glass. And it seems that this symptom did not happen to anyone at[119] all in the past, because no one followed this regimen of ease of life and the consumption of a large quantity of food. Therefore, we find that ancient physicians judge it to be necessary that rigor is followed by fever. But I personally have often seen, and other present-day physicians have seen, a rigor occurring without fever following it.

4. The fever which the Greeks call "'NPY'LYS" [= *epialos*] is composed from that dyscrasia from[120] which a rigor occurs that is not followed by fever and[121] from the dyscrasia that[122] occurs during fever. And[123] when I say "epialos," I mean by this term only that fever in which both always occur together. But the fever which is preceded by rigor and then followed by heat,[124] as happens in tertian and quartan fever, I do not call "'NPY'LYS" [= *epialos*]. It is thus clear that the[125] fever which is called "'NPY'LYS" [= *epialos*] is composed from two kinds of anomalous dyscrasia, and the same is the case with the remaining fevers, except for hectic fevers.

(Chap. 9)

1. And likewise the illnesses with a swelling that are peculiar to a single part of the body, for all of them originate from an anomalous dyscrasia, like the[126] hot swelling which is known as "PLĠMWNY" [= *phlegmonē*], and[127] the swelling known as "cancer," and[128] the swelling known as "erysipelas,"[129] and[130] the pustules known as "shingles," and[131] the swelling known as "tarahhul,"[132] and[133] the swelling known as "canker," which the

---

[116]"These fevers"; cf. ibid.: "the composed fevers."

[117]"In [certain] conditions"; cf. ibid.: "according to their condition" (missing in Kühn's Greek text, but added by GN following Ḥunayn's Arabic text).

[118]"Like the humor similar to glass"; cf. MS P: "which Praxagoras compared to glass"; Galen, trans. GN 169: "such a humour was first introduced by Praxagoras as vitreous."

[119]"At all"; cf. Galen, trans. GN 169; "this way."

[120]"From which a rigor occurs that is not followed by fever"; om. Galen.

[121]"And from the dyscrasia that occurs during fever"; cf. Galen, trans. GN 171: "and that of patients with fever."

[122]"That occurs during fever"; MSS **BE** translate: "from which fever arises."

[123]"And when I say 'epialos,' I mean by this term only that fever"; cf. Galen, trans. GN 171: "I call this way that fever."

[124]"Heat"; cf. ibid.: "fever."

[125]"The fever which is called "NPY'LYS' [= *epialos*]"; cf. ibid.: "*êpialos.*"

[126]"The hot swelling which is known as 'phlegmonē'"; cf. ibid.: "inflammation."

[127]"And the swelling known as 'cancer'"; cf. ibid.: "*cancer.*"

[128]"And the swelling known as 'erysipelas'"; cf. ibid.: "*erysipelas.*"

[129]"Erysipelas"; Galen, trans. GN 171, adds: "*anthrax*" (carbuncles).

[130]"And the pustules known as 'shingles'"; cf. ibid.: "*herpes.*"

[131]"And the swelling known as 'tarahhul'"; cf. ibid.: "swelling."

[132]"Tarahhul" (i.e. Arab. *tarahhul* [swelling]); cf. Galen, K7:751, 1.16; GN 170, 1.13: οἴδημα. Galen adds: φαγέδαινα, trans. GN: "*phagedaina.*"

[133]"And the swelling known as 'canker,' which the Greeks call Greeks call 'ĠNĠRYN'" [= *gangraina*]; cf. Galen, trans. GN 171: "*gangraina.*"

Greeks call "ĠNĠRYN'" [= *gangraina*], and[134] it occurs with the affected part proceeding on the path of death. For all these illnesses have in common that they originate from a moisture that streams to[135] a part of the body, and they differ because some of them originate from a phlegmatic humor, some from a[136] humor that is of the variety of yellow bile, and some of them from black <bile>, and some of them originate from blood. And[137] <of> those that originate from blood, some of them originate from hot, thin blood <and> boiling, and[138] some originate from cold, thick blood, and[139] some originate from blood that is of another disposition. I will give a detailed explanation of the different kinds of these diseases in another book.

2. In this book I am content with what I said about the[140] disposition of the moisture that[141] streams to a part of the body, and its afflictions, each of the mentioned illnesses which it causes which occurs in accordance with the earlier description of the occurrence of the swelling called "PLĠMWNY" [= *phlegmonē*] from a hot, bloody humor. And that every single homoiomerous part, simple and primary, when[142] that moisture dominates it, is brought to an anomalous dyscrasia; for at the outside, it is heated or cooled or dried or moistened according to the disposition of that moisture that[143] is close to it, while[144] its interior parts have not yet gotten into the same condition. If[145] both its exterior and interior were altered entirely and completely and it were made of one disposition totally, it would immediately and completely be relieved from pain, although the illness[146] would be more[147] hard and more difficult. If[148] someone has previous knowledge of this <account>, it will be sufficient for him, in my opinion, to understand my book *On Drugs*, and then, after that, my book *On the Therapeutic Method*.

This is the end of Galen's treatise *On the Anomalous Dyscrasia*. Thanks be to God for his help and his benefactions, may God bless Mohammed, the seal of the prophets, and grant him salvation.

---

[134]"And it occurs with the affected part proceeding on the path of death": om. Galen.

[135]"To a part of the body": om. Galen.

[136]"A humor that is of the variety of yellow bile"; cf. Galen, trans. GN 171: "the bilious . . . humor."

[137]"And <of> those that originate from blood, some of them originate from": om. Galen

[138]"And some originate from cold, thick blood"; cf. Galen, trans. GN 171: "or cold and thick."

[139]"And some originate from blood that is of another disposition"; cf. ibid.: "or in any other state."

[140]"The disposition of"; om. Galen.

[141]"That streams to a part of the body"; om. Galen.

[142]"When that moisture dominates it"; cf. Galen, trans. GN 173: "being affected by this flux."

[143]"That is close to it": om. Galen.

[144]"While . . . condition"; cf. Galen, trans. GN 173: "on the other hand, it will not yet be in an homogeneous state up to its depth"; ibid., n. 30: "i.e., completely."

[145]"If . . . totally"; cf. ibid.: "However, if the whole of it would wholly change and be altered."

[146]"Illness"; cf. ibid.: "condition."

[147]"More hard and more difficult"; cf. ibid.: "more difficult."

[148]"If . . . my book"; cf. ibid.: "That seems to me enough to be known in advance by those who are going to follow the thread of the study."

C. The Latin Text

SIGLA AND ABBREVIATIONS

A = Paris, BN n.a.l. 343, fols. 37–39v

H = London, British Library Harl. 5425, fols. 53v–56v

O = Vatican City, BAV Ottob. 1158, fols. 86v–88v

E = Erfurt, Amplon. F. 249, fols. 234rb–236vb

F = Paris, BN lat. 6865, fols. 152–154v

P = Cambridge, Peterhouse 33, fols. 23v–25

V = Vatican City, BAV Palat. Lat. 1095, fols. 51v–53v

Ar. = Arabic text, ed. G. Bos

Heb. = Hebrew text, ed. J Shatzmiller

add. = *addidit*

corr. = *correxit*

del. = *delevit*

eras. = *erasit*

illeg. = *illegibilis*

ins. = *inseruit*

m. r. = *manu recentiore*

mg. = *in margine*

om. = *omisit*

scr. = *scripsit*

scrips. = *scripsi*

tr. = *transtulit, transposuit*

Incipit liber Galieni De malitia complexionis diverse[1]

(**1.1**) Malitia[2] complexionis diverse quandoque in toto animalis corpore existit, sicut quod ei accidit inde[3] in specie ydropisis, notione[4] carnosa; et in febre in qua eger calorem et frigus in una invenit[5] dispositione, quam greci epialam[6] vocant, et in plerisque febribus aliis, preter febrem fixam dictam grece ethicam. (**1.2**) Malitia quoque[7] complexionis diverse in uno[8] membrorum erit,[9] quodcumque fuerit, cum in eo accidet mollicies que est apostema flegmaticum; aut fiet[10] in ipso apostema sanguineum calidum ad terminum tendens,[11] secundum quod erit[12] in semita corruptionis et mortis, et est apostema quod[13] greci nominant[14] cancrene; aut fit in ipso apostema aliud[15] erisipila[16] nominatum; et aliud apostema notione[17] cancer. Lepra quoque huius generis est, et similiter estiomenus[18] et formica. Omnes autem egritudines iste non evacuantur quin cum eis sit superfluitas membro infusa in quo fiunt.

Est tamen malitie[19] complexionis diverse modus alius absque infusione superfluitatis in membris, sed ipsorum qualitates tantum alterantur, cum in ipsis superat calor aut frigus ex sole, aut cum exercitium transcendit mensuram que[20] est decens, aut cum quies et tranquillitas pertranseunt quantitatem intentionis, aut alia hiis similia. In corporibus quoque nostris fit malitia complexionis diverse ex rebus que eis[21] exterius[22] occurrunt, si calefaciunt res ille aut infrigidant aut desiccant[23] aut humectant. Et hee quidem species malitie complexionis[24] sunt simplices et singulares, quemadmodum ostendi in libro de complexionibus.

(**1.3**) Eius quoque sunt alie quatuor species composite, que fiunt cum calefit corpus et humectatur simul, aut calefit et desiccatur simul, aut infrigidatur et humectatur simul, aut infrigidatur et desiccatur simul.[25] Et manifestum quidem est quod species iste[26] malitie

---

[1]incipit liber G. de malitia complexionis diverse O Liber G. de malitia complexionis diversa A *om.* H
[2]*add.* O etiam
[3]inde AHO (Ar.) *om.* **EFPV (Heb.)**
[4]notione AO vocatione H, *corr.* H *ad* vocatio **tamen non in omni sed in EFPV (Heb.)**
[5]in una invenit AO invenit nimia H **sustinet in una EFPV (Heb.)**
[6]epiliam H
[7]quoque AH etiam O
[8]uno AHO (Ar.) **unoquoque EFPV(Heb.)**
[9]in. . . erit AO erit in uno membrorum H
[10]fuerit O
[11]*add.* O *mg. m. r.* caliditatis
[12]erat H
[13]quam H
[14]nominant AO vocant H
[15]aliud apostema H
[16]trisipila H
[17]notione AHO **nominatum EFPV (Heb.)**
[18]estiomenus AHO **herpes estiomenus E herpestiomenus FPV (Heb.)**
[19]malitia AH
[20]quod H
[21]*om.* O
[22]extrinsecus O
[23]resiccant H
[24]malitie complexionis AO *tr.* H
[25]aut calefit et desiccatur . . . simul *om.* H
[26]ille HO

complexionis diverse non diversificantur a speciebus malitie complexionis equalis nisi quoniam ipse non consistunt[27] in omnibus partibus corporis cuius corrumpitur[28] complexio.

Mea igitur intentio (A37rb) in hoc libro[29] est enunciare quomodo fiat[30] generatio omnium specierum malitie complexionis diverse. Ut sit sermo meus in illo manifestus, iam ergo oportet ut te[31] recordari faciam dispositionis[32] membrorum omnium; et incipiam recordari maiorum[33] eorum, que nota sunt ei apud quem[34] medicine notitia[35] non existit. Manus enim[36] et pedes et venter et pectus et caput non sunt ex eis quorum esse secundum aliquem[37] evanescat.[38] **(2.1)** Ad unum[39] igitur ipsorum perveniamus et ipsum[40] in propinquiores partes ex quibus componitur dividamus. Exempli itaque causa:[41] pedem in coxam et crus[42] et pedem dividamus; et manum in[43] adiutorium et ulnam et palmam sequestremus; ipsam quoque palmam in membra sibi propria dividamus,[44] que sunt rasceta[45] et pecten et digiti. Et digitos etiam[46] dividamus in partes ex quibus sunt compositi,[47] et sunt ossa et[48] cartillagines et ligamenta et nervi et vene pulsatiles et non pulsatiles[49] et panniculi[50] et caro et corde et ungues et cutis et adeps.

(2.2) Hec ergo[51] membra que postremo nominavi non est possibile[52] dividere in speciem aliam post istam,[53] sed ipsa quidem sunt[54] membra similium partium prima—preter venas pulsatiles et non pulsatiles, nam hec duo composita sunt ex villis et panniculis,[55] sicut dixi in libro de medicatione[56] anothomie. Et in illo etiam libro[57] narravi

---

[27]consistunt AHO **introducte sunt E vincte sunt F vincentes sunt PV (Heb.)**

[28]corrumpitur *scrips.*: alteratur AHO, *mg.* A in alio corrumpitur

[29]est in hoc libro H

[30]sit H

[31]te AH (Ar.) *om.* **OEFP (Heb.)** *mg.* V

[32]dispositiones H

[33]*om.* H

[34]apud quem: quam H

[35]nocentia H

[36]etenim O

[37]aliquem A aliquam H aliquod O

[38]*add.* et O

[39]unum AHO (Ar.) **unumquodque EFPV (Heb.)**

[40]*del.* O prosequamur

[41]cum O

[42]et pedem AHOE *om.* **FPV (Heb.)**

[43]manum in: manus O

[44]*add.* O in partes ex quibus sunt composita

[45]rasceta A rascepta O rascheta H

[46]quoque O

[47]composita O, *corr.* A *ex* composita

[48]et *om.* A

[49]et non pulsatiles HEFPV *om.* A **(Heb.)** *mg.* O

[50]panniculus O

[51]ergo AHO

[52]possibile est O

[53]ista A

[54]sunt *ins.* A

[55]et panniculis: panniculosis O

[56]medicatione AOEV medicamine H **meditatione F iudicatione in al. medicatione P**

[57]libro AHO (Ar.) *om.* **EFPV (Heb.)**

quod inter membra prima[58] similium partium sunt foramina plura, et ex eis plura et[59] maiora existunt inter membra composita officialia. Quandoque tamen invenimus simile illis foraminibus in aliquo[60] membrorum similium partium, quemadmodum invenimus illud in osse et in cute. Verumtamen quodcumque[61] membrorum fuerit molle[62], quedam[63] partes ipsius[64] alias cooperient[65] et occultabuntur[66] sensui foramina que sunt inter eas; sed quodcumque membrorum fuerit durum et siccum, tu consequeris quicquid est in eo ex foraminibus et scissuris[67] sensu, sicut[68] reperimus in vacuitatibus ossium; et in illis quidem vacuitatibus ossium existit humiditas, natura[69] grossa,[70] alba, preparata[71] ossibus ut nutriantur ipsa. Quomodo autem pori qui[72] in cute sunt proveniant, iam ostendi in libro de complexionibus.

Hec ergo sunt quorum necessario[73] fuit rememorandum, ut per ipsa[74] verificetur quod in[75] sequentibus narrabo.

(2.3) Nunc autem oportet ut ad intentionem malitie complexionis diverse perveniamus et narremus que sit eius[76] natura et[77] secundum quot modos proveniat. Et[78] nos iam[79] quidem[80] in hiis que sunt premissa[81] diximus quod[82] in partibus corporis in quo accidit malitia complexionis diverse, non est complexio una, (A37va) quoniam hoc est[83] commune et participativum[84] omni malitie complexionis diverse; eius autem species sequuntur naturam corporum in quibus sunt.[85] Eventus namque malitie[86] complexionis diverse in carne nuda

---

[58]*om.* H

[59]ex eis plura et *scrips.*: in plura tamen et A et eis plura et H et ex eis parva et O

[60]illo H

[61]*add.* EFPV (Heb.) **illorum**

[62]molle fuerit H

[63]quedam AHO **quod EFPV**

[64]*corr.* A *ex* illius

[65]cooperient AH cooperiendo O

[66]occultabunt H

[67]sissuris H

[68]sensu sicut AHO (Ar.) **sicut sensu EFPV (Heb.)**

[69]humiditas natura: humidas H

[70]crossa A, *corr. m. rec. ad* crassa

[71]temperata H

[72]qui AH *om.* O

[73]necessaria H

[74]ipsam O *corr.* A *ex* ipsam

[75]in *om.* H

[76]sit eius *tr.* H

[77]*ins.* O

[78]proveniat et AO permanet H

[79]*om.* O

[80]iam quidem *tr.* A

[81]sunt premissa *tr.* H

[82]*del.* H sequitur naturam corporum

[83]hoc est *mg.* O

[84]participativum AHOEV, *corr.* A *ex* participate [*eras.*] **principatum P,** *mg.* **P** *m. rec.* **vel participatum participatum F "proprium(?)" Heb.**

[85]sunt H fiunt O fuerit A

[86]malitie *om.* H

est preter eventum ipsius in lacerto sicut est;[87] et unusquisque eorum existit secundum modum alium a modo secundum quem alter existit.

(**3.1**) Inde est quod, cum in[88] musculo calida effunditur superfluitas, tunc maiores[89] vene que in ipso sunt, pulsatiles et non pulsatiles, implentur primo et extenduntur; deinde, post illud, ille que sunt minores. Et incessanter procedit[90] sic[91] donec ad minores perveniatur[92] venas. Cum ergo superfluitas illa in illis redundat[93] venis et eam non continent, effluit aliquid eius[94] ex orificiis illarum venarum et resudat[95] ex ea aliquid et egreditur ex ipso corpore venarum. Postquam ergo fuerit illud, implentur foramina que inter prima existunt membra illa superfluitate, adeo donec[96] eis accidat calefieri et[97] humectari undique ex illa[98] humiditate quam continent.

Per membra autem[99] prima in hoc loco volo intelligi[100] nervos et ligamenta et panniculos et carnem; et ante hoc,[101] ipsas venas pulsatiles et non pulsatiles, in quibus iam proprie[102] dolor primo accidit secundum modos diversos, et illud ideo quoniam superfluitas, que in interioribus earum continetur, calefacit eas et extendit et disrumpit;[103] et superfluitas que est[104] extra eas calefacit ipsas[105] et constringit et coartat et gravat.[106] Aliorum vero[107] membrorum, quedam non egrotare facit nisi calefactio tantum, et quedam non facit pati nisi coartatio tantum, et quedam eorum egrotare[108] faciunt utreque[109] res simul. (**3.2**) Et hec quidem egritudo dicitur apud grecos flegmon,[110] que[111] est apostema calidum, et est malitia complexionis diverse accidens[112] lacerto, et illud ideo quoniam sanguis, qui est in ipso, iam calefactus est et evenit[113] ei similitudo ebullitionis. Deinde calefiunt primo proprie[114] eius

---

[87]sicut est AH sic O

[88]*om.* H

[89]maioris A

[90]procedunt H

[91]sic *om.* O

[92]perveniatur AH perveniantur O

[93]reduntiat? O

[94]eius *om.* O

[95]desudat H

[96]*post* donec *del. H* ad maiores perveniatur venas. cum ergo superfluitas illa in illis redundaret

[97]huius *del.* H, *tr.* H humectari *post* undique

[98]ipsa O

[99]*add.* H propria

[100]intelligere O

[101]et ante hoc AH (Ar.), et *corr.* A *mg.* ad post [*reads* ante *as* autem] **post hoc autem OEFPV "post" Heb.**

[102]*om.* O

[103]disrumpit et extendit H

[104]*om.* H

[105]ipsas AO eas H

[106]agravat O

[107]vero autem O

[108]*om.* O

[109]utrumque O

[110]flemon O

[111]quod H

[112]*tr.* H *post* lacerto / *add.* O in

[113]*corr.* A *ex* venit

[114]primo proprie: A *eras.* [*illeg.*], *scr. m. rec.* proprie

calefactione corpora[115] venarum pulsatilium et non pulsatilium;[116] postea omnia que sunt extra eas ex eis in quibus continetur,[117] donec ipsum submergant.[118]

Et impossibile quidem est quin res ad unum duorum modorum perveniat: aut ut[119] vincat superfluitas que in[120] lacerto effunditur,[121] et corrumpat[122] corpora in quibus vincit; aut vincatur illa superfluitas et redeat lacertus ad dispositionem suam naturalem. Pono itaque ut superfluitas vincatur, cum incipere ab eo quod est bonum sit melius et laudabilius. Dico quod[123] sanitas erit tunc[124] secundum unum duorum modorum: aut ut[125] resolvantur omnes humiditates que effuse sunt in lacerto, aut ut[126] decoquantur. Sed laudabilior du(A37vb)abus sanationibus[127] est que resolutione erit.[128] Decoctionem vero consequuntur[129] due res necessario, quarum una est generatio saniei et altera collectio. Et collectio[130] quidem quandoque in maiore foraminum[131] est viciniore loco et minoris timoris, et[132] hec est collectio laudabilior. Et quandoque est in maiore[133] foraminum[134] propinquiore,[135] sed foramen illud non est parvi timoris; aut est in foramine parvi timoris,[136] sed non est maius foraminum[137] neque propinquum.

(3.3) Quod si fuerit illud[138] in partibus stomachi, laudabilior erit collectio que erit in amplitudine que in interioribus eius existit, et ad quam secundum plurimum fit[139] saniei eruptio; collectio vero que fit sub siphac est mala. Et cum fuerit illud[140] in partibus cerebri, tunc collectio in duobus ventriculis eius anterioribus erit laudabilis,[141] sed collectio sub duabus matribus cerebri[142] et in ventriculo qui est in posterioribus cerebri facta est illaudabilis et mala. Exiturarum autem que fiunt in partibus costarum, eruptio erit ad amplitudinem pectoris, et[143]

---

[115]corpus O

[116]et non pulsatilium *om.* H

[117]continetur A continet HO

[118]submergant A submergat H submergatur O

[119]ut *ins.* A *om.* H

[120]in: est in O / *add.* H eo

[121]et funditur O

[122]corrumpit H

[123]*add.* H ad

[124]tunc *om.* H

[125]*ins.* O

[126]*om.* H

[127]duarum sanationum O

[128]ǫiutur(?) O

[129]decoctionem . . . consequuntur *om.* O, *mg.* O decoctionem vero secuntur

[130]et collectio: *ins.* O

[131]foramine H

[132]et *om.* H

[133]minore A

[134]foramine O

[135]**et quandoque est in minore foraminum et remotiore a loco exitus et est maioris periculi** *add.* V (Heb.) *mg.* **F (maiori F)** *add.* V *mg.* **in alio loco vacat**

[136]aut in . . . timoris *om.* H

[137]foramen H

[138]illud fuerit H

[139]fit *om.* H

[140]fuerit illud: facit illud H / illud *ins.* A

[141]laudabilior H

[142]*om.* O

[143]exiturarum autem . . . et *om.* O

exiturarum que fiunt in lacertis eruptio erit versus cutem; sed[144] exiturarum[145] que fiunt in visceribus eruptio erit aut[146] ad venas[147] que sunt in eis[148] pulsatiles et[149] non pulsatiles, aut versus panniculum qui continet ea et est eis[150] sicut cutis.

(**3.4**) Quod si superfluitas vincat[151] membra, tunc manifestum est quod oportet ex dominio malitie complexionis in eis ut ipsorum destruatur operatio et corrumpatur secundum temporis longitudinem.[152] Sed principium quietis egritudinis ab eis erit cum similabuntur[153] rei que resolvit ea et transmutat;[154] et illud est[155] quoniam membris non accidit dolor cum ipsorum complexio iam integre transmutata est, sed in dispositione permutationis eius— sicut[156] iam narravit[157] de esse eius mirabilis Ypocras, ubi dixit quod dolores non fiunt in membris nisi in dispositione alterationis eorum[158] et corruptionis et[159] exitus ipsorum[160] a naturis suis. Et unumquodque[161] membrorum non alteratur et egreditur a natura sua et corrumpitur, nisi calefiat aut infrigidetur aut desiccetur aut humectetur aut eius continuitas solvatur. In malitia autem[162] complexionis diverse, propterea quod membrum calefit aut infrigidatur, proprie; et illud ideo quoniam[163] hee due qualitates sunt fortioris operationis quam alie qualitates. Sed[164] iam fit[165] illud propterea quod membrum desiccatur aut humectatur in fame et siti; et[166] accidit passio propter penuriam substantie sicce in fame et[167] propter penuriam humiditatis in dispositione sitis. Cum autem in membro fit[168] operatio ab eo quod ipsum pungit aut corrodit aut extendit aut coartat aut disrumpit, (A38ra) tunc eventus passionis est propter solutionem continuitatis.

(**4.1**) Cumque calor sanguinis qui est in membro apostemoso fuerit calor quietus, et fuerit sanguis quem[169] totum continet corpus equalis complexionis, forsitan non accidet ei ut calefactione membri infirmi calefiat.[170] Et cum caliditas sanguinis qui est in membro

---

[144]exiturarum que . . . sed *mg.* O (est O)

[145]*add.* O etiam

[146]aut *om.* HO

[147]ad venas *om.* O

[148]que sunt in eis *tr.* HO *post* non pulsatiles

[149]aut H

[150]ei O

[151]vincat *om.* O, *ins. supra* vincit

[152]ipsius longitudinem H

[153]assimilabuntur H

[154]*add.* O ea

[155]est *om.* O

[156]sed H

[157]narravi H

[158]eorum AHO (Ar.) **corporis EFPV (Heb.)**

[159]et AO quia H

[160]eorum AO

[161]*add.* H quidem, *add. et eras.* A [*illeg.*]

[162]tamen H

[163]quoniam AO quod H

[164]si A

[165]iam fit: *eras.* [*illeg.*] A, *scr. m. r.* autem fiat

[166]et *om.* H

[167]et *om.* O

[168]fit AHOEFP, *eras.* A, *ins.* A *m. rec.* deficit **deficit V (Heb.)**

[169]qui O

[170]**totum corpus** *add.* P (Heb.)

apostemoso fuerit caliditas fortis, calefiet corpus fortitudine ebullitionis eius;[171] et cum fuerit ut sanguini, quem[172] totum continet[173] corpus, dominetur colera, tunc non stat quin calefactione eius superflua calefiat totum[174]—et quanto plus si[175] fuerit illud cum utreque res aggregantur,[176] scilicet ita[177] ut sit sanguis qui est in membro apostemoso fortis caliditatis, et in sanguine qui est in corpore[178] dominetur[179] colera.

(4.2) Primum vero quod[180] ex[181] sanguine[182] calefit, cum in eo superfluit calefactio,[183] est sanguis qui est in venis pulsatilibus, propterea quod in natura sui est[184] calidior et propinquior nature spiritus; deinde, post ipsum, sanguis qui est in venis non pulsatilibus. Si ergo membrum apostemosum propinquum fuerit aliquibus visceribus sanguine[185] habundantibus quem continent, erit caliditas eius[186] recurrens ad sanguinem velociter quem totum corpus continet.[187] Et universaliter dignius[188] est ut calefiat ante[189] omnis res que velox est ad resolvendum, aut in natura sua est calida, et similiter[190] primum quod[191] infrigidatur ante res etiam[192] est que[193] velox est[194] ad resolvendum aut est in natura sua frigida. Velocius autem ad resolvendum eis que in corpore sunt est[195] spiritus, propterea quod est subtilior eis[196] et tenuior; et calidius quod[197] in corpore est est[198] colera rubea, et frigidius[199] quod est in eo est flegma. De reliquis vero humoribus, sanguis calidus[200] est post coleram, et melancolia frigida[201] post flegma. Et colera quidem[202] facile resolvitur et velociter ab omni

---

[171]*om.* O

[172]qui O

[173]continet *tr.* HO *post* corpus

[174]totum AO totum corpus H

[175]**si *om.* EFPV (Heb.)**

[176]augeantur O

[177]scilicet ita *tr.* H

[178]*post* corpore *add.* O cui

[179]*del.* A corpore

[180]*mg.* O

[181]vero quod ex *om.* H

[182]sanguine AHO (Ar.) **eo EFPV (Heb.)**

[183]*add.* H a primus sanguis qui calefit adeo ut in eo superfluat

[184]*om.* H

[185]sanguinem O

[186]caliditas eius *om.* H

[187]continet corpus O

[188]*corr.* A *ex* dignus dignus O

[189]tantum H

[190]sit H

[191]quasi H

[192]et H

[193]*ins.* O

[194]velox est *tr.* H

[195]*om.* H

[196]eam H

[197]quod AO quam H

[198]in corpore est est A in corpore est HO

[199]feb' H

[200]calidus AH calidior O

[201]frigida H frigidior *mg.* AO

[202]quoque O

quod in eam agit,[203] melancolia[204] autem laboriose et violenter resolvitur. Et universaliter quidem omne quod est subtile et tenue est velocis resolutionis, et omne quod est[205] spissum et grossum est tarde resolutionis. (**4.3**) Quapropter oportet ut sit veniens[206] apostematum resolutio plurimum diversa propter diversitatem dispositionis corporum: primo autem quoniam humor a quo provenit apostema aut erit augmentate caliditatis aut diminute. Deinde post illud, quoniam putrefactio eius non erit nisi[207] secundum naturam ipsius, et secundum superfluitatem retentionis[208] eius aut parvitatem retentionis eius,[209] in interioribus scilicet.[210] Nam illius putrefactio quod expirationem non habet[211] velox erit,[212] et illud quidem[213] in omnibus rebus[214] extrinsecis invenitur.

Quod si convenerit cum hoc ut sit eius complexio calida et humida, erit illud[215] magis adiuvans[216] ad hoc ut eius[217] putrefactio sit velox. Et membrum etiam[218] in quo fit[219] apostema, aut erit propinquum vi(A38rb)sceribus sanguine habundantibus[220] aut ab eis remotum, nam et[221] in sanguine toto etiam[222] superhabundat colera aut melancolia aut flegma aut ventositas. Et omnes iste quidem[223] dispositiones diversificantur paucitate et multitudine. Oportet ergo necessario ut sit resolutio[224] plurime diversitatis, cum unum comparatur[225] alii et cum comparatur[226] sibi ipsi.

(**5.1**) Et hec quidem omnia sunt causa malitie[227] complexionis diverse. Et illud ideo quoniam in eis vincens[228] caliditas que est in sanguine est[229] in membro apostemoso; deinde post ipsum[230] in sanguine qui est in visceribus, et proprie sanguine qui est in corde et ex hoc

---

[203]ea ait O

[204]melancolie A

[205]*om.* H

[206]veniens HO evenies A eventus **EFPV**

[207]*ins.* O *m. r.*

[208]resolutionis H

[209]eius H *del.* A *om.* O

[210]in interioribus scilicet *ins.* A *mg.* tamen minoribus scilicet H in interioribus O *om.* Ar.

[211]illius putrefactio que expirationem non habet (putrefactio . . . habet *m. r.* over erasure) A quod exspirationem non habet putrefactio O illius quod experimentum non habet petrefactio H

[212]velox erit *tr.* O

[213]quem H

[214]rebus AHO (Ar.) **interioribus rebus et EFPV (Heb.)**

[215]*om.* O

[216]adiuvans magis H

[217]*om.* H

[218]etiam AO et H

[219]*om.* H

[220]sanguinem habentibus H

[221]*add.* O si *mg.* A in alio et si in sanguine toto etiam

[222]*om.* O

[223]quidem iste O

[224]resolutione H

[225]aperitur H

[226]cum comparatur: comparatur H

[227]causa malitie AO cause H

[228]vincet O

[229]*om.* O

[230]ipsam A

proprie qui est in ventriculo eius sinistro. Nam si ad hunc[231] veneris[232] ventriculum, dum animal adhuc vivit et nondum accidit ei febris, et intromiseris digitum tuum, sicut narravi in libro de medicatione anothomie, senties[233] ex eo fortiorem[234] caliditatem que est. Non est ergo longe, cum[235] corpus totum[236] calefactione naturam supergrediente[237] calefactum fuerit, quin perveniat ventriculus ille proprie[238] cordis ad finem[239] caliditatis. Et ex eis quidem[240] que[241] ad hoc[242] iuvant[243] est quod in ipso est sanguis[244] subtilior et nature spiritus vicinior et movetur etiam[245] motu assiduo.

(5.2) Verumtamen in huiusmodi febribus totum sanguinem invenitur comprehendisse[246] iam calefactio,[247] et recipit illam caliditatem egredientem cursum naturalem, generatam[248] a putrefactione[249] humorum, receptione perfecta. Corporum[250] vero venarum pulsatilium et[251] aliorum corporum complexio que eis sunt vicina et continent ea, non invenitur adhuc perfecte[252] et integre alterata, sed sunt adhuc[253] habentia[254] resolutionem et alterationem tendentem ad calefactionem.[255] Et si illud perseveraverit in eis[256] spatio longo, pervenient ad terminum in quo iam erunt[257] victa et resoluta penitus, ita ut tunc non sint in[258] termino in quo calefiant sed[259] sint in termino in quo iam integre[260] consecuta[261] sunt calefactionem a natura egredientem. Resolutionis autem terminus in unoquoque membrorum est

---

[231]ad hunc A adhuc HO

[232]veneris *scrips.*: veniens A innueris O, *corr.* O *ad* inveneris circitueris H

[233]sentiens A

[234]foramine H

[235]cum AO et H

[236]tuum H

[237]supergrediente A super egrediente O eggrediente H

[238]*corr.* A *m. r. ad* prius

[239]calefactum . . . finem *mg.* O

[240]*corr.* O *m. r. ex* qui

[241]*ins.* A

[242]ad huc H

[243]iuvat H

[244]sanguinis H

[245]etiam A *om.* O et H

[246]amph' vidisse H

[247]calefactio A caliditas O calefacto H

[248]generatam HO generata A

[249]putredine O

[250]corpore H

[251]etiam H

[252]perfecte adhuc H

[253]adhuc *om.* H

[254]habentia AHO (Ar.) **contrahencia EFPV, in al. habentia** *mg.* **P**

[255]*add.* **integram V (Heb.)**

[256]eo H

[257]e't A erant P *om.* H

[258]*ins.* A

[259]tunc non sint . . . sed AOH (Ar.) **tunc non E tunc iam F(Heb.) iam P tunc V,** *add. mg.* **V non sint in termino in quo calefiant sed**

[260]integre O integram AH

[261]consecuta HO c'secuta A

nocumentum operationis eius.[262] Tota autem intentio que est[263] apud principium rei[264] ad hoc ut perveniatur ad hunc terminum, non est[265] nisi via exeundi ad[266] dispositionem[267] egredientem a re naturali commixta, communis, media inter duo contraria,[268] scilicet inter dispositionem que vere[269] est natura eius[270] et inter dispositionem que a[271] natura penitus est egressa.[272] In toto ergo[273] hoc temporis[274] spatio inerit[275] corpori quod a dolore[276] calefit quantitas resolutionis que ipsum sequitur.[277] (5.3) Cum autem prima omnia[278] corporis membra integre et perfecte sunt calefacta, dicitur febris illa ethica,[279] que est fixa, et illud ideo quoniam eius essentia tunc non existit in humiditatibus et spiritu[280] tantum, sed est preter hoc in corporibus quibus adest fixio.

Et[281] cum hac febre non est[282] passio neque dolor, et estimat[283] patiens eam quod nullo modo[284] sit in eo febris, quoniam non (A38va) sentit eius caliditatem, nam membra eius iam omnia[285] calefacta sunt[286] equaliter[287] secundum dispositionem unam. Et iam quidem[288] convenerunt super hoc speculatores naturarum, apud considerationes suas[289] de sensibus, quod sensus non est[290] nisi[291] alteratione et non fit passio neque dolor in his[292] que iam[293] integre alterata sunt. Quapropter fit ut cum nulla febre[294] huius generis (quam paulo ante

---

[262]eius *tr.* H *post* autem

[263]*om.* H

[264]rei: ipsum rei O

[265]*add.* O enim

[266]ad *om.* H

[267]a dispositione O

[268]duo contraria AHO (Ar.) **hec duo EFPV (Heb.)**

[269]vere AO vera H

[270]natura eius: naturalis O

[271]*ins.* A

[272]*add.* O et

[273]*om.* O

[274]hoc temporis H corporis AO

[275]invenerint O

[276]dolore AHO (Ar.) **calore tali EFPV (Heb.)**

[277]que ipsum sequitur *om.* O

[278]omnia AO, *tr.* O *ante* prima *om.* H

[279]hethica A ectica O

[280]spiritu AH spiritibus O

[281]*om.* O

[282]*ins.* H

[283]existimat H extimat AO

[284]*om.* H

[285]iam omnia *tr.* AH omnia O

[286]sunt calefacta O

[287]*add.* O calefactione

[288]*corr.* O *m. r.* ex qui

[289]*om.* O

[290]sit O fit AH

[291]nisi A nisi ab O *om.* H

[292]ab his O

[293]*om.* O

[294]*om.* H

ethicam nominari diximus)[295] sit passio neque dolor neque patiens eam penitus sentiat:[296] et illud ideo quoniam membrorum eius dispositio non est dispositio qua quedam ipsorum[297] agant[298] et quedam patiantur, cum omnia iam[299] facta sint dispositionis unius, et facta sit eorum complexio una conveniens—(**6.1**) etsi sint quedam augmentate[300] calefactionis[301] et quedam[302] augmentate infrigidationis,[303] nam ex superfluitate calefactionis eorum que ex eis sunt calidiora non pervenit[304] eis[305] que ex[306] eis sunt frigidiora ut impediantur que vicina sunt calefactione. Quod si res ita[307] esset,[308] membra se ad[309] invicem impedirent naturali[310] dispositione. Membra namque in illa etiam dispositione[311] in[312] complexione sua diversificantur, et illud est quoniam caro est membrum calidum[313] et os est[314] membrum frigidum, verumtamen cum[315] diversitate[316] horum et similium non est dolor neque passio, propter parvitatem comparationis inter ea in[317] caliditate et frigiditate. Inde est quod aer corpora[318] circundans[319] non impedit ea, antequam alteretur[320] eo,[321] usque[322] superfluat in ipso calor aut frigus. Species autem diversitatis eius inter superfluitatem caloris et inter[323] superfluitatem[324] frigoris sunt secundum multitudinem[325] eorum et manifestationem comparationis[326] inter ea, nam corpora ipsum[327] sentiunt et non ab eo impediuntur.

---

[295]ethicam nominari diximus H diximus nominari ethicam A nominavimus ethicam O

[296]sentit O

[297]ipsarum O

[298]agunt H

[299]iam *ins.* A *m. r. et del. post* sint

[300]augmentate A augmentationis HO, *tr.* O *post* calefactionis

[301]calefactionis AO caliditatis H

[302]et quedam *om.* O

[303]augmentate infrigidationis A infrigidationis O augmentaris frigiditatis H

[304]provenit A

[305]eis *mg.* A

[306]*om.* O

[307]*om.* O *et ins. post* esset

[308]esset A essent O erunt H

[309]ad se H

[310]*add.* A entia *add.* H essentia **add. EF essentia et *add*. PV (Heb.) et essentia**

[311]membra . . . dispositione *mg.* A

[312]*om.* H

[313]calidum membrum H

[314]*om.* H

[315]etiam O

[316]*del.* A rerum

[317]*om.* H

[318]***add*. P (Heb.) nostra**

[319]corpora circundans A corpora dans H corpus circundans O

[320]alteretur A alterentur O alterantur H

[321]eo *ins. m. rec.* O

[322]usque AH quousque O, *add.* HO donec

[323]*om.* H

[324]caloris . . . superfluitatem *om.* O, *add.* O *mg. m. rec.* et inter superfluitatem caliditatis *post* frigoris

[325]multitudinem AH similitudinem O

[326]comparationum H

[327]ipsas H

(**6.2**) Ergo forsitan anima secundum hanc ratiocinationem acquiescet[328] sermoni illi qui dictus[329] est, quemadmodum dixit Ypocras in quibusdam libris suis, quod omnes egritudines non sunt nisi ulcera; et illud[330] ideo quoniam ulcus non est[331] nisi continuitatis solutio, et caliditas superflua et frigus superfluum fortasse continuitatem solvunt—caliditas quidem fortis, propterea quod solvit et secat continuitatem substantie in qua vincit; et frigiditas quidem superflua, propterea quod adunat et constringit substantiam[332] in qua vincit ad interiora, donec exuberet ex ea aliquid et[333] egrediatur[334] et[335] coartat[336] quod remanet ex eo[337] et disrumpit. Quod si aliquis ponat hunc terminum in superfluitate frigiditatis et[338] caliditatis,[339] dignum est[340] ut sit non[341] longe quod estimetur[342] de eo quod iam adinvenit. Verumtamen[343] si hoc[344] non est terminus in superfluitate, sed terminus[345] in illo est aliud,[346] tunc secundum manifestam dis(A38vb)positionem est quod omnis superfluitas non intelligitur nisi secundum semitam relationis ad[347] aliquid. Et illud ideo quoniam quod omni corpori advenit ex rebus que sunt unius dispositionis caliditatis et frigiditatis, non est res una.

(**6.3**) Quapropter[348] fit ut humores qui sunt in quibusdam animalibus ad invicem sint[349] convenientes et quorundam humores non ad invicem[350] conveniant, sed preter[351] hoc corrumpant se et interficiant[352], sicut homo et vipera, cuiusque cui eorum[353] saliva alterum perimit. Et ex hoc[354] quidem fit ut cum homo[355] super scorpionem expuit[356] dum est ieiunus interficiat[357] ipsum; homo autem hominem sibi similem non interficit cum eum mordet, neque[358]

---

[328]quiescens est O, *corr.* O *ad* adquiescens
[329]dicens O
[330]*add.* est H
[331]non est ulcus H
[332]substantia O
[333]aliquid et H aliquid A quidem O *mg. add.* AO et
[334]egreditur O
[335]et *om.* H
[336]coburatat O
[337]ex eo *ins.* A
[338]*ins.* O
[339]caliditatis et frigiditatis H
[340]est dignum H
[341]ut non sit H
[342]existimetur H
[343]verum O
[344]si hoc *mg.* O
[345]tunc H
[346]est aliud H aliud AO, *ins.* O est *ante* aliud
[347]*om.* O, *ins.* O *m. r.*
[348]quoniam propter H
[349]sint adinvicem H
[350]adinvicem non H
[351]preter AO propter H
[352]corrumpunt . . . interficiunt H
[353]cui eorum A ei (*ins.*) ipsorum O hec eorum H
[354]ex hoc: *om.* O, *ins.* O hoc
[355]et vipera . . . homo: *mg.* A
[356]expuit OH *om.* A, *mg.* A expuit
[357]interficiat A interficit HO
[358]*om.* H

vipera sibi similem neque draco draconem, et illud ideo quoniam simile est conveniens et amicum, et contrarium est[359] inimicum[360] impediens. Et ex eis quidem que hoc significant est quod omnia que augmentantur et nutriuntur, non augmentantur et nutriuntur[361] nisi suo simili et sibi convenienti, et omne quod[362] moritur et minuitur, non moritur et minuitur nisi suo contrario. Et propter hoc conservatio[363] sanitatis non fit nisi[364] rebus convenientibus et similibus corporibus sanis; sanitas quoque et curatio ab egritudinibus non fit[365] nisi a rebus sibi[366] contrariis. Verumtamen loqui de[367] hoc est preter illud in quo[368] sumus.

(**6.4**) Illam autem febrem[369] fixam que substantie animalis[370] fixe inheret non sentit qui ea laborat. Nulla vero reliquarum[371] febrium existit quam eam patiens non sentiat; verumtamen quasdam earum sentit et[372] ab eis impeditur plus et quasdam[373] minus. Earum preterea sunt quedam cum quibus est tremor, et hoc etiam[374] accidens, tremor scilicet,[375] sicut et plura[376] alia accidentia, non fiunt[377] nisi ex[378] malitia complexionis diverse. Et neque quidem possibile est ut narrem qualiter[379] hoc accidens generetur[380] in hoc sermone in quo sumus, nisi ostendam de virtutibus naturalibus quot sint, et que sint,[381] et quid sit illud[382] quod uniuscuiusque earum[383] proprium est[384] efficere.[385] Ego autem narrabo esse omnium accidentium in libro de morbis et accidentibus.

(**7.1**) Redeamus autem ad species malitie complexionis diverse. Iam quidem dixi in hiis[386] que sunt premissa[387] qualiter generetur febris ab[388] apostemate calido quod flegmon

---

[359]et contrarium est AO contrarium autem est H

[360]*add.* O et

[361]non . . . nutriuntur *mg.* A

[362]quidem H, *ins.* H quod

[363]generatio H

[364]*add.* H ex

[365]fiunt O

[366]a rebus sibi A rebus sibi H a rebus O

[367]*ins.* A

[368]illud in quo A id in O

[369]febrem autem H

[370]*ins.* O

[371]*corr. m. r.* H *ex* vel

[372]sentit et AHO **cum sentit EFPV (Heb.)**

[373]quasdam AHOF **a quibusdam EPV (Heb.)**

[374]*om.* H

[375]tremor scilicet AO *tr.* HEFV *om.* **P (Heb.)**

[376]plurima O

[377]fit A sit H fiunt O

[378]a AO *om.* H, *ins.* H a

[379]qualiter: equaliter unde O

[380]*add.* O et

[381]et que sint *om.* H

[382]illud A id O *om.* H

[383]eorum H

[384]proprium est A *tr.* HO

[385]efficitur H

[386]eis O

[387]*del.* A s.

[388]ex O

nominatur, et quod omne apostema huius generis et omnis febris, preter febrem fixam nominatam,[389] sunt ex[390] egritudinibus in quibus complexio est diversa. Et iam quidem fiunt febres ex putrefactione humorum tantum absque apostemate, et illud ideo quoniam non quod[391] putrefit est illud[392] quod iam adheret vel retentum est[393] et privatur expiratione[394] tantum, sed velocissime fit in hoc[395] putrefactio et fortissime;[396] et iam quidem putrefiunt res alie multe que sunt preparate ad putrefiendum.[397] Sed narrabo esse preparationis[398] eius quod preparatum[399] est[400] putrefactioni in alio libro ab isto. (7.2) Et malitia quidem complexionis diverse fit[401] secundum modum alium in corpore toto: et[402] quandoque quidem est illud, cum vapor calidus in ipso (A39ra) constrictione[403] retinetur; et quandoque est propter[404] augmentum caliditatis causa[405] exercicii pluris[406] mensura[407] que conveniens est,[408] et quandoque est propterea[409] quod sanguis calefit et fervet ebullitione superflua propter iram aut calefit[410] superflue propter moram in sole calido. Et manifestum quidem est apud me quod omnes febres iste provenientes ab apostematibus, sunt secundum virtutem cause operantis[411] in corpore et secundum dispositionem cuiusque corporum; erit febris in quibusdam corporibus fortior et in quibusdam debilior et quedam eorum[412] penitus non febriunt.

(7.3) Et manifestum etiam est[413] quod malitia complexionis quandoque provenit in spiritu tantum et quandoque[414] pertransit eum[415] etiam usque ad humores. Et ex eis quidem †que non sunt inferiora[416] illo in declaratione[417] est† quod omnes febres, cum prolongantur,

---

[389]nominata O

[390]ex *ins.* A

[391]quod H quod iam O *eras.* A

[392]est illud O est H *eras.* A

[393]vel retentum est OH *mg.* A

[394]exspiratione H experitationem A respiratione O

[395]in hoc: h' H

[396]et fortissime *om.* H

[397]putrefaciendum O putrefiendum A putrefiunt H

[398]preparationis AH putrefactionis O

[399]apparatum O

[400]est *om.* H

[401]fit diverse H

[402]etiam O

[403]constitutione O

[404]per H

[405]causa *om.* O

[406]pluris AO plura nihil H

[407]mensura A mensure O gurtur H

[408]est conveniens H

[409]quandoque est propterea A quandoque est propter O propterea quandoque est H

[410]calelefit A

[411]virtutem cause operantis AHO (Ar.) **esse virtutum (virtutum esse V) operantium EFPV "esse virtutis cause operantis" Heb.**

[412]*corr.* A *ex* eo

[413]etiam est AH est etiam O

[414]*ins.* O *m. rec.*

[415]eum AHO **cum hoc EFPV (Heb.)**

[416]inferiores O

[417]declaratione *corr.* A *m. rec. ex* [*illeg.*] declinatione HO

consequitur[418] eas febris fixa. Et ex hoc quidem sermone quasi iam declaratum est[419] quod malitia complexionis diverse quandoque provenit ab humiditate calida aut frigida[420] currente ad aliquod membrorum, quemadmodum narravi de esse membrorum in quibus fiunt apostemata; et quandoque non est res[421] ita, sed est cum alteratur complexio corporis in qualitate sua; et quod quedam occasiones[422] que alterant ipsum[423] consurgunt[424] ex ipso corpore, et quedam eveniunt[425] exterius. Cum febris quidem[426] fit[427] a putrefactione solum,[428] et cum quedam[429] a quibusdam apostematibus, ex ipso corpore. Et eventus quidem febris[430] a calefactione solis[431] aut a[432] superfluitate exercitii, exterius. Et illud quidem narrabo latius quam in hoc sermone in libro de causis accidentium.[433]

Et[434] quemadmodum febris accidit a caliditate solis cum alteratur complexio corporis, similiter accidit[435] quibusdam hominibus ex frigore[436] aeris multotiens ut vincat in eis vehementer frigus in toto corpore donec moriantur quidam eorum.[437] Et res quidem in hiis etiam omnibus[438] manifesta est quod[439] accidit eis[440] passio et dolor. (8.1) Et[441] passio et dolor etiam accidit ei[442] cui[443] dominatur frigus vehemens ex forti frigore; deinde nititur calefacere[444] corpus suum velociter[445] approximando ipsum[446] igni. Et multi illorum[447] quibus evenit illud, cum appropinquant corpora sua igni[448] subito, sentiunt dolorem vehementissimum[449]

---

[418]consequntur H

[419]declinatum est *del. A et post scr.* declaratum est

[420]aut frigida *mg.* O

[421]res non est O

[422]occasiones A alterationes O, *mg.* O al. occasiones secationes H

[423]alterant ipsum AO *tr.* H

[424]consurgent H

[425]eveniunt quidem O

[426]*corr. A m. rec. ad* quedam

[427]quidem fit: que sit H

[428]putrefactione solum AH (Ar.) **calefactione solis** (solius O) O**EFPV (Heb.)**

[429]quibus (*del.*) quidam A

[430]exterius cum febris. . . febris AH febres O

[431]solum H solius O

[432]ex O

[433]*add.* O eorum

[434]*om.* O

[435]*add.* H in

[436]frigiditate O, *add.* O solius

[437]eorum quidam H

[438]hiis etiam omnibus A omnibus hiis etiam H hiis omnibus O **hiis hominibus EFPV (Heb.)**

[439]et H

[440]*corr. A ex* ei

[441]passio et dolor et *om.* O

[442]passio et dolor etiam accidit AHO(Ar.), *mg.* V (**accidunt V**) *om.* EFP (Heb.)

[443]cui AHO, *corr. A m. rec. ad* cum eis

[444]calefactione H

[445]*om.* O

[446]ipsi approximando H

[447]aliorum H

[448]*ins.* O

[449]vehementem O

in radicibus unguium.[450] Quis ergo, cum sensibiliter videat[451] in hac dispositione quod causa passionis et doloris non est nisi malitia complexionis diverse, audeat respondere illud[452] in doloribus qui intrinsecus accidunt? Et miretur qualiter accidat dolor multotiens[453] hominibus absque apostemate, aut in intestino[454] quod nominatur colon, aut in[455] extremo testiculorum, aut in reliquis membris, et illud ideo quoniam nichil horum est mirabile.

Et neque etiam[456] qualiter accidat febris et tremor in[457] quibus(A39rb)dam hominibus in dispositione una, propterea quod[458] multiplicatur in corpore[459] humor frigidus flegmaticus similis vitro, et humor calidus qui est de genere colere,[460] donec in ipso simul[461] dominentur[462] et moveantur[463] in corpore, et proprie in membris sensibilibus, non est mirandum si sentiat cuius hec[464] est[465] dispositio utraque[466] simul. Nam si[467] ad hominem veneris[468] et in sole calido eum[469] stare[470] feceris, deinde super ipsum[471] aquam frigidam effunderis,[472] non erit inconveniens si sentiat caliditatem solis et frigiditatem aque. Verumtamen hec duo simul habenti[473] hanc dispositionem non adveniunt nisi exterius, et advenit ei etiam unumquodque eorum[474] in partibus corporis sui magnis.

(8.2) In febre autem[475] quam greci nominant[476] epialam, quod advenit ei[477] ex calido et frigido[478] non advenit[479] ei nisi intrinsecus,[480] et advenit ei etiam[481] unumquodque eorum in

---

[450]lignium H

[451]videat O vid'at A *om.* H, *ins.* H viderat

[452]respondere illud AO illud respicere H respicere illud **F respuere illud EPV (Heb.)**

[453]*om.* O

[454]aut in intestino O aut intestina A aut intestino H

[455]*om.* H

[456]*add.* **mirabile est P (Heb.)**

[457]*om.* A

[458]*add.* **cum HEFV (Heb.)**

[459]in corpore *tr.* O *post* humor

[460]qui est . . . colere *om.* O

[461]simul *om.* A *et ins. ante* in ipso / simul in eo O

[462]dominatur simul H

[463]dominetur et moveatur O

[464]si sentiat cuius hec: cum O

[465]est hec H

[466]utrorumque O

[467]si: cum O

[468]veneris *scrips.*: vieris(?) A inveris O vehementer hanc dispositionem *del.* H, meris H

[469]in . . . eum A eum in sole calido O in sole calido H

[470]constare H

[471]ipsam H

[472]effunderis AH infunderis O

[473]habenti AO habent H

[474]*ins.* A

[475]*om.* O

[476]nominant O vocant H vocant vel nominant A

[477]ei AHO, *scr. supr.* A id est patientis

[478]ex calido et frigido AH ex calido et ex frigido O

[479]advenienti H

[480]extrinsecus H

[481]ei etiam *tr.* O

partibus corporis sui[482] parvis. Et ita fit ut non sint partes magne corporis primi[483] quibus adveniat frigus,[484] nisi[485] ad latus cuiusque earum[486] sit pars magna cui adveniat calor; et non sit pars parva corporis secundi cui[487] adveniat frigus, nisi et ad latus eius sit alia[488] pars parva cui[489] adveniat[490] calor. Et propter hoc fit ut iste secundus[491] estimet[492] se sentire utraque simul in suo corpore. Et illud ideo[493] quoniam cum unumquodque quod infrigidat et[494] calefacit sit sparsum in partibus parvis, quarum una est post aliam, et non[495] sit post eas[496] in parvitate ultima,[497] non est possibile ut inveniatur pars[498] ex istis parvis in qua sit sensus unus[499] caloris et frigoris[500] absque alia.[501] **(8.3)** Et cuidam eorum[502] qui[503] febriunt accidit,[504] cum primo[505] febris eum invadit, in unaquaque accessionum suarum, ut sentiat cum ea frigus superfluum et calorem superfluum, sed nullum eorum sentit in loco in quo sentit alterum. Ille tamen[506] cui illud[507] advenit potest discernere manifeste inter membra sua que calefiunt et inter ea[508] que infrigidantur, et illud ideo quoniam sentit calorem[509] quod[510] interius est in ipsis suis[511] visceribus et sentit frigus in omnibus membris que sunt in manifesto[512] sui corporis.

---

[482]sui *om.* O

[483]primi *tr.* H *ante* corporis

[484]calor O

[485]*add.* A et

[486]eorum O

[487]adveniat . . cui *om.* O

[488]alia sit AO

[489]cum H

[490]adiuvat O

[491]secundus AHE (Ar.) partes O **sensus FPV**

[492]estimet *scrips.*: existimet AH exstimant O

[493]*ins.* O

[494]aut O

[495]*om.* O

[496]eam O

[497]*add.* et O

[498]*add.* aliqua FP

[499]unus P

[500]*add.* F simul *add.* V et

[501]pars . . . alia FP (Heb.) *mg.* A (A *add. apud principium* in alio), *mg.* V / *post* alia *add.* AHOEFP aliqua (aliquam AH altera F aliquando EP *om.* V) harum (*om.* HO) minimarum partium sensus (sensu O aliquando sensus V) in aliquo (alio H quo sit EFPV) frigido et calido (frigus et calor simul F calor et frigus P frigus et calor EV) absque alia

[502]cuidam eorum: eiusdem earum H

[503]que H

[504]accidit A accidunt H *om.* O

[505]primo AOP (Ar.) prius H **post EFV (Heb.)**

[506]tantum O

[507]*om.* H

[508]membra H

[509]calidum H

[510]*ins.* O

[511]*om.* H

[512]sub manifesto H

Et ex febribus preterea est febris quam greci vocant[513] synochum numquam remota ab hac dispositione, et similiter est genus febrium adurentium[514] mortificantium.[515] Et illud quidem quod accidit in hiis febribus in partibus maioribus est quod accidit in febre quam greci vocant epialam in partibus minoribus, malitia namque complexionis in hiis febribus etiam est diversa, et est etiam diversa in eo cui advenit tremor, preter quod ipsum sequatur febris. Hoc autem accidens raro accidit; sed tamen secundum dispositionem accidit quibusdam mulieribus et quibusdam viris. Verumtamen oportet proculdubio ut ipsum iam precesserit regimen quietis, aut patiens[516] spatio[517] longo assidue sit usus multitudine cibi generantis humorem frigidum crudum flegmaticum sicut humor[518] similis vitro. Et videtur quidem quod accidens hoc[519] non accidit ante[520] alicui penitus quoniam non fuit aliquis hominum usus hoc regimine quietis et multi(A39va)tudinis cibi. Et propter hoc invenimus antiquos medicorum iudicantes quod necesse est ut tremorem consequatur febris. Nos tamen[521] iam vidimus multotiens et viderunt[522] alii novorum medicorum tremorem provenire[523] quem postea febris non est consecuta.[524]

(8.4) Febris autem quam greci vocant[525] epialam est composita ex hac malitia complexionis a qua provenit tremor quem non sequitur febris, et ex malitia complexionis a qua[526] provenit febris. Cum autem dico epialam, nolo intelligi per hoc nomen nisi febrem in qua utraque semper[527] accidunt. Febrem vero quam tremor precedit et quam postea[528] sequitur calor, sicut accidit in tertiana et quartana, non nomino[529] epialam. Iam igitur[530] manifestum est quod febris[531] que epiala[532] nominatur est composita[533] ex duobus modis[534] malitie complexionis diverse, et similiter est dispositio in reliquis[535] febribus preter febres fixas.

(9.1) Et similiter sunt[536] egritudines que sunt proprie alicui membrorum cum apostemate: omnes enim[537] fiunt a[538] malitia complexionis diverse, sicut apostema quod nominatur flegmon et

---

[513]vocant AHO

[514]*add.* H et

[515]mortificativum A

[516]*om.* H

[517]tempore O .

[518]homī H

[519]accidens hoc *tr.* O

[520]ante A (Ar.) inde H *om.* OFVEP (Heb.)

[521]autem O

[522]videtur O

[523]provenire HO pervenire A

[524]consecuta est O

[525]vocant AO nominant H

[526]*add.* H non

[527]*add. et del.* H est

[528]post H

[529]voco O

[530]ergo O

[531]quod febris *om.* O

[532]epialos A

[533]composita est O

[534]*mg.* A

[535]omnibus O

[536]*ins.* A

[537]autem A

[538]cum H

nominatur[539] cancer et nominatur formica, et pustule que per erisipilam noscuntur,[540] et apostema nominatum[541] mollicies et nominatum estiomenus et illud quod nominant greci[542] cancrene,[543] et est[544] accidens perducens[545] membrum in semitam mortis. Omnibus enim egritudinibus istis est commune quod ab humiditate proveniunt[546] ad aliquod membrorum effusa; et diversificantur quoniam quedam eorum[547] proveniunt[548] ab humore flegmatico, et quedam ab humore qui est de genere colere rubee,[549] et quedam eorum a colera nigra, et quedam[550] a sanguine; et eorum que proveniunt[551] a sanguine, quedam fiunt a sanguine calido subtili ebulliente et quedam proveniunt[552] a sanguine frigido spisso[553] et quedam fiunt a sanguine cuius dispositio est alia.

Perscrutabor igitur subtilissime ut exponam species harum egritudinum in libro alio. **(9.2)** In hoc autem libro contentus sum ut dicam qualiter sit dispositio in humiditate que ad membrum effunditur et[554] eventu suo, quo provenire[555] facit unamquamque egritudinum quas[556] nominavimus; quod est secundum ratiocinationem quam in eis que premissa sunt narravimus de proventu apostematis quod nominatur flegmon ab humore calido sanguineo. Et quod unumquodque membrorum similium partium, simplicium, primorum,[557] cum in eo vincit humiditas illa, provenit[558] ad malitiam complexionis diverse; et illud ideo quoniam manifestum est et apparens quod calefit aut infrigidatur aut desiccatur aut humectatur secundum quod in ipso dominatur illa humiditas que ei appropinquat, eius vero interiora nondum conversa sunt ad similem[559] illius eiusdem dispositionis. Quod si totum resolvatur ab ultimo exterius sive interius[560] et fiat totum dispositionis unius, sedabitur ab eo subito dolor penitus; egritudo tamen tunc[561] erit spissior et difficilior et siccior.

Et qui antecedit quidem et scit quod narro[562] de hoc,[563] sufficit ei donec intelligat librum meum de medicinis; deinde, post ipsum, librum de ingenio sanitatis.[564]

---

[539]nominatur O nominatum AH

[540]noscuntur A (Ar.) nascuntur HOFEPV (Heb.)

[541]nominatum AH quod nominatur O

[542]greci vocant O

[543]cancrena A

[544]est *om.* A

[545]producens A

[546]proveniunt: *om.* O, *ins.* O procedunt

[547]eorum AO earum H

[548]ad aliquod membrorum . . . proveniunt *om.* H

[549]rubeo H

[550]*add.* H enim

[551]*del.* H ab humore flegmatico et quedam ab humore

[552]*om.* O

[553]frigido spisso A *tr.* O spisso H

[554]et AH *om.* O

[555]provenire O pervenire AH

[556]quam O

[557]priorum H

[558]provenit OH pervenit A

[559]similem AH simile O

[560]exterius sive interius AO exterius sive et interius H **exteriorum suorum et interiorum EFPV (Heb.)**

[561]adhuc O

[562]quod narro AH quod narratio O

[563]de hoc *tr.* H *post* ei

[564]*add.* A completus est liber G. de malitia complexionis diversa [*sic*] *add.* O deo gratias ammen

D. The Hebrew Text

Editorial Policies and Conventions

The edition we offer of this text is based on a study of a digitized copy made for us by the Bodleian Library, Oxford; our transcription of the text has been informed but not constrained by simultaneous reference to the text of the prior Latin translation. We have also examined the manuscript itself, in the Bodleian Library, in order to try to clear up a few remaining problems in our reading. Yeḥi'el of Genzano's semicursive script is not particularly difficult to read, but the ink with which he wrote has occasionally penetrated through the paper page and caused problems with particular words; other words have been corrected and made hard to read as a result. He framed his text with lines at the top and bottom and at either side of the page, and when he wrote over these lines, his text is again sometimes not entirely clear.

We had originally expected to publish the text of the Bodleian manuscript as it stood, and to point out omissions, offer corrections, and suggest additions in footnotes, but there proved to be too many problems with the text to make this feasible; as written, it is often impossible to understand, and sometimes can only be understood in a sense opposite to what Galen wrote. Some of these problems have arisen in the process of copying, as scribes slipped in their writing to another similar word further on in the text; others are likely to have originated with the translator himself. Ideally, we would like to offer a text that would represent as closely as possible the version that David Caslari himself completed, without disguising the fact of that version's probable corruption in the nearly two hundred years that separate it from its only surviving copy, in the process conveying to present-day readers a sense of the difficulties that medieval readers of Hebrew medical texts were likely to encounter.

We have tried to meet these two goals with the following compromise. Misunderstandings and omissions that are likely to have originated with the translator and his collaborator have been left as they stand in the text and identified in the notes. On the other hand, when there was reason to attribute the errors to the scribes who copied and recopied the text over the course of its history (such as casual misspellings), we have corrected them in the text itself and have given the actual reading of the manuscript in the notes. A few words that seem to be textual intrusions (i.e., they are not necessary to sense and have no correspondence to the Latin) have been left in the text but set off in square brackets. Editorial additions to the text, whether to expand abbreviations or to supply words we felt were needed for sense, have been placed in angle brackets. Ellipses in angle brackets (thus: < . . . >) indicate the omission in the Hebrew text of significant passages from the Latin original; the missing Latin is supplied in the notes and translated into Hebrew. (Minor divergences from the Latin have not been signaled; they will in any case appear in a close comparison of the two texts.) The copyist occasionally indicated the proper vocalization for Hebrew words, and whenever he did so, we have reproduced his vocalizations. It should thus be possible to read the Hebrew text essentially as it appears on the page.

Two other editorial interventions in the text should be acknowledged. We have of course maintained the chapterization of the Hebrew text, but we have also continued the division of the text into the arbitrary chapters and numbers introduced editorially into the Arabic version and maintained in the Latin translation. These numbers, placed within parentheses, should facilitate a comparison of the three versions of Galen's treatise. We have also given the folio numbers of the Bodleian manuscript in boldface type, both recto and verso, and placed them in square brackets at the corresponding place in our edition.

SIGLA AND ABBREVIATIONS

א   = MS Oxford, Bodl. Opp. Add. Fol. 18, fols. 19v–27r

ᵃא   = א note in the margin of MS

L   = Galen, *De malicia complexionis diverse*, tr. Gerard of Cremona, ed. Michael McVaugh

add.   = added by

del.   = deleted by

ditt.   = dittography

om.   = omitted by

[...]   = conjectural deletion

<...> = conjectural addition

(!)   = corrupt reading

(?)   = doubtful reading

ספר רוע מזג מתחלף לגליאינוס

העתקת החכם ר' דוד ב"ר אברהם הקשלרי מלשון נוצרי אל לשון הקודש

[19r] פרק ראשון שישים בו חילוק רוע מזג מתחלף. אמר גליאינוס רוע מזג מתחלף לפעמ' יהיה

בכל הגוף החי כמו מה שיקרה לאיזה איש באחד ממיני השיקוי, לא בכל שיקוי אלא באחד ממיניו ר"ל

בבשרי ובאות⟨ה⟩ הקדחת שיסבול החולה קור וחום בתכונה אחת שקורין היוונים¹ איפילא

ובהרבה מהקדחות אחרות זולת הקדחת הנקבעת הנקראת שידפון. (1.2) ורוע מזג מתחלף יהיה בכל

אחד ואחד מן האיברים, אי זה שיהיה, כמו שיהיה לו רכות שהוא מורסא לחיית, או שתהיה מורסא

דמיית חמה הולכת אל הקץ באותו שיהיה בדרך הפסד ומות והיא מורסא שקורין הנוצרים קַקְרֵיבֵּי,

או תהיה בו מורסא אחת שקורין אֵירֵיסִיפֵּילָא או מורסא אחת שקורין קרָנְקוֹ ובאמת צרעת היא מזה

הסוג וכן אֵישְׁפֵּירְטִי אומינוש ונמלה. והנה אלו החליים אינם מורקים עד שלא יהיה עמהם מותר

נקבע באבר אשר הם בו. ויש עניין אחר מרוע מזג מתחלף שהוא בלא שפיכת מותר באיברים אלא

שאיכויותיהם לבד משתנים, אם שיקוררו מקור או יחוממו מחום השמש, או שפעולותיהם עוברות

השיעור הניאות והראוי, או שהמנוחה או **[19v]** העצלה עוברים השיעור הנאות והראוי וזולת זה

ממה שדומה לאלו. בגופים באמת נעשה רוע מזג מתחלף מסבות יבואו מחוץ ואותם העניינים

מחממים או מקררים או מלחלחים. ומיני רוע המזג אלו הם פשוטות ופרטיות כמו שהראיתיך בספר

המזג. (1.3) וממנו באמת יש ארבעה מינים אחרים מורכבים שיתהוו כשיחוממם ויתלחלח הגוף יחד

או שיחוממם ויתיבש הגוף יחד או שיקורר ויתלחלח יחד או שיקורר ויתיבש יחד. ומפורסם הוא באמת

שאלו המינים מרוע מזג מתחלף אינם מתחלפים מרוע מזג נקבע לפי שהם אינם מנצחות אבל חלקי

הגוף אותו שנשתנה מזגו.

פרק שני². אם כן שכוונתי בזה הספר היא הידיעה באי זה דרך נעשה הווית כל מיני רוע מזג

מתחלף. בעבור שיהיה דברי בכאן מבואר לכן ראוי שאזכור בכונת כל האיברים ואתחיל לדבר

---

¹ היוונים : הנוצרים א   בנוסח הנוצרי כתוב שקורין היוונים אֵיפִּילא א¹

² שני : emendation editors שיני א

מהגדולים מהם הנודעים[3] לאותו שאין לו[4] ידיעה ברפואה, שהיד והרגל והבטן והחזה והראש הם

אותם שלא יסכול שום אדם בישותם. (2.1) לכן נעיין בדבר[5] כל אחד מהם, וכל אחד ואחד נחלק

לחלקים הקרובים אליו שהוא מורכב מהם. המשל בזה הרגל נחלק אל הרגל והשוק, והיד אל הזרוע

והקנה והכף, והכף נחלק אל האיברים [20r] הקרובים לו שהם הסבוכיות[6] והגב והאצבעות יחלקו

עוד לחלקים שהורכבו מהם והם העצמות והסחוסים וקשרים ועצבים וגידים דופקים וקרומים ובשר

ומיתרים וציפרנים ועור ושומן.

(2.2) כי אלה האיברים אשר זכרתי באחרונה אי איפשר לחלקם בשום חלוקה אחרי זאת, אבל הם

באמת איברים ראשונים דומי החלקים, זולתי הגידים הדופקים והנחים, כי אלה שני האיברים

מורכבים מליפים וקרומים כמו שזכרתי באו<דות>[7] הנתוח. והודעתי בו עוד כי בתוך האיברים

הראשונים דומי החלקים יש נקבים רבים שמהם גדולים ורבים שיש בתוך האיברים הכליים. ולפעמ'

נמצא באי זה אבר דומה החלקים נקבים דומים להם כמו שאנחנו רואים בעצמות והעור. אבל מאותם

האיברים יש שהוא רפה החלקים, כי ממנו מתהוים חלקים שנקביהם יעלמו לחושים. אך יש אבר מן

האברים שהוא קשה ויבש תוכל להשיג כל הנקבים והסדקים אשר הם בו, כמו שנשיג בחוש ריקות

העצמות; ובאותו הריקות יש לחות שמניית לבנה בטבע מוכנה לעצמות שיזונו בה ממנה. אולם באי זה

צד יתילדו אלו הנקבים שהם בעור כבר הודעתי בספר המזג. ואלו הדברים ההכרח חייב זכרונם לפי

שבעבורם יתאמת מה שנמשיך לזכור.

(2.3) **פרק שלישי** שילמד בו [20v] כל מהות רוע מזג מתחלף וישים חילוק בין מיניו. ועתה יאות

שנבוא אל ידיעת רוע מזג מתחלף ושנזכור טבעו וכמה מ<י>ניו. הנה כבר אמרנו בהרבה מקומות זולת

זה שחלקי[8] הגוף שבהם יקרה רוע מזג מתחלף אינו מזג אחד. וזה נאות שוה לכל מיני מזג מתחלף,

אבל מיניו[9] הולכים אחרי טבע הגופות אשר יתילדו, כי כשיקרה רוע מזג מתחלף בבשר הוא זולת

הקרותו בקשרים בלבד, ומקרה כל אחד מאלה עניינו בזולת עניינו.[10]

---

[3] הנודעים : emendation editors passim   הנועדים א
[4] לו : emendation editors   לא א
[5] בדבר : emendation editors   בדיבור א
[6] הסבוכיות : rasceta L
[7] באו<דות> : De . . . anotomie L
[8] שחלקי : emendation editors   שחליק א
[9] מיניו : emendation editors   מינים א
[10] בזולת עניינו : מזה נמשך א add

(3.1) **פרק רביעי** שיבאר בו איך יתילד רוע מזג מתחלף חם כשהחומר יהיה בעצל. מזה נמשך[11] שאם ישפך מותר חם בעצל או בגידים הגדולים ממנו הדופקים והבלתי דופקים מתמלאים בתחילה ומתפשטים, ואחריהם בקטנים. וזה לא יעצור עד שיבוא אל הגידים היותר קטנים. ואחר שאותו המותר מפעפע מהגידים ולא יכילוהו, ישפך ממנו כמות מה מפיות אותם הגידים ומתדיית[12] מה, ויורקו ממנו מגופות הגידים. ואח<ר> שיהיה זה הנה יתמלאו מאותו המותר הנקבים אשר בתוך האברים הראשונים עד שיקרה להם שיתחממו ויתלחלחו מכל צדדיהם מאותו המותר אשר יכילו. ורצוני באברים הראשונים שיובן העצבים והקשרים והקרומים והבשר, ואחר אלה גידים דופקים ובלתי דופקים, ובהם בייחוד יקרה הכאב בראשונה לפי ענינים מתחלפים. והיה זה[13] [21r] לפי שהמותר אשר בפנימיותם יחממם וימתחם <ויבקעם, והמותר אשר בחוץ יחממם> ויקבץ ויבצר ויכביד. ואמנם בשאר האברים בקצתם לא יחלו ממנו אם לא בחום לבד, וקצתם לא יחלו ממנו רק במתיחה לבדה, וקצתם יחלו בשני ענינים יחד. (3.2) והחולי הזה הוא הנקרא בלשון היוונים "פליגמוני", שהוא מורסא חמה, והוא רוע מזג מתחלף יקרה בעצל, ובעבור הדם אשר בו הנה נתחמם ויקרהו כדמות רתיחה. ואחר יתחממו ראשונה מחומו גופות הגידים הדופקים והבלתי דופקים, ואחר זולתם משאר האברים אשר יכילו אותו הדם עד שיושקע בו.

ובאמת הוא בלתי אפשר שזאת העלה לא תבוא לאחד משני אלו הפנים : או שהמותר ינצח ויהיה נשפך<לעצל> ויפסיד הגופות אשר ינוצחו ממנו, או שהמותר מנוצח וישוב העצל לתכונתו הטבעית. נציע שהמותר יהיה מנוצח, שזה ראוי יותר ונאות יותר להקדים מה שהוא טוב. אני אומ' שהבריאות תהיה לפי אחד משני אלו הפנים : או שיפסידו כל הלחיות שנשתפכו בעצל או שיתבשלו. אולם הבריאות היותר משובחת משני אלו היא אותה שהיא בכליון. אמנם אחר בישול אותו המותר ימשכו שני אלו עניינים : האחד הוא התילדות מוגלא ואחר קיבוץ. וזה הקבוץ לפעמים יהיה בנקבים הגדול היותר קרוב ליציאה, ובמעט פחד ; וזה קבוץ יותר משובח לפי שהוא בנקב יותר רחב ויותר קרוב. ולפעמ' [21v] יהיה בנקב קטן ויותר רחוק ממקום היציאה והוא יותר מסוכן[14] ; ואותו הנקב אינו

---

[11] מזה נמשך : om. א
[12] ומתדיית : resudat L
[13] "והיה זה לפי ענינים מתחלפים" חוזר בכה"י.
[14] מסוכן : emendation editors : מסוקן א

במעט פחד. ולפעמ' יהיה בנקב מעט הפחד ואינו מהנקבים הגדולים ולא מהקרובים לצאת[15], (3.3)

והוא בהיותו בחלקי האסטומ' יהיה יותר משובח שהוא בחללו מאותו שהוא בפנימיות עצמיותו

<...>[16]. אמנם הקיבוץ המתהווה בקרום הנקרא "ציפאק" הוא רע. וכשיהיה הקבוץ בחלקי המוח,

בהיותו בשני החדרים המוקדמים יהיה יותר משובח, והקבוץ המתחדש תחת השני קרומים כשיהיה

בחדר האחרוני מהמוח הוא מגונה ורע. אמנם הקבוצים אשר בחלקי הצלעות תהיה בקיעתם לחללי

החזה, והקבוצים המתחדשים בעצלים בקיעתם אל העור, והקבוצים המתחדשים באברים הפנימיים

בקיעתם בגידים הדופקים והבלתי דופקים אשר בהם, או אצל הקרום[17] אשר יקיפם אשר הוא להם

במקום העור.

(3.4) ושהמותר ינצח האברים הוא באמת, אז מתבאר שזה לתגבורת רוע מזג אשר בהם הוא בטול

פעולתם, ושהיא תיפסד לאורך הזמן. אמנם התחלת מנוחת החולי בהם יהיה כשידמו האיברים אל

העניין המתחלף ומשנה אותם, וזה יהיה כשלא ירגישו האברים הכאב לפי שטבעם נשתנה תכלית

השתנות, אלא בעת השתנות הטבע, כמו שכבר זכר זה העניין המעולה אפוקראט באומרו שהכאבים

אינם מורגשים לאיברים [22r] אלא בתכונת השתנות הגוף ומהפסדו ויציאתו מטבעו. וכל אחד ואחד

שתרצה מהאברים לא ישתנה ולא יצא מטבעו ולא יפסד אם לא יחומם או לא יקורר או לא יתלחלח

או לא ינוגב או שיפורק חיבורו. ואמנם ברוע המזג המתחלף, לפי שהאבר נתחמם או נתקרר יקרה

הכאב בייחוד, ויהיה זה לפי שפעולת שני האיכיות חזק משאר האיכיות. אמנם יתחדש הכאב גם כן

<כ>שיתלחלח האבר או כשיתיבש כמו בעת הרעב והצמא, ויקרה זה החולי ברעב לחסרון עצם יבש

ובעת הצמא לחסרון עצם לח. אמנם כשפעולת האבר תחדל בסבת מה שיעקצהו או מה שיפסידהו או

מה שימתיחהו או שיפרקנו, אז יקרה החולי הזה בסבת פרוק החבור.

(4.1) **פרק החמישי**. וכשחום הדם אשר באבר אפוסטומושא ר״ל בעל מורסא יתחדש חום נח,[18]

ויהיה הדם אשר בכל הגוף שוה המזג, [ו]אולי לא יתחדש חום בכל הגוף מחום האבר העלול.

---

[15] לצאת : om. L
[16] et ad quam secundum plurimum fit saniei eruptio   חסר בכה״י ותרגומנו : "ועל הרוב נשפכת לתוכו מוגלא"
[17] הקרום : emendation editors הקורום א
[18] וכשחום הדם אשר באבר אפושטומושא ר״ל בעל מורסא, יתחדש חום נח   emendation editors : כשיתמגל הדם אשר באבר יתחדש חום נח א   כשיתמגל נ״א וכשיתמרסם נ״א וכשחום הדם אשר באבר אפושטומושא ר״ל בעל מורסא יהיה החום נח א[1]

וכשיתחממם הדם אשר באבר המת<מ>גל[19] חם חזק, יתחמם [ב]כל הגוף מחוזק רתיחת הדם אשר בו.
וכשתגבר האדומה בדם העובר בכל הגוף אז לא יכלא <יוכל (?)> שלא יתחמם הגוף חום חזק. וכאשר
ישתתף התגבורת בשני האכיות האלו ר״ל שהדם אשר באבר המתגמל יהיה חזק החום והדם הכולל
כל הגוף תגבר עליו האדומה, יהיה זה היותר חזק.

(4.2) אמנם מה שיתחמם ראשונה, כשיגבר החום, יתחמם הדם אשר בגידים הדופקים, מפני שהוא
בטבעו יותר חם ויותר קרוב לטבע הרוח, ואחריו הדם אשר בגידים הבלתי דופקים. וכשהאבר
המתגמל יהיה [22v] קרוב לאותם האיברים הפנימיים המתגברים בדם אשר יכילם, ילך החום
מהרה אל הדם העובר בכל הגוף. ובכלל יותר ראוי שיתחמם ראשונה כל מה שהוא נקל להשתנות[20] או
שבטבעו יותר חם; וכן, הראשון שיתקרר הוא מה שהוא נקל להשתנות או שבטבעו יותר קר. ומה
שהוא יותר קל ההשתנות בגופותינו הוא הרוח מפני שהוא יותר דק והיותר רקיק. והיותר חם
בגופותינו המרה האדומה, והיותר קר הליחה הלבנה. ואמנם בשאר הליחות חום הדם הוא אחר חום
האדומ׳, וקור המרה השחורה הוא אחר קור הליחה הלבנה. האדומ׳ משתנה מהרה ובנקלה ממה
שיפעל בה, והשחורה משתנה בקושי. ובכלל: כל מה שהוא דק ורקיק קל ההשתנות, ומה שהוא גס
ועבה מתפעל בקושי ובאיחור.

(4.3) ולכן ראוי שיהיה הקרוב מהמורסה הראשונה השתנותו מתחלף מאד להתחלפות תכונות
הגופות ממנו, לפי שהליחה אשר תחדש ממנה המורסא היא מתוספת חום או מחסרונו. ועוד סבה
אחרת -שעיפושה אינו אלא לפי [ש]טבעה, ולפי יתרון גודל כמות התאספה או מיעוטה <ב>פנימיות
האברים. כי עיפוש ממה שאין לו התנשמות נקל מאד וממהר, וזה נמצא בדברים הפנימיים
והחיצוניים. ואם יראה עם זה שמזגה חמה ולחה, הנה העפוש המתחדש ממנה יהיה יותר מהרה.
והאבר גם כן אשר בו המורסא או [23r] הוא קרוב לאברים אשר הם רבי הדם או רחוק מהם. ועוד, כי
הדם שתגבר בו האדומ׳ או השחורה או הליחה או הרוח [ו]יתחלפו אלו התכונות בריבוי או במיעוט.
ויתחייב אם כן בהכרח שיהיה גבול[21] המורסא רב התחלפויות לפי התיחס[22] כל אחד ואחד מאלה זה
עם זה וכפי התיחסו לעצמו.

---

[19] המת<מ>גל : מורסי בל׳ אפושטומושא א[1]
[20] להשתנות : להשנות א emendation editors
[21] גבול המורסא : resolutio L
[22] התיחס emendation editors : חתיסם א

(5.1) הנה התאמת שכל אילו העניינים הם סבת רוע מזג מתחלף [23] אשר בדם

היותר מנצחת היא באבר המתמגל, ואחריו באברים אשר הם רבי הדם, ואחריו בדם אשר בלב,

ובייחוד אותו שהוא בחלל השמאלי ממנו. שאם תכניס האצבעות בזה החלל בעוד שהאיש חי, ושהוא

בלתי מוקדח, <...>[24] תרגיש חום מופלג ביותר בתכלית. לכן אינו רחוק שהגוף כשיתחמם מחום חזק

מתגבר על הטבע, שהחלל ההוא יתחמם תכלית החום. וממה שיעזור לפועל הזה הוא לפי שבו יהיה

הדם היותר דק והיותר קרוב לטבע הרוח, ואחר לפי שהוא מתנועע תנועה תמידית.

(5.2) אמנם בקדחות ימצא שהחום מתלקח בכל הדם, ושהוא מקבל קבול שלם החום העובר

המנהג הטבעי המתיל מעיפוש הליחה. אמנם בגופות הגידים הדופקים ושאר הגופים השכנים אליהם

והמקיפים אותם אינו נמצא עדין דין שלימות השתנות המזג, אבל הם מתאחרים ההשתנות ההולך אל

החום השלם. ואם יותמד זה לאורך זמן, [23v] יגיע אל התכלית אשר בו יונצחו וישתנו מכל וכל, ואז

הם כבר הגיעו לקץ אותו החום היוצא מהטבע <...>.[25] אמנם אי זו תכונה כשהיא אצל תכלית העניין

הגעת זה התכלית אינו אלא דרך לצאת התכונה ההיא מהעניין הטבעי המורכבת בשיווי ובמצוע בין

שני אלו ר"ל בין התכונה הטבעית באמת ממנו ובין התכונה כשהיא יוצאת מהטבע לגמרי.

פרק ששי. ואם כן בכל זמן ארוך יקרה שהגוף יתחמם מזה החום כמות מהשתנות הולך אחריו.

(5.3) אבל לפי שאברי הגוף הראשונים בשלמות נתחממו מחום אותה הקדחת הנקראת[26] שדפונית

ובלעז "איטיקא" שהיא נקבעת, והיה כן לפי שהעצם ממנה אינו עומד בליחיות וברוחות[27] לבד, אבל

היא בזולת אלו והיא בגופים הקיימים. ובזאת הקדחת <לא> יהיה ציר, וידמה אז החולה שאין בו

קדחת לפי שלא ירגיש חום, וזה לפי שאבריו ניתחממו בשיווי בתכונה אחת.[28] והנה נסכמו על זה

הפילוסופים הטבעיים בעיונם בחושים ואמרו, שאין הרגש אם לא בהפכיות, ושלא יהיה ציר וכאב

באותם אשר נשתנו בתכלית השלימות. ולזה הוא שאין בעל אחת הקדחות מזה הסוג שקדם זכרה

בסמוך, ר"ל קדחת השדפון, מרגיש בכאב וחולי ואין החולה מרגיש בה כלל, [24r] והסבה בזה לפי

---

[23] שהאיכות qualitas) =) : L caliditas

[24] <...> : L - Sicut narravi in libro de medicatione anathomie - ותרגומו:"כפי שאמרתי בספר אודות רפואת האנטומיה"

[25] <...> : L - Resolutionis autem terminus in unoquoque membrorum est nocumentum operationis eius - ותרגומו: "סיומו של כל שינוי באבר מן מהאברים גורם נזק לפעולתו"

[26] הנקראת : איטיקא add. and del. א

[27] וברוחות : emendation editors וברוחוד א

[28] בתכונה אחת emendation editors : בתכונות אחרית א

שתכונת אברי הגוף בעלי זאת הקדחת אינה תכונה שתפעל בקצתם ויתפעלו ממנה קצתם, כי כולם

כבר נעשו מתכונה אחת ומזגם נעשה אחד נאות [29] (6.1) ואע״פ שהיה קצתם, <ר״ל> האברים [30], הם

חמים ביותר וקצתם קרים קור מופלג ולא יקרה לאותם החמים השכנים לאותם הקרים שיתבלבלו

מקור אותם האברים הקרים השכנים להם. שאלו היה כן, הנה לאברים בעצמם יקרה כמו זה הבלבול

בישות מהותם ותכונתם. שהאברים שהם בתכונתם הטבעית יש בהם הפכיות, והוא שהבשר ממנו הוא

אבר חם והעצם ממנו קר, והנה אין בהתחלפות [31] אלה והדומים להם ציר וחולי למיעוט יחס <החום >

והקור ביניהם. ולזה הוא שהאויר [32] המקרה גופותינו אינו משנה גופותינו עד שישתנה שינוי מתגבר

בחום או בקור. ואמנם המינים המתחלפים [33] ממנו ברוב חום או ברוב קור יהיו לפי התרבותם [34] ולפי

הערך אשר בינו ובין הגופות, כן גופותינו ירגישוהו ולא יתבלבלו ממנו.

(6.2) ואם כן אולי איזה בעל נפש יודה לפי זה העיון למה שנאמר, כמו שזכר אפוקרט בספריו, שכל

החוליים אינם אלא חבורות. והיה זה בעבור שהחבורות אינם [35] אלא פירוק חבור, וחום מופלג או קור

לעתים מחדשים פירוק חבור ; החום המופלג מפני שיתיך וישבור חבור הגשם שינצח, [24v] והקור

המופלג יחבר ויקבץ בפנים העצמיות ממה שינצח עד שיתגבר איזה ענין ממנו, ויוציא ויקובץ מה

שנשאר ממנו ויפורק. ואם אחד שישים זה הגבול בתגבורת חום או בתגבורת קור, יצדק הענין שלא

יהיה רחוק מלחשוב ממנו שימצא הסבה. אמנם אם זה הגבול אינו בתגבורת, בזה יהיה גבול אחר

בו, והנה לפי תכונה נגלית ששום תגבורת אינה מובנת אלא דרך היחס לאיזה דבר. ולזה יהיה שמה

שיקרה לגוף מהדברים שהם מתכונה אחת בחום ובקור אינו בצד אחד.

(6.3) ומפני זה היה שהליחות שהם בקצת בעלי חיים יש ביניהם נאותות, ומקצת בעלי חיים הליחות

אשר ביניהם אינם ניאותות, אבל מפסידים והורגים זה את זה, כמו האדם והנחש שכל אחד מהם

ממית חברו ברוקו. ולזה הוא שהעקרב ימות ברוק האדם הצם, והאדם אינו ממית הדומה לו ממנו

ולא האפעה אפעה אחר. והסבה שהדומה הוא נאות ואוהב והפך שונא ומבלבל. וממה שיור<ה> על

זה הוא שכל הצמחים הגדלים לא יצמחו ולא יקבלו גידול אלא במה שידמה להם הנאות להם, והנפסד

נאות [29] emendation editors : שנאות א

האברים [30] : om. L

המתחלפים [31] emendation editors : מתחלפות א

שהאויר [32] emendation editors : שהאבר א

המתחלפים [33] emendation editors : המתחליקים א

התרבותם [34] : התרכבותם(?) א

אינם [35] emendation editors : אינה א

או הנתך לא יפסד ולא יתך אלא מהפכו. ולזה היה ששמירת הבריאות אינה אלא בדברים נאותים

ודומים לגופים הבריאים וטובים[36] לבריאות, ורפואת החליים אינה אלא בעניינים ההפכיים. ואולם

[25r] הדבור מזה הוא בזולת כוונתינו במה שאנחנו בו.

(6.4) ואולם אותה הקדחת הקיימת אשר היא מבואשה קיימת קיום חזק[37] לא ירגישנה מי

שיסבול אותה. ומשאר הקדחות אין אחת מהם שלא תהיה מוחשת לסובלה; אבל בקצתם כשירגישוה

הגופות יהיה מאד מבולבל וקצתם במעט בלבול. ומהם עדיין יש בקצתם שיחדשו סמור, וזה

המקרה[38] הוא בשאר המקרים הרבים שלא יהיו אלא מרוע מזג מתחלף. ואי אפשר[39] שאזכור באיזה

מן המינים יתחדש זה המקרה במאמרי זה, אם לא אודיעך כמה הם הכחות הטבעייות ומהותם, ומה

הוא מה שהוא מיוחד בפועל כל אחד ואחד מהם. אבל אזכור סבות המקרים כולם והוייתם בספר

החליים והמקרים.

(7.1)   **פרק שביעי**. ונשוב למיני רוע מזג מתחלף. הנה כבר זכרתי במה שקדם באי זו דרך תתיילד

הקדחת ממורסא החמה הנקרא<ת> "פלגמוני", ושכל מורסה מהסוג הזה וכל קדחת, זולת קדחת

שדפון, הם מהחוליים אשר בהם רוע מזג מתחלף. והנה יתיילדו קדחות מעפוש ליחות, ואמנם בלא

מורסא, והיה זה מפני כי מה שיתעפש אינו מתקבץ שיהיה מוסף נעצר, והוא נעדר ההתנשמות לבד,

אבל יותר מהרה יתילד עפוש בזה ובחוזק. ואמת הנה יתעפשו דברים אחרים רבים שהם מוכנים

להתעפש. אבל אני אזכור הוית ההכנה ממה שהוא מוכן להתעפש בספר אחר זולת זה.

(7.2)   ואולם רוע מזג מתחלף יתחדש בדרך אחרת בכל הגוף; ולפעמים יהיה בהיות האיד החם[40] בו

מקובץ ועצור, [25v] ולפעמים יהיה מרוב חום בסבת תנועה גדולה מהשיעור הראוי, ולפעמ' מפני

שהדם יתחמם ויורתח רתיחה רבה בסבת הכעס, או שיתחמ' מאד בסבת העמידה בשמש החם.

ומבואר הוא אצלי שכל אלו הקדחות הבאות מחמת מורסא הם לפי הוית כח הסבות הפועלות בגוף,

ולפי תכונת כל אחד הגופות תהיה הקדחת בקצת הגופות יותר חזקה ובקצת הגופות יותר חלושה,

וקצת הם בלא שום קדחת כלל.

---

[36] וטוב<>ים <ס> : emendation editors ושוב : א

[37] מבואשה (מבושאה א) קיימת קיום חזק : א que substantie animalis fixe inheret L

[38] המקרה : emendation editors   המקה א

[39] אפשר : emendation editors איפשר א

[40] החם : emendation editors החום א

(7.3) ואמנם הנה הוא מבואר שרוע מזג מתחלף הווה לפעמי' ברוחות לבד ולפעמים יעבור עם זה אל הליחה. ובאמת מהדברים שאינם למטה מזה בבאור שכל הקדחות המתארכות ימשך אחריהם קדחת שדפונית. ומזה העניין הנה נתבאר שרוע מזג מתחלף לפעמי' הוא מליחה חמה או קרה נאגרת⁴¹ לאי זה אבר, כמו שביארתי מהיות האיברים אשר בהם המורסות. ולפעמים לא יהיה כן, אבל הוא בהשתנות מזג הגוף משווה,⁴² ושקצת עילות אשר ישנו אותו או באות מתוך הגוף, וקצת באות מחוץ. ויקרה שקדחת מתילדת מחום השמש ולפעמים מקצת מורסות הגוף. והתילד קדחת מחום השמש או בתנועה מופלגת חיצונה אזכור בבאור יותר רחב מזה החבור בספרי בסבות והמקרים. וכמו שהתחדש קדחת מחום השמש בהשתנות מזג הגוף, כן יקרה גם כן לקצת האנשים פעמים רבות לקרירות האויר שינצח בהם קור⁴³ מופלג עד שימותו [26r] קצתם. והעניין באמת באלו האנשים הוא מבואר שיקרה להם חולי וכאב (8.1) כשיגבר בהם קור רב מקור חזק, ואחר יתחזק ויתחמם גופם מהרה בהתקרב⁴⁴ הגוף אל האש. ורב מהם אשר יקרם זה ויקריבו גופם מהרה אל האש, ירגישו כאב חזק בשרשי הצפרנים .

פרק שמיני אם כן מי שרואה במוחש בזה הדרך שסבת ציר וכאב אינו אלא רוע מזג מתחלף איך יטיח דברים לבזות אותו העניין בכאבים אשר יקרו בפנימיות הגוף. ושיתמה באיזה צד⁴⁵ יקרה כאב פעמי' רבות בלא מורסא לאנשים, אם במעי הנקרא "קולון" אם בקצ<ו>ת הבצים או בשאר האברים, ואומר אני בזה שאחד מאלו העניינים אין ראוי להפלא עליהם בזה. ואחר שהוא כן אין זה מן הפלא מה שיקרה לקצת האנשים קדחת ופלצות בתכונה אחת, כי זה העניין הוא כן כאשר תגבר ליחה קרה ליחיית דומה לזכוכית, וליחה חמה שהיא מסוג האדומה, בכדי שתהיינה גוברות יחד בגוף ומתנועעות בגוף, וביחוד באברים המרגישים, ואין מן התמה אם מי שהוא בזאת התכונה ירגיש שני העניינים האלה יחד. שאם תעמיד האדם בשמש חמה ואחר תשפוך עליו מים קרים, אינו בלתי נאות אם ירגיש חום השמש וקור המים . אמנם אלו השנים יש להם זאת התכונה ושלא יקרו מחוץ, ויקרה כל אחד ואחד בחלקים הגדולים מהגוף.

(8.2) אמנם בקדחת שקורין היונים "איפיאלא" יקרה הפעלות חום [26v] <וקור>, ויקרה זה ממה שבפנים, ויקרה לזה גם כן כל אחד ר"ל חום וקור בחלקי הגוף הקטנים ממנו. והסבה בהיות זה שאין

---

⁴¹ נאגרת : emendation editors   נגארת א

⁴² משווה א (= equalitate) : L qualitate

⁴³ קור : emendation editors   חום א

⁴⁴ בהתקרב : emendation editors   בהתקרר א

⁴⁵ צד : emendation editors   זד א

חלקי הגוף הראשון הגדולים אשר להם יקרה הקור, שלא יהיה בצד כל אחד חלק גדול שלא יקרה
אליו חום. והגוף השני אין בו חלק אחד קטן שיקרה לו הקור אשר לא יהיה בצדו חלק אחר קטן שלא
יקרה לו חום. ומפני זה חוש הגוף השני ידמה שירגיש שניהם יחד. והיה זה לפי שכל אחד ואחד ממה
שיחומם ויקורר הוא עובר בחלקים קטנים קרובים האחד אצל האחר, ולא ימצא אחר קוטן החלקים
האלה חלקים קטנים מהם, ואי אפשר[46] שימצא איזה חלק שבו יהיה חוש חמימות וקרירות יחד בלתי
האחר. (8.3) וקצת מהגופות אשר תקרה להם קדחת, אחר שאחזו הקדחת בכל אחת ואחת מהעונות
יקרה שירגיש עמה קור או חום חזק, אבל לא ירגיש אחד מאלה האכויות במקום שבו ירגיש האחר.
ומי שיקרה אליו זה יוכל לברר להכיר בין האברים שלו איזה מהם הוחם ואיזה מהם נתקרר, והיה
זה מפני שהוא ירגיש חום באברים הפנימיים וירגיש <קור> בכל האברים החיצוניים מגופו.

ומהקדחות עוד יש קדחת שקורין היונים ״שינוקא׳ שאינה נופלת וחסירה מזה העניין, וגם יש
מהקדחות השורפות . ומה שיקרה לאלו הקדחות בחלקים גדולים הוא מה שיקרה בקדחת שקורין
היונים ״איפילא״ בחלקים הקטנים, כי רוע מזג באלו הקדחות הוא מתחלף <והוא מתחלף גם>
באותה שתקרה אליו פלצות מבלי שיקרה לו קדחת. אולם זה המקרה מעט הוא [27r] שיקרה, אבל
אמנם לפי התכונה יקרה לקצת האנשים ולקצת הנשים. ובאמת יתחייב לפני זה, ר״ל הפלצות,[47] קדם
ההנהגה במנוחה, או שהחולה הרגיל זמן ארוך בהתמדת רב אוכל מוליד ליחה פגה ליחיית כמו הליחה
הדומה לזכוכית. הנה נראה שזה המקרה לא יתחדש כל כך באותם אנשים שלא הרגילו הנהגת המנוחה
ורוב אוכל. ולזה נמצא שקדמוני הרופאים גוזרים שהוא מוכרח שהפלצות ימשוך אחריו קדחת.
ובאמת אנו כבר ראינו, וראו אחרים מהרופאים החדשים, פלצות יבוא אבל לא תמשך אחריו קדחת.

(8.4) אמנם הקדחת שקורין היוונים ״איפילא״ מורכבת מרוע מזג שממנו יתחדש פלצות זה מוסף
בספר אחר[48] זה הוא שלא ימשך עמו קדחת, ומרוע מזג שממנו תקרה קדחת. ואמנם אמרינו
״איפילא״ איני רוצה להבין מזה השם אלא הקדחת שבה יקרה האחר לעולם, אבל הקדחת שילך
לפניה הפלצות ואחריו ימשך <חום> כמו שיקרה בשלישית וברביעית איני קורא אותה ״איפילא״.
הנה כבר התבאר שהקדחת הנקרא<ת> ״איפילא״ מורכבת משני מיני רוע מזג מתחלף, וגם כן היא
זאת התכונה בשאר הקדחות מלבד קדחת איטיקא.

---

[46] אפשר א : emendation editors אפשר א

[47] ר״ל הפלצות : L .om

[48] זה מוסף בספר אחר : L .om

(9.1) וכן יש חוליים שהם מיוחדים בקצת איברים, עם מורסא, וכולם מתהווים מרוע מזג מתחלף,

כמו המורסא הנקראת "פלגמון" ונקראת "סרטן" ונמלה, והנאצורים הנולדים בעבור איירישיפילא,

והמורסא הנקראת "מוליסִיאוני" והנקראת "אישטיאומינוש", ואותה שיקראו היונים " קַקְרִינִי "[49],

והוא מקרה יביא האבר לדרך המות. שכל אלו החוליים שוים לכל אחד מהאברים בהשפך אחת

מהליחות בהם, אבל הם מתחלפות, כי בקצת יתחדשו בסבת ליחה [27v] <ליחיית ובקצת בסבת

ליחה> אדומיית צהובה. וקצת מהם <...>[50] מדם חם דק רותח, וקצת מהם מדם עבה קר. וקצת מהם

נעשות משאר מיני הדם.

(9.2) אומנם אני אחקור ואבאר בעיון דק מיני הקדחות אילו בספר אחר. אבל בזה הספר יספיק לי

שאזכור באיזה דרך הוא תכונה בליחה הנשפכת באבר במקרה אשר לו, שבעבורו יתחדש כל אחד מן

החוליים שזכרתי, שהדבר ההוא לפי העיון[51] שקדם מדברינו ממקרה המורסא הנקראת "פלגמון"

שהיא מליחה חמה ודמיית. ושכל אחד ואחד מהאברים דומי החלקים, <ה>פשוטים <ו>הראשונים,

כשינצח אותם לחות הזה , מזגו יבוא לרוע מזג מתחלף. והסבה בזה בעבור שהוא ידוע אם שהוא

יתחמם[52] או שיתקרר או שיתנגב או שיתלחלח לפי התגברות[53] אותו הלחות הקרובה אליו בו, אמנם

מה שבפנים מאותו האבר עדיין אינו משתנה למה שידמה לאותה התכונה. ואע"פ שהוא ישתנה כולו

תכלית ההשתנות באחרונה מה שבפנימיותו ובשטחו החיצון ויהיה כולו מתכונה אחת, וישקוט ויקל

ממנו הכאב לגמרי. אבל החולי אז הוא יותר קיים ויותר כבד ויותר קשה. ומי שהיטיב בעיון מה שעבר

ומה שקדם יבין מה שנזכר מזה ויספיק לו עד שיבין ספרי ברפואות ואחריו בספר תחבולת [28r]

הבריאות.

ותהילה לאל חי שלי יחיאל מקיינצאנו בכמ' מרדכי הרופא זלה"ה מגרוסיטו כתבתי פה בקיינצאנו

[מ]חדש סיו[ו]ן רל"ה ליציר<ה>

---

[49] קַקְרִינִי : קַקְרִיבִי א

[50] A colera nigra et quedam a sanguine et eorum que proveniunt a sanguine quedam fiunt L : <...>
ותרגומנו : "מתוך המרה השחורה ומהם מן הדם ומאלה אשר נובעים מהדם יש היוצרים "

[51] העיון : emendation editors   העניין א

[52] יתחמם : או יתחמם א add

[53] התגברות : emendation editors   התגבורת א

III. GLOSSARIES

The primary glossary gives Latin, Hebrew, and English equivalents for the principal Arabic terms and phrases occurring in Hunayn's translation of *Fī sū' al-mizāğ al-muḫtalif*. Latin and Hebrew *indices verborum* follow separately.

A. Arabic–Latin–Hebrew

The following paragraphs describe the arrangement of entries in the primary glossary and explain its use of symbols:

Arabic entries:

1) Order of entries: The glossary is arranged according to the Arabic roots. Within each root, the following order has been applied: verbs are listed first, followed in second place by the derivative nominal forms in order of their length and complexity, followed thirdly by the verbal nouns of the derived stems, and fourthly by the participles, both in the order of their verbal stems.
2) Verbs: Verbs are listed according to the common order of the verbal stems (I, II, III. . .). If the first stem does not appear in the text, the first derived stem to do so is introduced by the first stem set in parentheses. When more complex expressions headed by a verb are listed, they directly follow the corresponding verb.
3) Nouns: The different numbers of a noun (sg., du., pl., coll., n. un.) are listed as separate entries and are usually given in their indeterminate state. However, the article is supplied if the noun is commonly used with the article in general, or if it always appears in the text with the article in a nominalized usage.
4) Complex expressions: Each entry may have subordinate entries featuring complex expressions that contain the term from the superordinate entry in some place. Complex expressions may be listed in the indeterminate as well as the determinate state.
4) Foreign words: Foreign words are listed in a strictly alphabetical order unless they are arabicized.
5) Vocalization: Only such words that might be confused with each other are vocalized. For the main part, this applies to the verbal nouns of the first stem that might be confused with the verb. In these cases, only the verbal noun is vocalized. Nouns that are distinguishable from each other by their vowel structure only are likewise vocalized, unless only one of them appears in the glossary.
6) Numbers: The numbers indicate the chapter and paragraph of the Arabic text in which the respective entry may be found.

Symbols employed in the Arabic entries:

1) - The dash is used in subentries to represent the superordinate entry. If this superordinate entry is a complex one, the dash represents only its first element.
2) : A word followed by a colon may have two functions. A singular with a colon introduces a plural or dual, when the corresponding singular does not figure in the

text. Any word followed by a colon may be used to introduce complex verbal or nominal expressions containing the word preceding the colon when this word itself does not figure in the text as an isolated item. The two functions of the colon may be combined.

3) < The angled bracket refers to other entries either containing the word in question or representing a different orthography thereof.

Hebrew equivalents:

1) Every word is given in the spelling (either defective or plene or both) in which it appears in the text.
2) Nouns are given in the indeterminate state, unless the corresponding Arabic term is given in the determined state for some reason; in the latter case, the Hebrew equivalents are given in the state in which they figure in the text.
3) Sometimes Pi'el verbs are written with an additional yud that does not necessarily appear in the texts, with the purpose of distinguishing the Pi'el from the corresponding Qal.

English equivalents:

The English translation corresponds to the Arabic entry as it is translated in the English text. Therefore, it does not necessarily correspond to the Hebrew equivalents, nor does it necessarily represent the common usage of the Arabic word independently from the text. This practice may result in a lack of symmetry between the different translations of the singular, dual, and plural of one single word.

when the part of the body is affected	ואמנם כשפעולת האבר תחדל	cum autem in membro fit operatio	تأثير: عند تأثير ما يؤثِّر في العضو 3.4	1
			مؤخّر > تجويف	
to harm	התבלבל, קרה הבלבול, משנה	impediri; impedire	أذي: آذي 6.1	2
to suffer harm	היה מבולבל	impediri	تأذّى 6.4	3
harmful	מבלבל	impediens	مؤذ 6.3	4
the roots of the nails	שרשי הצפורנים	radices unguium	أصل: أصول الأظفار 8.1	5
			أصلي > أعضاء	
'QTYQWS [= hektikos]	שידפון, שדפונית ובלעז "איטיקא"	ethica	اقطيقوس 1.1; 5.3	6
to corrode	הפסיד	corrodere	أكل 3.4	7
canker	אישטיאומינוש	herpestiomenus; estiomenus	أكلة 1.2; 9.1	8
composed	הורכב	compositus	مؤلَّف 2.1	9
to hurt	חלה	egrotare facit; facit pati	ألم: آلم 3.1	10
pain	חולי, כאב, ציר	egritudo, dolor, passio	ألــم 3.4; 5.3; 6.1; 7.3; 8.1	11
			آلي> أعضاء	
meninges	השני קרומים	duae matres	أمّ: أمّا الدماغ 3.3	12
testicles	בצים	testiculi	الأنثى: الأنثيان 8.1	13
'NPY'LYS [= epialos]	איפילא, איפיאלא, איפילא	epiala	انفياليس 1.1; 8.2,3,4	14
scattered	עובר	sparsus	مبثوث 8.2	15
pustules	נאצורים	pustule	بثر 9.1	16
vapor	איד	vapor	بخار 7.2	17

English	Hebrew	Latin	Arabic	#
body	גוף	corpus	بدن ‏;1.2; 4.1,2; 5.1; 6.2;‏ ‏7.2,3; 8.1,2,3 < أعضاء‏	18
in the entire body of the animal	בכל הגוף החי	in toto animalis corpore	‏-: فــي الــبـدن كـلّــه مـن‏ ‏الحيوان 1.1‏	19
bodies; body	גופים, גופות	corpora; corpus	أبـــدان ‏;1.2; 3.1,2; 5.2;‏ ‏6.1,3; 7.2‏	20
healing	בריאות	sanitas	برء 3.2; 6.3‏	21
			برئان > أحمد‏	
to cool; to be cooled	מקרר, קורר, התקרר, נתקרר	infrigidare, infrigidari	بــرد ‏;1.2,3; 3.4; 4.2; 8.3;‏ ‏9.2‏	22
to cool	קורר	infrigidare	أبرد 8.2‏	23
cold	קור, קרירות	frigus; frigiditas; frigor	بَــــرْد ‏;1.1,2; 6.1,2; 7.3;‏ ‏8.1,2,3 < غلب‏	24
a severe chill	קור חזק	fortis frigor	‏-: شديد 8.1‏	25
cold	יותר קר, קור	frigidus, frigidior	بــارد ‏;4.2; 6.1; 7.3; 8.1,3;‏ ‏9.1‏	26
coldest; colder	יותר קר, קר	frigidius, frigidior	أبردُ 4.2; 6.1‏	27
to spit	רוק	exspuere	بزق 6.3‏	28
simple	פשוט	simplex	بسيط 1.2 < الأعضاء‏	29
slow to be changed	מתפעל בקושי ובאיחור	tarde resolutionis	بطيء: بطيء الاستحالة‏ ‏4.2‏	30
to be abolished	בטול	destrui	بطل 3.4‏	31
belly	בטן	venter	بطن 1.3‏	32
to become moist	התלחלח	humectari	بلّ: ابتلّ 3.1‏	33
phlegm	ליחה לבנה, ליחה	flegma	بلغم 4.2,3‏	34
phlegmatic	ליחיי	flegmaticus	بلغمي ‏;9.1‏ ‏8.1,3< ورم‏	35
white	לבן	albus	أبيض: بيضاء 2.2‏	36

English	Hebrew	Latin	Arabic	#
fixed	נקבע	fixus	ثابت 5.3 > جوهر, حمّى, حمّيات	37
			ثبات > أجسام	
thick	גס	spissus	ثخين 4.2	38
serpent	-	draco	ثعبان 6.3	39
to bear down	הכבי[ד]	gravare	(ثقل) أثقل 3.1	40
elephantiasis	-	lepra	جذام 1.2	41
body	גוף	corpus	جرم 2.3	42
<parts>	גופות	corpora	أجرام 2.3	43
			مجرى > الحرارة	
part	חלק	pars	جزء 8.2	44
parts	חלוק, חלקים	partes	أجـــزاء 8.1,2,3; 2.3 > أعضاء	45
body	גוף	corpus	جسم 5.2	46
bodies	גופות	corpora	أجسام 3.2; 4.3; 5.2,3	47
bodies that have firmness	הגופים הקיימים	corpora quae adest fixio	الأجسام: الأجسام التي لها ثبات 5.3	48
to dry	התיבש, נוגב, התנגב	desiccare, desiccari	جفّ 1.2,3; 3.4; 9.2	49
skin	עור	cutis	جلد 2.1,2; 3.3	50
to contract and compress	חיבר וקיבץ	adunare et constringere	جمع: جمع وعصر 6.2	51
concentration	קיבוץ	collectio	جَمْع 3.2,3	52
kind, kinds	סוג	genus	جـــنـــس 1.2; 5.3; 7.1; 8.1,3 > خِلَط	53
to be near, to be adjacent, to be close	שכן, קרוב	vicinus; vicinior; appropinquare	(جـور) جـاور 5.2; 6.1; 9.2	54
close	קרוב	propinquum	مجاور 4.2	55

to pass	עבר	pertransire	(جاز) جاوز 7.3	56
immoderate	עבר השיעור הניאות והראוי	transcendere mensuram que est decens	تجاوز المقدار الذي ينبغي 1.2	57
hunger	רעב	fames	جوع 3.4	58
ventricle	חלל	ventriculus	تجويف 5.1	59
the posterior ventricle of the brain	החדר האחרוני מהמוח	ventriculum qui est in posterioribus cerebri	التجويف: التجويف الذي في مؤخّر الدماغ 3.3	60
the anterior ventricles	שני החדרים המוקדמים	ventriculi anteriores	التجويفان المقدّمان 3.3	61
substance	עצמיות	-	جوهر 6.2	62
the moist substance	עצם לח	humiditas	الجوهر الرطب 3.4	63
the dry substance	עצם יבש	substancia sicca	الجوهر: الجوهر اليابس فرق > 3.4	64
the fixed substance of an animal	?	substantia animalis fixa	الـثـابـت مـن جـوهـر الحيوان 6.4	65
beloved	אוהב	amicus	محبوب 6.3	66
degree; definition; limit	קץ, תכלית, גבול	terminus	حدّ 6.2 ;5.2 ;1.2	67
present-day physicians	הרופאים החדשים	novi medici	حدث: الحدث من الأطبّاء 8.3	68
afflictions	מקרה	eventus	أحداث 9.2	69
heat	חום	calor; caliditas	حرّ 1.1,2; 6.1,2; 8.2,3	70
hot	חם, יותר חם	calidus, calidior	حـــــارّ ;6.1 ;4.2,3 ;3.1 ورم > 7.2,3; 8.1; 9.1,2	71
heat; hot	חום	calor	حـــــرارة ;5.1,3 ;4.1,2,3 أقوى > 6.2; 7.2; 8.1	72
strong heat	חום חזק	caliditas fortis	قوية 4.1 -	73
quiet heat	חום נח	calor quietus	هادنة 4.1 -	74

English	Hebrew	Latin	Arabic	#
unnatural heat	החום העובר המנהג הטבעי	caliditas egrediens cursum naturalem	الحرارة: الحرارة الخارجة عن المجرى الطبيعي 5.2	75
			محرق > حمّى	
to move	מתנועע	moveri	حرك: تحرّك 8.1	76
it moves with a constant motion	מתנועע תנועה תמידית	movetur...motu assiduo	تحرّك...حركة دائمة 5.1	77
			حركة > حرك	
to feel, to be felt; to sense	מרגיש, הרגיש, היה מוחש ל-	sentire	حسّ 5.3؛ 6.1,4؛ 8.1,2,3	78
to feel	הרגיש	sentire	أحسّ 5.1؛ 8.1	79
sense; sensation	חוש, הרגש	sensus	حِسّ 2.2؛ 5.3؛ 8.2	80
sensation	חושים	sensus	حواسّ 5.3	81
sensitive	מרגיש	sensibilis	حسّاس 8.1	82
viscera; intestines	האברים הפנימיים, באברים אשר הם רביי הדם	viscera	حشا: أحشاء 3.3؛ 5.1؛ 8.3	83
the intestines abounding in blood	האיברים הפנימיים המתגברים בדם, האברים אשר הם רבי הדם	viscera sanguine habundantia	الأحشاء: الأحشاء الغزيرة الدم 4.2,3	84
the preservation of health	שמירת הבריאות	conservatio sanitatis	حفظ: حفظ الصحّة 6.3	85
to be congested	מקובץ ועצור	in ... constrictione retineri	احتقان 7.2	86
perfectly	שלמות	perfectus	مستحكم 5.3 > سخن	87
to be dissolved	הפסיד	resolvere	حلّ: تحلّل 3.2	88
dissolution	כליון	resolutio	تحلّل 3.2	89
to be feverish; fever patient	קדחת	febrire	حمّ 7.2؛ 8.3	90
fever	קדחת, מוקדח	febris	حـــمّــى 1.1؛ 5.1؛ 5.3؛ 7.1,2,3؛ 8.1,2,3,4	91

hectic fever	הקדחת הקיימת, קדחת שדפונית	febris fixa	الحمّى: الحمّى الثابتة 6.4؛ 7.3	92
the fever known as hectic	קדחי שדפון?	febris fixa nominata	ـ التي تعرف بالثابتة 7.1	93
the fever known as "hectic fever"	הקדחת הנקבעת	febris fixa	ـ المعروفة بالثابتة 1.1	94
fevers	קדחות	febres	حمّيات 1.1؛ 5.2؛ 6.4؛ 7.2؛ 8.4	95
hectic fevers	קדחת איטיקא	febres fixe	الحمّيات: الحمّيات الثابتة 8.4	96
ardent fever	הקדחות השורפות	febres adurentes	ـ المحرقة 8.3	97
laudable	יותר משובח	laudabilis	محمود 3.3	98
better; best; laudable	יותר משובח	laudabilius, laudabilior	أحمد 3.2,3	99
the best healing	הבריאות היותר משובחת	laudabilior duabus	أحمد البرئين 3.2	100
erysipelas	אירישיפֵלַא, נמלה	formica	حمرة 1.2؛ 9.1	101
to overwhelm	מתלקח	comprehendere	(حوذ) استحوذ 5.2	102
to surround	הקיף, מקיף	continere	حاط: أحاط 3.3؛ 5.2	103
surrounding	הכיל	continere	محيط 3.1 <> هواء	104
to transform	מתחלף	resolvere	(حول) أحال 3.4	105
to be changed; to be altered	משתנה, השתנה	resolvi; resolutus esse; alterare; alterari	استـحـال 4.2؛ 5.2؛ 6.1؛ 7.3؛ 9.2	106
to change and alterate	מתאחר ההשתנות	habens resolutionem et alterationem	ـ وتغيّر 5.2	107
the change ... has been completed; the alteration ... has been completed	נשתנה תכלית ההשתנות, נשתנה בתכלית השלימות	transmutatus est; integre alteratus esse	ـ وفرغ 3.4؛ 5.3	108
transmutation; change; alteration	השתנות, התחלפויות, הפכיות	permutatio; resolvendum; resolutio; alteratio	استحالة 3.4؛ 4.2,3؛ 5.2,3 <> بطيء	109

time; disposition; condition	תכונה, עניין	dispositio	حــــال 5.3; 7.2; 8.1,3,4; 9.1,2	110
the unnatural disposition	התכונה ההיא מהעניין הטבעי	dispositio egrediens a re naturali	الحال: الحال الخارجة عن الأمر الطبيعي 5.2	111
the disposition that is truly natural	התכונה הטבעית באמת	dispositio que est vere natura	- التي هي بالحقيقة طبيعية 5.2	112
the disposition that is fundamentally unnatural	התכונה כשהיא יוצאת מהטבע לגמרי	dispositio que est a natura penitus egressa	- التي هي خارجة عن الطبيعة أصلا 5.2	113
a natural disposition	תכונתם הטבעית	naturalis dispositio	- الطبيعية 6.1	114
dispositions	תכונות	dispositiones	أحوال 4.3	115
			حيلة: حيلة البرء > كتاب	
alive	חי	vivere	حيّ 5.1	116
animal, animals	איש, בעלי חיים	animal; animalia	حيـوان 5.1; 6.3 > بــدن, جوهر	117
to stream forth; to emerge	הורק, הוציא	egredi	خرج 3.1; 6.2	118
departure	יציאה	exiture	خروج 3.4 > طريق	119
abscesses	קבוצים	exiturae	خراج: خراجات 3.3	120
in all external things	בדברים הפנימיים והחיצוניים	in omnibus rebus extrinsecis	خـارج: في جميع الأشياء الـخـارجـة 4.3 > حـرارة, حال	121
idleness; ease of life	מנוחה	quies	خفض 1.2; 8.3	122
gaps	סדקים	scissure	خلل 2.2	123
humor	ליחה	humor	خِلْط 4.3; 8.1,3; 9.1,2	124
a humor that is of the variety of yellow bile	ליחה אדומיית צהובה	humor qui est de genere colere rubee	- من جنس المرار الأصفر 9.1	125
humors	ליחות, ליחה	humores	أخــــلاط 4.2; 5.2; 6.3; 7.1,3	126

English	Hebrew	Latin	Arabic	No.
to vary; to differ	התחלף, מתחלף	diversificari	خلف: اختلف 4.3; 9.1	127
diversity	התחלפות, מתחלף	diversitas	اختلاف 4.3; 6.1	128
to vary; to differ; different; anomalous	הפכיות, מתחלף	diversus; diversificari	مختلف 4.3; 6.1; 7.1; 8.3 > سوء	129
to follow	הרגיל	usus esse	دبر: تدبّر 8.3	130
regimen	הנהגה	regimen	تدبير 8.3	131
inside	פנימיות	interiora	داخل 3.3	132
to reject	הטיח דברים לבזות אותו העניין	respondere	دفع 8.1	133
to indicate	הורה	significare	دلّ 6.3	134
blood	דם	sanguis	دم 3.2; 4.1,2,3; 5.1,2; 7.2; 9.1 > أحشاء	135
bloody	דמיי	sanguineus	دموي 9.2 > ورم	136
			دماغ > أمّ؛ تجويف؛ نواحي	
to apply oneself	הרגיל	assidue esse	أدمن 8.3	137
to bring close	הקריב	appropinquare	دنا: أدنا 8.1	138
			أدوية > كتاب	
reprehensible	מגונה	illaudabilis	مذموم 3.3	139
head	ראש	caput	رأس 1.3	140
ligaments	קשרים	ligamenta	رباط: رباطات 2.1; 3.1	141
quartan fever	רביעית	quartana	ربع 8.4	142
foot	רגל	pes	رجل 2.1	143
legs	רגל	pedes	رجل: رجلان 1.3	144
wrist	סבוכיות	rasceta	رسغ 2.1	145

English	Hebrew	Latin	Arabic	№
to sprinkle	שפך	effundere	رشّ 8.1	146
to exude	מתדיית	resudare	رشح 3.1	147
to moisten, to be moist, to be moistened	מלחלח, התלחלח	humectare, humectari	رطب 1.2,3; 3.4; 9.2	148
fluid; moisture; residue	לחות, מותר,ליחה, אחת מהליחות	humiditas	رطـوبــة 2.2; 3.1,2; 7.3; 9.1,2	149
moistures	לחיות	humiditates	رطوبات 5.3	150
moist	לח	humidus	رَطِب 4.3 < جوهر	151
thin	רקיק, דק	tenuis; subtilis	رقيق 4.2; 9.1	152
thinnest	יותר רקיק, היותר דק	tenuior; subtilior	أرقّ 4.2; 5.1	153
compound; composed	מורכב	compositus	مركّب 1.3; 2.1,2; 8.4 < أعضاء	154
swelling; "tarahhul"	רכות, מוֹלִיסִיאוֹנִי	mollicies	ترهّل 1.2; 9.1	155
spirit	רוח, רוחות	spiritus	روح 4.2; 5.1,3; 7.3	156
ventosity	רוח	ventositas	ريح 4.3	157
exercise	פעולות, תנועה	exercitium	رياضة 1.2; 7.2 < إفراط	158
to have an empty stomach	צם	ieiunus	ريق: على الريق 6.3	159
glass	זכוכית	vitrum	زجاج 8.1,3	160
to push against	קיבץ	constringere	زحم 3.1	161
to increase	רוב	augmentum	(زيد) تزيّد 7.2	162
cause	סבה	causa	سبب 8.1 < قوة	163
cause, causes	סבה, עילות	causa; occasiones	أسباب 5.1; 7.3 < كتاب	164
to heat; to be hot; to be heated	מחמם, חומם, התחמם, נתחמם	calefacere; calefieri; calefactus esse	سخــن 1.2,3; 3.1,2,4; 4.1,2; 5.1,2; 7.2; 8.3; 9.2	165

English	Hebrew	Latin	Arabic	No.
to become hot equally	נתחמם [בשיווי]	calefactus esse equaliter	ـ سخونة مستوية 5.3	166
to be heated excessively	התחמ' מאד	calefieri superflue	ـ سخن سخونة مفرطة 7.2	167
to be fully and perfectly heated	בשלמות נתחמם	integre et perfecte calefactus esse	ـ الـسـخـونـة الـتـامـة المستحكمة 5.3	168
to be fully heated	-	integre calefactus esse calefactionem	ـ وفرغ 5.2	169
to heat	חימם, התחמם	calefacere; calefieri	أسخن 3.1; 4.1; 8.2	170
to warm quickly	התחמם מהרה	calefacere velociter	ـ إسخانا سريعا 8.1	171
heat; to become hot	חום	calefactio	سخونة 3.1,2; 4.1,2; 5.2; 6.1; 7.3	172
unnatural heat	החום היוצא מהטבע	calefactio a natura egrediens	ـ خـارجـة عـن الأمـر الطبيعي 5.2	173
unnatural heat	חום חזק מתגבר על הטבע	calefactio naturam supergrediens	ـ خارجة عن الطبع 5.1	174
to be exceedingly hot	חום חזק	calefactio superflua	ـ مفرطة 4.1	175
hottest; hotter	יותר חם, חם	calidior	سُخن: أسخن 4.2; 6.1	176
cancer	סרטן, קַרַנְקֹו	cancer	سرطان 1.2; 9.1	177
fast; quick	נקל, קל	velox	سريع 4.2 > أسخن	178
quickly; quicker; fastest; very fast	מהרה, יותר קל, נקל מאד וממהר, יותר מהר	velociter; velocius; velox; velocissime	أسرع 4.2,3; 7.1	179
rapidity	מהר	velox	سرعة 4.3 > سهولة	180
forearm	קנה	ulna	ساعد 2.1	181
dropsy	שיקוי	ydropisis	استسقاء 1.1	182
to rely upon; to be relieved from	הודה, שקט	acquiescere; sedari	سكن 6.2; 9.2	183
to ease	מנוחה	quies	سكون 3.4	184

pores	נקבים	pori	مسامّ 2.2	185
easily and quickly	מהרה ובנקלה	velociter	سهولة: بسهولة وسرعة 4.2	186
dyscrasia	רוע מזג מתחלף, רוע מזג	malitia complexionis diverse; malitia complexionis	سوء: سوء المزاج 1.3; 7.3; 8.3,4	187
anomalous dycrasia	רוע מזג מתחלף	malitia complexionis diverse	- مزاج مختلف 3.2; 9.1,2	188
anomalous dycrasia	רוע מזג מתחלף, חילוק רוע מזג מתחלף, רוע מזג	malitia (malitie) comple- xionis diverse; malitia complexionis	- المزاج المختلف 0; 1.1,2; 2.3; 3.4; 5.1; 6.4; 7.1,2,3; 8.1,4; 9.2	189
the uniform [kinds] of anomalous dycrasia	רוע מזג נקבע	malitie complexionis diverse	- المزاج المستوي 1.3	190
black bile	שחורה	melancolia	سوداء 4.2,3	191
lower leg	שוק	crus	ساق 2.1	192
			مستوي> سخن, سوء	
to flow	נגאר	currens	(سيل) سال 7.3	193
to be inherent to	קיים קיום?	inherere	شبث: تشبّث 6.4	194
to resemble	דומה	similis	مشابه 6.3	195
to become similar	דמה	similari	شبه: تشبّه 3.4	196
			متشابه > أعضاء	
fat	שומן	adeps	شحم 2.1	197
			شدّة > كدّ	
severe	מופלג	fortis	شديد 6.2	198
			تشريح > كتاب	
cure	רפואה	curatio	شفاء 6.3	199

127

similar	נאות	conveniens	مشاكل 6.3	200
common; combined	שוה, בשיווי	participativus; communis	مشترك 5.2 ;2.3	201
finger	-	digitus	إصبع 5.1	202
fingers, finger	אצבעות	digiti	أصابع 2.1	203
to stream	נקבע, שפיכה, נשפך, היה נשפך, נשתפך, השפך	infusus; infusio; effundi	صبّ: انصبّ ;3.1,2 ;1.2 9.1,2	204
			صحّة > حفظ	
healthy	בריא	sanus	صحيح 6.3	205
chest	חזה	pectus	صدر 1.3 > فضاء	206
to split	-	disrumpere	صدع 3.1	207
yellow bile	אדומה	colera	صفراء 8.1; 4.3	208
			أصفر > خلط	
peritoneum	הקרום הנקרא ציפאק	siphac	صفاق 3.3	209
hard	קשה	durus	صلب 2.2	210
heat	<חום>	calor	صالب 8.4	211
to bring close to the fire	בהתקרב הגוף אל האש	approximando ipsum igni	اصطلاء: بالاصطلاء 8.1	212
kind	עניין	modus	صنف 1.2	213
kinds	מינים	species	أصناف ;6.1 ;2.3 ;1.2,3 7.1	214
to be right; to happen; to occur	מצא הסבה, קרה	adinvenire; evenire; advenire	(صوب) أصاب 6.2; 8.1,3	215
to contain	הכיל	continere	ضبط 3.1	216
opposite	הפך	contrarium	ضدّ 6.3 > متوسّط	217
contrary	הפכיי	contrarius	مضادّ 6.3	218
harm	-	nocumentum	ضرر 5.2	219

English	Hebrew	Latin	Arabic	No.
weaker	יותר חלש	debilior	أضعف 7.2	220
to put pressure on; squeeze; to be squeezed	מתח, קובץ	coartare; coartari	ضغط 6.2؛ 3.1,4	221
pressure	מתיחה	coartatio	ضَغْط 3.1	222
			ضلع > نواحي	
relation	יחס	relatio	إضافة 6.2	223
medical	רפואה	medicina	طبّ 1.3	224
			طبيب: أطبّاء > حدث، قديم	
nature	טבע	natura	طبع 2.2 > سخونة	225
nature	טבע	natura	طبيعة 2.3؛ 3.4؛ 4.2,3؛ 5.1	226
natures, nature	טבע, טבעי	natura; nature	طبائع 2.3؛ 3.4؛ 5.3	227
natural	טבעי	naturalis	طبيعي 3.2 > حرارة, حال, سخونة, قوى	228
the way [process] that leads to	דרך לצאת	via egrediens	طريق: طريق الخروج 5.2	229
			طعام > إكثار	
to be prolonged	מתארך	prolongari	(طول) تطاول 7.3	230
nails	ציפרנים	ungues	ظفر: أظفار 2.1 > أصول	231
ĠNĠRYN‘ [= *gangraina*]	קַקְרִיבֵי	cancrene	عبقريا 1.2	232
balanced	שוה	equalis	معتدل 4.1	233
hostile	שונא	inimicus	عدو 6.3	234
range (latitude)	תכונה	intentio	عرض 5.2	235
symptoms	מקרים	accidentia	أعراض 6.4 > كتاب	236
symptom	מקרה	accidens	عارض 6.4؛ 8.3؛ 9.1	237

English	Hebrew	Latin	Arabic	№
knowledge	ידיעה	notitia	معرفة 1.3	238
vessels	גידים	vene	عرق: عروق 3.1	239
the pulsating vessels	הגידים הדופקים	vene pulsatiles	الـعـروق: الـعـروق الضوارب 5.2; 4.2	240
the nonpulsating vessels	הגידים הבלתי דופקים	vene non pulsatiles	- غير الضوارب 4.2	241
pulsating and non-pulsating vessels	גידים דופקים, הגידים הדופקים והנחים, גידים דופקים ובלתי דופקים	vene pulsatiles et non pulsatiles	- الـضـوارب وغـيـر الضوارب 2.1,2; 3.1,2	242
the largest pulsating and nonpulsating vessels	בגידים הגדולים ממנו הדופקים והבלתי דופקים	maiores vene que in ipso sunt, pulsatiles et non pulsatiles	- التي هي أعظم عروقها الـضـوارب وغـيـر مـنـها الضوارب 3.1	243
the vessels there, <that is> the pulsating and non-pulsating <vessels>	הגידים הדופקים והבלתי דופקים אשר בהם	vene que sunt in eis pulsatiles et non pulsatiles	- التي فيها الضوارب وغير الضوارب 3.3	244
more difficult	יותר קשה	difficilior	عسر: أعسر 9.2	245
nerves	עצבים	nervi	عصب 2.1; 3.1	246
			جمع <عصر	
to bite	-	mordere	عضّ 6.3	247
upper arm	זרוע	adiutorium	عضد 2.1	248
muscle	קשרים, עצל	lacertus; musculus	عضلة 2.3; 3.1,2	249
part	אבר	membrum	عضو 1.2; 3.4; 4.3; 6.1; تأثير <9.1	250
some part	אי זה אבר	aliquod membrum	- من الأعضاء 7.3	251
in any part of the body, whatever part it is	בכל אחד ואחד מן האיברים אי זה שיהיה	in uno membrorum erit, quodcumque fuerit	-: فـي عـضـو واحـد مـن الأعضـاء أيّ عضـو كـان 1.2	252
the affected part	האבר העלול	membrum infirmum	العضو: العضو العليل 4.1	253

English	Hebrew	Latin	Arabic	#
the swollen part	האבר המתמגל, אבר אפושטומושא	membrum apostemosum	العضو الوارم 5.1; 4.1,2	254
part, parts; organs	איברים	membra	أعضاء 1.2,3; 2.1,2; 3.1,4; 5.3; 6.1; 7.3; 8.1,3; 9.1	255
homoiomerous, primary parts	איברים ראשונים דומי החלקים	membra similium partium prima	متشابهة الأجزاء أوّليّة 2.2	256
the main parts of the body	אברי הגוף הראשונים	prima corporis membra	الأعضاء: الأعضاء الأصلية من البدن 5.3	257
first parts	האברים הראשונים	prima membra	الأوّل 3.1	258
the primary, homoiomerous parts	האיברים הראשונים דומי החלקים	membra prima similium partium	الأوّل المتشابهة الأجزاء 2.2	259
the composite, instrumental parts	האיברים הכליים	membra composita officialia	المركّبة الآلية 2.2	260
homoiomerous part, simple and primary	אברים דומי החלקים <ה>פשוטים <ו>הראשונים	membra similium partium simplicia prima	المتشابهة الأجزاء البسيطة الأوّل 9.2	261
one [particular] homoiomerous part	אי זה אבר דומה החלקים	aliquod membrorum similium partium	-: الواحد من الأعضاء المتشابهة الأجزاء 2.2	262
to be destroyed	נפסד	mori	عطب 6.3	263
thirst	צמא	sitis	عطش 3.4	264
bone	עצמות, עצם	os	عظم 2.2; 6.1	265
bones	עצמות	ossa	عظم: عظام 2.1,2	266
to putrefy	התעפש	putrefieri	عفن 7.1	267
putrefaction	עיפוש, עפוש	putrefactio	عفونة 4.3; 5.2; 7.1,3	268
scorpion	עקרב	scorpio	عقرب 6.3	269
illness	חולי	egritudo	علّة 3.2; 9.2	270
afflictions	חליים	egritudines	علل 1.2; 9.2 > كتاب	271

			عليل > عضو	
			علاج> كتاب	
to act	פעל	agere	4.2 عمل	272
ĠNĠRYN [= *gangraina*]	קַקְרִינִי	cancrene	9.1 عنقرانا	273
tertian fever	שלישית	tertiana	8.4 غبّ	274
to feed; to be nourished	זן, קבל גידול	nutriri	2.2; 6.3 اغتذى	275
to immerse	הושקע	submergere	3.2 (غرق): استغرق	276
membrane	קרום	panniculus	3.3 غشاء	277
membranes; tunics	קרומים	panniculi	2.1,2; 3.1 أغشية	278
anger	כעס	ira	7.2 غضب	279
cartilages	סחוסים	cartillagines	2.1 غضروف: غضاريف	280
to overpower; to dominate; to be dominated; to be dominant; to be overcome	ניצח, נוצח, מנוצח, גבר	vincere; vinci; dominare; superhabundare; victus esse	3.2,4; 4.1,3; 5.2; 6.2; 7.3; 8.1; 9.2 غـلـب	281
domination	תגבורת	dominium	3.4 غلبة	282
thick; gross	שמני, עבה	grossus; spissus	2.2; 4.2; 9.1 غليظ	283
more hard	יותר קיים	spissior	9.2 أغلظ	284
most dominating	היותר מנצח	vincens	5.1 أغلب	285
to boil	הורתח, רותח	fervere; ebulliens	7.2; 9.1 غلى	286
cooking; boiling; to boil	רתיחה	ebullitio	3.2; 4.1; 7.2 غليان	287
to enter	מפעפע	redundere	3.1 غاص	288
to transmute; to alter	משנה, שינה	transmutare; alterare	3.4; 7.3 غيّر (غير)	289
to change	משתנה, השתנה	alterari	1.2; 3.4 تغيّر > استحال	290

English	Hebrew	Latin	Arabic	No.
to be altered completely	שלימות השתנות	perfecte et integre alteratus	وفرغ 5.2 -	291
transmutation; to change	השתנות	alteratio; alterari	تغيُّر 3.4; 7.3	292
to be discharged	-	fit saniei eruptio	فجر: انفجر 3.3	293
eruption; to erupt	בקיעה	eruptio	انفجار 3.3	294
thigh	-	coxa	فخذ 2.1	295
hollow space	נקב	foramen	فرجة 3.2	296
spaces; space	נקבים	foramina	فرج 2.2; 3.1,2	297
noncompound	פרטי	singularis	مفرد 1.2	298
to be exceedingly...; extreme...	גבר, מתגבר	superfluere	فرط 4.2; 6.1	299
excessive	מופלג, רב, חזק	superfluus	مـفـرط 6.2; 7.2; 8.3 > سخن, سخونة	300
excess; excessive	רוב, תגבורת	superfluitas	إفراط 6.1,2	301
excessive exercise	תנועה מופלגת	superfluitas exercitii	الرياضة 7.3 -	302
			فرغ > استحـال, سـخـن, تغيّر	
to dissolve the continuity	חידש פירוק חבור	continuitatem solvere	فرّق: فرّق الاتّصال 6.2	303
to dissolve and cut the continuity	התיך ושבר חבור הגשם	solvere et secare continuitatem substantie	فرّق وقطع اتّصال الجوهر 6.2	304
its continuity is dissolved	שיפורק חיבורו	eius continuitas solvatur	تفرّق: بأن يتفرّق اتّصاله 3.4	305
to distinguish clearly	ברר להכיר	discernere manifeste	فرّق: فرّق تفرقة بيّنة 8.3	306
the continuity is dissolved; dissolution of continuity	פרוק החבור, פירוק חבור	solutio continuitatis	تفرُّق: تفرّق الاتّصال 3.4; 6.2	307
to tear; to be torn	פרק, פורק	disrumpere	فسخ 3.4; 6.2	308

English	Hebrew	Latin	Arabic	№
to be corrupted	נפסד, נשתנה	corrumpi	فسد 1.3; 3.4	309
to corrupt	הפסיד	corrumpere	فسد: أفسد 3.2	310
decay; corruption	הפסד	corruptio	فساد 1.2; 3.4	311
corrupting	מפסיד	corrumpere	مفسد 6.3	312
residue; excess	מותר, יתרון גודל כמות	superfluitas	فضل 1.2; 3.1,2; 4.3; 6.1	313
disparity	יחס, ערך	comparatio	تفاضل 6.1	314
empty space	חלל	amplitudo	فضاء 3.3	315
the hollow space of the chest	חללי החזה	amplitudo pectoris	ـ الصدر 3.3	316
to act; to effect	פעל, פועל	agere; efficere	فعل 5.3; 6.4	317
to be acted upon	התפעל	pati	انفعل 5.3	318
activity; effect; functioning	פעולה	operatio	فِعْل 3.4; 5.2	319
			فاعل > قوة	
viper	נחש, אפעה	vipera	أفعى 6.3	320
lack	חסרון	penuria	فَقْد 3.4	321
PLĠMWNY [= *phlegmonē*]	פלגמוני, פלגמון	flegmon	فلغموني 3.2; 7.1; 9.1,2	322
openings	פיות	orificia	فم: أفواه 3.1	323
to kill	מת	interficere	قتل 6.3	324
destroying; fatal	הורג	interficere; perimere	قاتل 6.3	325
mortifying	-	mortificans	قتّال 8.3	326
immoderate; measure	שיעור, כמות	mensura, quantitas	مقدار 1.2; 5.2; 7.2	327
foot	-	pedes	قدم 2.1	328
ancient physicians	קדמוני הרופאים	antiqui medicorum	قديم: القدماء من الأطبّاء 8.3	329

wound	חבורות	ulcus	قرحة 6.2	330
wounds	חבורות	ulcera	قروح 6.2	331
			قطع > فرق	
paucity; a smaller extent; a small measure	מיעוט	parvitas; paucitas	قلّة 6.1 ;4.3	332
heart	לב	cor	قلب 5.1	333
colon	קולון	colon	قولون 8.1	334
spirit	עצם	essentia	قوام 5.3	335
strength	חוזק	fortitudo	قوة 4.1	336
to the strength of the efficient cause	כח הסבות הפועלות	virtutem cause operantis in corpore	- السبب الفاعل 7.2	337
faculties	-	-	قوى 6.4	338
the natural faculties	הכוחות הטבעיות	virtutes naturales	القوى: القوى الطبيعية 6.4	339
strong	חזק	fortis	قوي 4.1 > حرارة	340
very strong; stronger	בחוזק, יותר חזק	fortior; fortissime	أقوى 7.1,2	341
the strongest heat there is	חום מופלג ביותר בתכלית	fortior caliditas que est	- ما يكون من الحرارة 5.1	342
to be compared	התיחס	comparari	(قيس) قاس: قيس 4.3	343
argument	עיון, ענין	ratiocinatio	قياس 9.2 ;6.2	344
my book *On the Causes and Symptoms <of Diseases>*	בספר החליים והמקרים	in libro de morbis et accidentibus	كتاب: كتابي في العلل والأعراض 6.4	345
my book *On Temperaments*	ספר המזג	liber de complexionibus	كتابي في المزاج 1.2 ;2.2	346
my book *On Anatomical Procedures*	בא[ודות] הנתוח	in libro de medicatione anathomie	كتابي في علاج التشريح 2.2 ;5.1	347
my book *On Drugs*	ספרי ברפואות	librum meum de medicinis	كتابي في الأدوية 9.2	348

English	Hebrew	Latin	Arabic	№
my book *On the Therapeutic Method*	ספר תחבולת הבריאות	librum de ingenio sanitatis	كتابي في حيلة البرء 9.2	349
my book *On the Causes of Symptoms*	ספרי בסבות והמקרים	liber de causis accidentium	كتابنا أسباب الأعراض 7.3	350
the consumption of a large quantity of food	התמדת רב אוכל, רוב אוכל	multitudo cibi	إكثار: الإكثار من الطعام 8.3	351
a larger extent; excessive	ריבוי	multitudo	كثرة 6.1 ;4.3	352
by exertion and strain	בקושי	laboriose et violenter	كذ: بكذّ وشدّة 4.2	353
hand	כף	palma	كف 2.1	354
quality	איכיות, משווה	qualitates	كيفية 7.3 ;1.2	355
two qualities	שני האיכיות	due qualitates	كيفيتان 3.4	356
(qualities)	איכיות	qualitates	كيفيات 3.4	357
to be for a long time	עמידה	mora	لبث 7.2	358
to flee	הלך מהרה	recurrere	لجأ 4.2	359
to be obstructed	מתקבץ שיהיה מוסף	adherere et retentus esse	لحج 7.1	360
tightness [constrictedness]	התאסף, פנימיות האברים	retentio	لحوج 4.3	361
to be joined by; to follow	נמשך, קרה	consecutus esse; consequi	لحق 8.3,4 ;7.3	362
flesh	בשר	caro	لحم 6.1 ;3.1 ;2.1,3	363
of the flesh	בשרי	carnosa	لحمي 1.1	364
fine	דק	subtilis	لطيف 4.2	365
finest	יותר דק	subtilior	ألطف 4.2	366
saliva	רוק	saliva	لعاب 6.3	367
to affect	בא	occurrere	لقي 1.2	368
LYPWRY'S	שינוקא	synochus	ليثورياس 8.3	369

fibers	ליפים	villus	ليف 2.2	370
soft	רפה החלקים	mollis	ليّن 2.2	371
to stretch	מתח	extendere	مدّ: مدّد 3.1,4	372
to stretch	מתפשט	extendi	تمدّد 3.1	373
pus	מוגלא	sanies	مدّة 3.2,3	374
black bile	המרה השחורה	melancolia	مرّة: المرّة السوداء 4.2	375
yellow bile	המרה האדומה, האדומ'	colera rubea, colera	- الصفراء 4.2	376
bile	אדומה	colera	مرار 4.1 < خِلْط	377
illnesses, illness	חוליים, חליים	egritudines	مـــرض: أمـــراض 6.2,3; 7.1; 9.1	378
temperament; composition	מזג, טבע	complexio	مـــــزاج 1.3; 2.3; 3.4; 4.1,3; 5.3; 6.1; 7.1,3 > سوء	379
mixed	מורכב	commixtus	ممزوج 5.2	380
marrow	ריקות	vacuitates	مشاش 2.2	381
metacarpus	גב	pecten	مشط 2.1	382
			معدة < ناحية	
intestine	מעי	intestinum	معى 8.1	383
to be filled	מתמלא, התמלא	impleri	ملأ: امتلأ 3.1	384
to die	מת	mori	(موت) مات 7.3	385
to die off; death	מות	mors	موت 1.2; 9.1	386
water	מים	aqua	ماء 8.1	387
the region of the stomach	חלקי האסטומ'	partes stomachi	ناحية: نواحي المعدة 3.3	388
the region of the brain	חלקי המוח	partes cerebri	نواحي الدماغ 3.3	389
the region of the ribs	חלקי הצלעות	partes costarum	نواحي الأضلاع 3.3	390

to sting	עקץ	pungere	نخس 3.4	391
to emerge; to protrude	נשפך; התגבר	effluere; exuberare	ندر 6.2; 3.1	392
to be concocted	התבשל	decoqui	نضج 3.2	393
coction	בישול	decoctio	نَضْج 3.2	394
study	עיון	considerationes	نظر 5.3	395
natural philosophers	הפילוסופים הטבעיים	speculatores naturarum	-: أصحاب النظر 5.3	396
mind	בעל נפש	anima	نفس 6.2	397
perspiration; to breathe [exhale]	התנשמות	expiratio	تنفّس 4.3; 7.1	398
rigor	סמור, פלצות	tremor	نافض 6.4; 8.1,4	399
to be annihilated	נתך	minui	نقص 6.3	400
shingles	איריסיפילא	erisipila	نملة 9.1	401
to grow	צמח	augmentari	نمى 6.3	402
every paroxysm	כל אחת ואחת מהעונות	unaquaque accessionum suarum	نوبة: كل نوبة من نوائبها 8.3	403
fire	אש	ignis	نار 8.1	404
crude	פג	crudus	نيئ 8.3	405
			هادئ > حرارة	
air	אויר	aer	هواء 7.3	406
the air which surrounds	האויר המקרה	aer circundans	الهواء: الهواء المحيط 6.1	407
disposition	הכנה	preparatio	تهيّؤ 7.1	408
to be disposed	מוכן	preparatus	متهيئ 7.1	409
to arise	בא	consurgere	(هيج) هاج 7.3	410
tendons	מיתרים	corde	وتر: وترات 2.1	411

English	Hebrew	Latin	Arabic	No.
pain	כאב	dolor	وجع ;3.1; 5.2,3; 6.1; 7.3; 8.1; 9.2	412
pains	כאבים	dolores	أوجاع 8.1	413
restfulness	עצלה	tranquillitas	دعة 1.2	414
swelling	מורסא, מורסה, מורסות	apostema; apostemata; apostematio	ورم ;1.2; 4.3; 7.1,3; 8.1; 9.1,2	415
inflamed swelling; hot swelling	מורסא (ה)חמה	apostema calidum	الورم: الورم الحارّ ;3.2; 7.1; 9.1	416
the hot sanguine swelling	מורסא דמיית חמה	apostema sanguineum calidum	- الدموي الحارّ 1.2	417
swellings, swelling	מורסא, מורסות	apostemata	أورام 7.2,3	418
			وارم > عضو	
in the middle between two opposites	בשיווי ובמצוע בין שני אלו	media inter duo contraria	متوسّط: متوسّط في ما بين الضدّين 5.2	419
			اتّصال > فرق؛ تفرُّق	
place	מקום	locus	موضع 8.3	420
to be fitting	נאות	conveniens esse	وفق: وافق 6.3	421
compatible	נאות, ניאות	convenire	موافقة 6.3	422
fitting	נאות	conveniens	موافق 6.3	423
to originate; arise	התחדש, התיילד	generari	تولّد 6.4; 7.1	424
to originate; generation	הוויה, התילדות	generatio	تولّد 1.3: 3.2	425
producing	מוליד	generans	مولّد 8.3	426
to originate	מתילד	generatus	متولّد 5.2	427
dry	יבש	siccus	يابس 2.2 > جوهر	428
arms	יד	manus	يد: يدان 1.3	429

B. Latin

With the exception of a few very common words (mostly pronouns, numerals, and prepositions), every occurrence of every word in *De malitia* has been entered below and referred to the chapters in which they are found. Verbs are usually given under the infinitive form, and nouns under the nominative. Most of these words have also been listed in the preceding Arabic–Latin–Hebrew glossary; in the index that follows, the number in parentheses at the end of an entry refers readers to the word's location (or locations) in the glossary, and will allow them to identify the word's Arabic or Hebrew equivalent in a specific passage. Particles and other simple words in the Latin text that do not appear in the glossary are usually given here followed by their normal Arabic equivalent in Ḥunayn's translation.

absque, 1.2, 7.1, 8.1 (من غير), 8.2 (دون)

accesio, 8.3 **(403)**

accidens, 3.2, 6.4, 6.4, 6.4, 6.4, 6.4, 7.3, 8.3, 8.3, 9.1 **(236, 237, 350)**

accidere, 1.1, 1.2, 2.3, 3.1, 3.1, 3.4, 3.4, 4.1, 5.1, 7.3, 7.3, 7.3, 8.1, 8.1, 8.1, 8.1, 8.3, 8.3, 8.3, 8.3, 8.3, 8.3, 8.4, 8.4

acquiescere, 6.2 **(183)**

adeo, 3.1

adeps, 2.1 **(197)**

adesse, 5.3

adherere, 7.1 **(360)**

adhuc, 5.1, 5.2, 5.2 (بعد)

adinvenire, 6.2 **(215)**

adiutorium, 2.1 **(248)**

(magis) adiuvans, 4.3 (أعون)

adunare, 6.2 **(51)**

adurens, 8.3 **(97)**

advenire, 6.2, 8.1, 8.1, 8.2, 8.2, 8.2, 8.2, 8.2, 8.2, 8.2, 8.3, 8.3 **(215)**

aer, 6.1, 7.3 **(406, 407)**

agere, 4.2 **(272)**, 5.3 **(317)**

aggregantur, 4.1 (اجتمع)

albus, 2.2 **(36)**

aliquis, 1.3, 6.2, 8.3, 9.1 (أحد)

alius, 1.1, 2.2, 7.1, 8.2 (آخر) , 2.3, 4.3, 6.2, 7.1 (غير), 3.1 (سائر); 1.2, 1.2, 1.2, 1.2, 1.3, 2.2, 3.4, 5.2, 6.4, 7.2, 8.2, 8.2, 8.3, 9.1, 9.1

alter, 2.3, 3.2 (آخر)

alterare, 1.2, 3.4, 5.2, 5.3, 6.1, 7.3, 7.3, 7.3 **(106, 289, 290, 292)**

alteratio, 3.4, 5.2, 5.3 **(107, 109, 292)**

amicus, 6.3 **(66)**

amplitudo, 3.3, 3.3 **(315)**

anima, 6.2 **(397)**

animal, 1.1, 5.1, 6.3, 6.4 **(19, 117)**

anothomia, 2.2, 5.1 **(347)**

ante, 3.1, 5.3 (في المتقدّم), 4.2, 4.2 (قبل من), 8.3 (قبل)

antecedere, 9.2 (تقدّم)

antequam, 6.1 (دون)

anterior, 3.3 **(61)**

antiquus, 8.3 **(329)**

apostema, 1.2, 1.2, 1.2, 1.2, 1.2, 3.2, 4.3, 4.3, 4.3, 7.1, 7.1, 7.1, 7.2, 7.3, 7.3, 8.1, 9.1, 9.1, 9.1, 9.2 **(415–418)**

apostemosus, 4.1, 4.1, 4.2, 4.1, 5.1 **(254)**

apparens, 9.2

appropinquare, 8.1, 9.2 **(54, 138)**

approximando, 8.1

apud, 1.3, 3.2, 5.3, 7.2 (عند), 5.2 (منذ)

aqua, 8.1, 8.1 **(387)**

assidue esse, 8.3 **(137)**

assiduo, 5.1 **(77)**

audere, 8.1 (قدم)

augmentari, 4.3, 6.1, 6.1, 6.3, 6.3 **(402)**

augmentum, 7.2 **(162)**

autem, 1.2 (إلا), 2.2, 2.3, 4.3, 5.2, 6.1, 7.1, 8.2 (أما), 6.4 (لكن); 2.3, 3.1, 3.3, 3.4, 3.4, 4.2, 4.2, 5.2, 5.3, 6.3, 6.4, 8.3, 8.4, 8.4, 9.2

bonus, 3.2

calefacere, calefieri, 1.2, 1.3, 1.3, 3.1, 3.1, 3.1, 3.2, 3.2, 3.4, 3.4, 4.1, 4.1, 4.1, 4.2, 4.2, 5.1, 5.2, 5.2, 5.2, 5.3, 5.3, 7.2, 7.2, 8.1, 8.2, 8.3, 9.2 **(165, 170)**

calefactio, 3.1, 3.2, 4.1, 4.1, 4.2, 5.1, 5.2, 5.2, 5.2, 6.1, 6.1, 6.1, 7.3 **(172)**

caliditas, 4.1, 4.1, 4.1, 4.2, 4.3, 5.1, 5.1, 5.1, 5.2, 5.3, 6.1, 6.2, 6.2, 6.2, 6.2, 7.2, 7.3, 8.1 **(70, 73)**

calidus, calidior, 1.2, 3.1, 3.2, 4.2, 4.2, 4.2, 4.2, 4.3, 6.1, 6.1, 7.1, 7.2, 7.2, 7.3, 8.1, 8.1, 8.2, 9.1, 9.2 **(71, 176)**

calor, 1.1, 1.2, 4.1, 4.1, 6.1, 6.1, 8.2, 8.2, 8.2, 8.3, 8.3, 8.4 **(70, 72, 74, 211)**

cancer, 1.2, 9.1 **(177)**

cancrene, 1.2 **(232)**, 9.1 **(273)**

caput, 1.3 **(140)**

carnosus, 1.1 **(364)**

caro, 2.1, 2.3, 3.1, 6.1 **(363)**

cartillagines, 2.1 **(280)**

causa, 2.1, 5.1, 7.2, 7.2, 7.3, 8.1 **(163, 164, 337, 350)**

cerebrum, 3.3, 3.3, 3.3 **(60, 389)**

cibus, 8.3, 8.3 **(351)**

circundans, 6.1 **(407)**

coartare, 3.1, 3.4, 6.2 **(221)**

coartatio, 3.1 **(222)**

colera, 4.1, 4.1, 4.2, 4.2, 4.2, 4.3, 8.1, 9.1, 9.1 **(125, 208, 375, 376, 377)**

collectio, 3.2, 3.2, 3.2, 3.3, 3.3, 3.3, 3.3 **(52)**

colon, 8.1 **(334)**

commixtus, 5.2 **(380)**

communis, 2.3, 5.2 **(201)**, 9.1

comparari, 4.3, 4.3 **(343)**

comparatio, 6.1, 6.1 **(314)**

complexio, 1.2, 1.2, 2.2, 2.1, 2.1, 2.3, 3.4, 3.4, 4.1, 4.3, 5.2, 5.3, 6.1, 7.1, 7.3, 7.3, 7.3, 8.3, 8.4, 8.4 **(187, 189, 379)**

complexio diversa, 1.1, 1.2, 1.2, 1.2, 2.1, 2.1, 2.3, 2.3, 2.3, 2.3, 3.2, 3.4, 5.1, 6.4, 7.1, 7.2, 7.3, 8.1, 8.4, 9.1, 9.2 **(187–190)**

componi, 2.1 (مركّب)

compositus, 1.3, 2.1, 2.2, 2.2, 8.4, 8.4 **(9, 154)**

comprehendere, 5.2 **(102)**

consequi, 2.2, 3.2, 7.3, 8.3, 8.3 **(362)**

conservatio, 6.3 **(85)**

consideratio, 5.3 **(395)**

consistere, 1.3

constrictio, 7.2 **(86)**

constringere, 3.1, 6.2 **(161)**

consurgere, 7.3 **(410)**

continere, 3.1, 3.1, 3.1, 3.2, 3.3, 4.1, 4.1, 4.2, 4.2, 5.2, 9.2 **(103, 104, 216)**

continuitas, 3.4, 3.4, 6.2, 6.2, 6.2 **(303, 304, 305, 307)**

contrarius, 5.2, 6.3, 6.3, 6.3 **(217, 218, 419)**

conveniens, 5.3, 6.3, 6.3, 6.3, 6.3, 7.2 **(200, 421, 423)**

convenire, 4.3, 5.3, 6.3 **(422)**

conversus esse, 9.2 (صار)

cooperire, 2.2 (انطبق)

cor, 5.1, 5.1 **(333)**

corda, 2.1 **(411)**

corpus, 1.1, 1.2, 1.3, 1.3, 2.3, 2.3, 3.1, 3.2, 3.2, 4.1, 4.1, 4.1, 4.1, 4.2, 4.2, 4.2, 4.3, 5.1, 5.2, 5.2, 5.2, 5.3, 5.3, 6.1, 6.1, 6.2, 6.3, 7.2, 7.2, 7.2, 7.2, 7.3, 7.3, 7.3, 7.3, 7.3, 8.1, 8.1, 8.1, 8.1, 8.1, 8.2, 8.2, 8.2, 8.2, 8.3 **(18, 20, 43, 46, 47)**

corrodere, 3.4 **(7)**

corrumpere, 1.3, 3.2, 3.4, 3.4, 6.3 **(309, 310, 312)**

corruptio, 1.2, 3.4 **(311)**

costa, 3.3 **(390)**

coxa, 2.1 **(295)**

crudus, 8.3 **(405)**

crus, 2.1 **(192)**

cum (adv. or conj.), 1.3, 3.1, 3.1, 3.3, 3.4, 4.3, 4.3, 5.3, 6.3, 6.3, 7.3, 7.3, 8.1, 9.2 (إذا), 5.3 (إذ) , 4.1, 4.1, 5.1, 8.4 (متى); 1.2, 1.2, 1.2, 1.2, 3.2, 3.4, 3.4, 4.1, 4.2, 5.3, 7.2, 7.3, 7.3, 7.3, 8.1, 8.2, 8.3

cum (prep.), 1.2, 4.3, 5.3, 6.1, 6.4, 9.1 (مع); 8.3

cumque, 4.1 (متى)

curatio, 6.3 **(199)**

currens, 7.3 **(193)**

cursus, 5.2 **(75)**

cutis, 2.1, 2.2, 2.2, 3.3, 3.3 **(50)**

debilior, 7.2 **(220)**

decens, 1.2 **(57)**

declaratio, 7.3

declaratum est, 7.3 (قول)

decoctio, 3.2 **(394)**

decoqui, 3.2 **(393)**

deinde, 3.1, 3.2, 4.2, 4.3, 5.1, 8.1, 8.1, 9.2 (ثمّ)

desiccare, 1.2, 1.3, 1.3, 3.4, 3.4, 9.2 **(49)**

destrui, 3.4 **(31)**

dicere, 1.1, 2.2, 2.3, 3.2, 3.2, 3.4, 5.3, 6.2, 7.1, 8.4, 9.2 (قال)

difficilior, 9.2 **(245)**

digitus, 2.1, 2.1, 5.1 **(202, 203)**

dignius, 4.2

dignum, 6.2 (خليق)

diminutus, 4.3 (أنقص)

discernere, 8.3 **(306)**

dispositio, 1.1, 1.3, 3.2, 3.4, 3.4, 3.4, 4.3, 4.3, 5.2, 5.2, 5.2, 5.3, 5.3, 5.3, 5.3, 6.1, 6.1, 6.2, 6.2, 7.2, 8.1, 8.1, 8.1, 8.1, 8.3, 8.3, 8.4, 9.1, 9.2, 9.2, 9.2 **(110, 111, 115)**

disrumpere, 3.1 **(207)**, 3.4, 6.2 **(308)**

diversificare, 1.3, 4.3, 6.1, 9.1 **(127, 129)**

diversitas, 4.3, 4.3, 6.1, 6.1 **(128)**

diversus, 3.1, 7.1, 8.3, 8.3, and see complexio **(129)**

dividere, 2.1, 2.1, 2.1, 2.1, 2.2 (قسم)

dolor, 3.1, 3.4, 3.4, 5.2, 5.3, 5.3, 5.3, 6.1, 7.3, 8.1, 8.1, 8.1, 8.1, 8.1, 9.2 **(11, 412, 413)**

dominare, 4.1, 4.1, 8.1, 8.1, 9.2 **(281)**

dominium, 3.4 **(282)**

donec, 3.1, 3.1, 3.2, 6.2, 7.3, 8.1, 9.2 (حتّى)

draco, 6.3, 6.3 **(39)**

dum, 5.1, 6.3

durus, 2.2 **(210)**

ebulliens, 9.1 **(286)**

ebullitio, 3.2, 4.1, 7.2 **(287)**

efficere, 6.4 **(317)**

effluere, 3.1 **(392)**

effundere, 3.1, 3.2, 3.2, 8.1, 9.1, 9.2 **(146, 204)**

eger, 1.1 (صاحبه)

egredi, 3.1, 3.4, 5.2, 5.2, 5.2, 5.2, 6.2 **(75, 118, 173, 229)**

egritudo, 1.2, 3.2, 3.4, 6.2, 6.3, 7.1, 9.1, 9.1, 9.1, 9.2, 9.2 **(11, 270, 271, 378)**

egrotare, 3.1, 3.1 **(10)**

enim, 1.3, 9.1, 9.1

enunciare, 1.3 (أخبر)

epiala, 1.1, 8.2, 8.3, 8.4, 8.4, 8.4, 8.4 **(14)**

equalis, 1.3, 4.1 **(233)**

equaliter, 5.3 (مستوية)

ergo, 1.3, 2.2, 2.2, 3.1, 3.1, 4.2, 4.3, 5.1, 5.2, 6.2, 8.1

erisipila, 1.2, 9.1 **(401)**

eruptio, 3.3, 3.3, 3.3, 3.3 **(293, 294)**

essentia, 5.3 **(335)**

estimare, 5.3, 6.2, 8.2 (ظنّ)

estiomenus, 1.2, 9.1 **(8)**

ethica, 1.1, 5.3, 5.3 **(6)**

etiam, 2.1, 4.3, 5.1, 7.3, 8.1 (أيضا); 2.2, 4.2, 4.3, 6.1, 6.4, 7.3, 7.3, 8.1, 8.1, 8.2, 8.3, 8.3

etsi, 6.1 (وإن)

evacuare, 1.2 (خلا)

frigor, 6.1, 7.3, 8.1, 8.2 **(24)**
frigus, 1.1, 1.2, 6.1, 6.2, 7.3, 8.1, 8.2, 8.2, 8.3, 8.3 **(24, 25)**

generare, 5.2, 8.3 **(424, 426, 427)**
generatio, 1.3, 3.2 **(425)**
genus, 1.2, 5.3, 7.1, 8.1, 8.3, 9.1 **(53, 125)**
gravare, 3.1 **(40)**
grece, 1.1 (باليونانية)
greci, 1.1, 1.2, 3.2, 8.2, 8.3, 8.3, 8.4, 9.1 (يونانيون)
grossus, 2.2, 4.2 **(283)**

habere, 4.3, 5.2, 8.1
habundans, 4.2, 4.3 **(84)**
homo, 6.3, 6.3, 6.3, 6.3, 7.3, 8.1, 8.1, 8.1, 8.3 (إنسان)
huiusmodi, 5.2 (أمثال هذه)
humectare, 1.2, 1.3, 1.3, 3.1, 3.4, 3.4, 9.2 **(33, 148)**
humiditas, 2.2, 3.1, 3.2, 3.4, 5.3, 7.3, 9.1, 9.2, 9.2, 9.2 **(63, 149, 150)**
humidus, 4.3 **(151)**
humor, 4.2, 4.3, 5.2, 6.3, 6.3, 7.1, 7.3, 8.1, 8.1, 8.3, 8.3, 9.1, 9.1, 9.2 **(124, 125, 126)**

ieiunus, 6.3 **(159)**
igitur, 1.3, 2.1, 8.4, 9.1
ignis, 8.1, 8.1 **(404)**
illaudabilis, 3.3 **(139)**
ille, 1.2, 2.2, 3.1, 5.2, 6.1 (تلك); and passim
impediens, 6.3 **(4)**
impedire, 6.1, 6.1, 6.1, 6.1, 6.4 **(2, 3)**
impleri, 3.1, 3.1 **(384)**
impossibile ... quin, 3.2 (لا بدّ)
incessanter, 3.1 (لا يزال)
incipere, 3.2 (ابتداء); 1.3
inconveniens, 8.1 (من المحال)
inde, 1.1, 3.1, 6.1 (من ذلك)
inesse, 5.2
inferior, 7.3 (بدون)
infirmus, 4.1 **(253)**
infrigidare, 1.2, 1.3, 1.3, 3.4, 3.4, 4.2, 8.2, 8.3, 9.2 **(22, 23)**
infrigidatio, 6.1 (برد)
infusio, 1.2 **(204)**
infusus, 1.2 **(204)**
ingenium, 9.2 **(349)**
inherere, 6.4 **(194)**
inimicus, 6.3 **(234)**
integre, 3.4, 5.2, 5.2, 5.3 (ألتامة) 5.3, (وفرغ) 5.3
intelligere, 3.1, 6.2, 8.4, 9.2 (فهم)
intentio, 1.2, 1.3, 2.3, 5.2 **(235)**
inter, 2.2, 2.2, 2.2, 3.1, 5.2, 5.2, 5.2, 6.1, 6.1, 6.1, 6.1, 8.3, 8.3 (بين)
interficere, 6.3, 6.3, 6.3 **(324, 325)**

interiora, 3.1, 3.3, 4.3, 6.2, 9.2 **(132)**
interius, 8.3 (باطن), 9.2 (من داخل)
intestinum, 8.1 **(383)**
intrinsecus, 8.1, 8.2 (من داخل)
intromittere, 5.1 (أدخل)
invadere, 8.3 (أخذ)
invenire, 1.1, 2.2, 2.2, 4.3, 5.2, 5.2, 8.2, 8.3 (وجد)
(ad) invicem, 6.1, 6.3, 6.3 (بعضها بعضا)
ira, 7.2 **(279)**
iste, 1.2, 1.3, 4.3, 7.1, 7.2, 8.2, 8.2, 9.1 (هذا)
ita, 6.1, 7.3 (كذلك); 4.1, 5.2, 8.2 (حتّى)
itaque, 2.1, 3.2
iudicare, 8.3 (حكم)
iuvare, 5.1 (أعان)

laborare, 6.4
laboriose, 4.2 **(353)**
lacertus, 2.3, 3.2, 3.2, 3.2, 3.3 **(249)**
latius, 7.3 (بأكثر)
latus, 8.2, 8.2 (جانب)
laudabilis, 3.2, 3.2, 3.2, 3.3, 3.3 **(98, 99, 100)**
lepra, 1.2 **(41)**
liber, 1.2, 1.3, 2.2, 2.2, 2.2, 5.1, 6.2, 6.4, 7.1, 7.3, 9.1, 9.2, 9.2, 9.2 **(345–350)**
ligamenta, 2.1, 3.1 **(141)**
locus, 3.1, 3.2, 8.3 **(420)**
longe (adv.), 5.1 (بالبعيد), 6.2 (بعيد)
longitudo, 3.4 (طول)
longus, 5.2, 8.3 (طويل)
loqui, 6.3 (الكلم)

magis, 4.3
magnus, 8.1, 8.2, 8.2 (عظيم)
maior, maius, 1.3 (أكبر), 2.2, 3.1, 3.2, 3.2, 3.2 (أعظم), 8.3 (كبار)
malitia, 1.1, 1.2, 1. 2, 1.2, 1.2, 1.3, 1.3, 1.3, 2.3, 2.3, 2.3, 2.3, 3.2, 3.4, 3.4, 5.1, 6.4, 7.1,
    7.2, 7.3, 7.3, 8.1, 8.3, 8. 4, 8.4, 8.4, 9.1, 9.2 (سوء)
malus, -a, -um, 3.3 (ردئ), 3.3 (مذموم)
manifestatio, 6.1 (بيان)
manifeste (adv.) , 8.3 **(306)**
manifestus [est], 1.3, 7.2, 7.3 (من البيّن), 1.3 (بيّن), 6.2, 7.3 (واضع), 8.3 (بيّنة),
    3.4 (ظاهر), 9.2 (بان); 8.4
manus, 1.3, 2.1 **(429)**
mater, 3.3 **(12)**
medicatione, 2.2, 5.1 **(347)**
medicina, 1.3, 9.2 **(224, 348)**
medicus, 8.3, 8.3 **(68, 329)**
medius, 5.2 **(419)**
melancolia, 4.2, 4.2, 4.3 **(191, 375)**
melius, 3.2 (أحمد)

membrum, 1.2, 1.2, 1.2, 1.3, 2.1, 2.2, 2.2, 2.2, 2.2, 2.2, 2.2, 2.2, 3.1, 3.1, 3.1, 3.4, 3.4, 3.4, 3.4, 3.4, 3.4, 3.4, 4.1, 4.1, 4.1, 4.1, 4.2, 4.3, 5.1, 5.2, 5.3, 5.3, 5.3, 6.1, 6.1, 6.1, 6.1, 7.3, 7.3, 8.1, 8.1, 8.3, 8.3, 9.1, 9.1, 9.1, 9.2, 9.2 **(250–255)**

mensura, 1.2, 7.2 **(57, 327)**

minor, 3.1, 3.1 (أصغر), 3.2 (أقلّ), 8.3 (صغير)

minus (adv.), 6.4 (أقلّ)

minui, 6.3, 6.3 **(400)**

mirabilis, 3.4 (عجيب), 8.1 (بعجب)

mirari, 8.1, 8.1 (تعجّب)

modus, 1.2, 2.3, 2.3, 2.3, 3.1, 3.2, 3.2, 5.3, 8.4, 7.2 **(213)**

mollicies, 1.2, 9.1 **(155)**

mollis, 2.2 **(371)**

mora, 7.2 **(358)**

morbus, 6.4 **(345)**

mordere, 6.3 **(247)**

mori, 6.3, 6.3 **(263)**, 7.3 **(385)**

mortificans, 8.3 **(326)**

mortis, 1.2, 9.1 **(386)**

motus, 5.1 **(77)**

moveri, 5.1, 8.1 **(76)**

mulieres, 8.3 (نساء)

multiplicare, 8.1 (كثر)

multitudo, 4.3, 6.1, 8.3, 8.3 **(351, 352)**

multotiens, 7.3, 8.1, 8.3 (كثيرا)

multus, 7.1, 8.1 (كثير)

musculus, 3.1 **(249)**

nam, 2.2, 4.3, 4.3, 5.1, 5.3, 6.1, 6.1, 8.1

namque, 2.3, 6.1, 8.3

narrare, 2.2, 2.2, 2.3, 3.4, 5.1, 6.4 , 6.4, 7.1, 7.3, 7.3, 9. 2, 9.2 (وصف)

natura, 2.2, 2.3, 2.3, 3. 4, 3.4, 4. 2, 4.2, 4.2, 4. 2, 4.3, 5.1, 5.1, 5.2, 5.2, 5.2, 5.3 **(225, 226, 227, 396)**

naturalis, 3.2, 5.2, 5.2, 6.1, 6.4 **(228, 339)**

necessario, 2.2, 3.2, 4.3 (ضرورة)

necesse, 8.3 (لا بدّ)

neque, 3.2, 5.3, 5.3, 5.3, 5.3, 6.1, 6.3, 6.3, 6.4, 8.1

nervi, 2.1, 3.1 **(246)**

nichil, 8.1 (ليس شيء)

niger, 9.1 (أسود)

nisi, 5.3 (غير), 6.4 (دون), 8.2 (إلّا); 1.3, 3.1, 3.1, 3.4, 3.4, 4.3, 5.2, 6.2, 6.2, 6.2, 6.3, 6.3, 6.3, 6.3, 6.4, 8.1, 8.1, 8.2, 8.2, 8.4

niti, 8.1 (رام)

nocumentum, 5.2 **(219)**

nolle, 8.4

nomen, 8.4 (اسم)

nominare, 2.2, 5.3, 9.2 (ذكر) , 8.1, 9.1 (سمّى); 1.2, 1.2, 7.1, 8.2, 8.4, 8.4, 9.1, 9.1, 9.1, 9.1, 9.2

nominari, 7.1, 9.1 (عرف)

non, 2.2, 3.4 , 5.1 (ليس), 3.1 (لم), 3.1, 6.3 (ما), 6.4 (لا); and passim
nondum, 5.1, 9.2
noscere, 1.3, 9.1 (عرف)
notio, 1.1, 1.2 (معروف)
notitia, 1.3 (**238**)
novus, 8.3 (**68**)
nudus, 2.3 (مجرّد)
nullus, 5.3, 5.3, 6.4, 8.3
numquam, 8.3
nunc, 2.3 (الآن)
nutrire, 2.2, 6.3, 6.3 (**275**)

occasio, 7.3 (**164**)
occultare, 2.2 (خفي)
occurrere 1.2 (**368**)
officialia, 2.2 (آل)
omnes, 1.2, 1.3, 1.3, 2.3, 3.2, 4.3, 5.3, 5.3, 6.2, 6.3, 6.4, 7.1, 7.3, 9.1 (جميع), 1.3, 3.2, 4.2,
    4.2, 4.2, 4.2, 4.3, 5.1, 5.3, 6.2, 6.2, 6.3, 7.1, 7.2, 7.3, 8.3, 9.1 (كل)
operans, 7.2 (**337**)
operatio, 3.4, 3.4, 3.4, 5.2 (**1, 319**)
oportet, 1.3, 2.3, 3.4, 4.3, 4.3, 8.3 (يجب)
orificia, 3.1 (**323**)
os, ossis, 2.1, 2.2, 2.2, 2.2, 2.2, 6.1 (**265, 266**)
ostendere, 1.2, 2.2, 6.4 (بيّن)

palma, 2.1, 2.1 (**354**)
panniculus, 2.1, 2.2, 3.1, 3.3 (**277, 278**)
pars, 1.3, 2.1, 2.1, 2.2, 2.2, 2.2, 2.2, 2.3, 3.3, 3.3, 3.3, 8.1, 8.2, 8.2, 8.2, 8.2, 8.2, 8.2, 8.2,
    8.3, 8.3, 9.2 (**44, 45, 388–390**)
participativus, 2.3 (**201**)
parvitas, 4.3, 6.1, 8.2 (**332**)
parvus, 3.2, 3.2, 8.2, 8.2, 8.2, 8.2, 8.2 (صغير)
passio, 3.4, 3.4, 5.3, 5.3, 5.3, 6.1, 7.3, 8.1, 8.1 (**11**)
pati, 3.1, 5.3 (**10, 318**)
patiens, 5.3, 5.3, 6.4, 8.3 (صاحبه)
paucitas, 4.3 (**332**)
paulo, 5.3
pecten, 2.1 (**382**)
pectus, 1.3, 3.3 (**206, 316**)
pedes, 1.3, 2.1, 2.1 (**143, 144, 328**)
penitus, 5.2, 5.2, 5.3, 7.2, 8.3, 9.2 (أصلا)
penuria, 3.4, 3.4 (**321**)
per, 2.2, 8.4, 9.1 (ب); 3.1
perducens, 9.1 (مع سلوك)
perfecte (adv.), 5.2, 5.3 (**87, 291**)
perfectus, 5.2 (**87**)
perimire, 6.3 (**325**)
permutatio, 3.4 (**109**)

perscrutari, 9.1 (تلخيص)
perseverare, 5.2 (دام)
pertransire, 1.2, 7.3 (**56**)
pervenire, 2.1 (عمد), 2.3 (قصد), 3.1, 5.1, 6.1 (بلغ), 5.2 (صار); 3.2, 5.2
plerisque, 1.1
plurime, 4.3 (كثيرة)
plurimum, 3.3 (في أكثر الأمر), 4.3 (كثيرة)
plus, 2.2, 2.2, 4.1, 6.4, 6.4, 7.2 (أكثر)
ponere, 3.2 (أنزل), 6.2 (جعل)
pori, 2.2 (**185**)
posse, 8.3 (قدر)
possibile, 2.2, 6.4, 8.2
post, 2.2, 3.1, 4.2, 4.2, 4.2, 4.3, 5.1, 8.2, 8.2, 9.2 (من بعد)
postea, 3.2, 8.3, 8.4 (ثمّ)
posterior, 3.3 (**60**)
postquam, 3.1
postremo, 2.2 (بآخرة)
precedere, 8.3 (قدم), 8.4 (تقدّم)
premissus, 2.3, 7.1, 9.2 (تقدّم)
preparatio, 7.1 (**408**)
preparatus, 2.2, 7.1, 7.1 (**409**)
preter, 1.1, 2.2, 8.4 (خلا), 2.3, 6.3 (غير), 5.3, 6.3 (مع ذلك), 7.1 (من خلا), 8.3 (من)
preterea, 6.4, 8.3
principium, 3.4, 5.2 (أوّل)
privare, 7.1 (عدم)
procedere, 3.1 (سرى)
proculdubio, 8.3 (لا محالة)
prolongari, 7.3 (**230**)
propinquus, 2.1, 3.2, 3.2, 4.2, 4.2, 4.3 (**55**)
proprie (adv.), 3.1, 3.2, 3.4, 5.1, 5.1, 5.1, 8.1 (خاصّة)
proprius, 2.1, 6.4, 9.1
propter, 6.1, 3.4, 3.4, 3.4, 4.3, 6.3, 7.2, 7.2, 7.2, 8.2, 8.3 (من قبل)
propterea, 3.4, 4.2, 4.2, 6.2, 6.2, 7.2, 8.1 (من قبل); 3.4
provenire, 2.2, 2.3, 4.3, 7.2, 7.3, 7.3, 8.3, 8.4, 8.4, 9.1, 9.1, 9.1, 9.1, 9.2, 9.2 (حدث)
proventus, 9.2 (حدوث)
pungere, 3.4 (**391**)
pustula, 9.1 (بثر)
putrefactio, 4.3, 4.3, 4.3, 5.2, 7.1, 7.1, 7.1, 7.3 (**268**)
putrefieri, 7.1, 7.1, 7.1 (**267**)

qualitas, 1.2, 3.4, 3.4, 7.3 (**355, 356, 357**)
qualiter, 6.4, 7.1, 8.1, 8.1, 9.2 (كيف)
quandoque, 1.1, 2.2, 3.2, 3.2, 7.2, 7.2, 7.2, 7.3, 7.3, 7.3, 7.3 (ربّما)
quantitas, 1.2, 5.2 (مقدار) (**327**)
quanto, 4.1
quapropter, 4.3 (لذلك), 5.3, 6.3 (من ذلك)
quartana, 8.4 (ربع) (**142**)
quasi, 7.3 (كأنّه)

quemadmodum, 1.2, 2.2, 6.2, 7.3, 7.3 (كما)

quidem, 1.2, 1.3, 2.2, 2.2, 2.3, 3.2, 3.2, 3.2, 4.2, 4.2, 4.3, 4.3, 5.1, 5.1, 5.3, 6.2, 6.2, 6.3, 6.3, 6.4, 7.2, 7.2, 7.2, 7.3, 7.3, 7.3, 7.3, 7.3, 7.3, 8.3, 8.3, 9.2

quies, 1.2, 3.4, 8.3, 8.3 **(122, 184)**

quietus, 4.1 (هادئة)

quin, 1.2, 3.2 (من أن), 4.1, 5.1 (أن)

quodcumque, 1.2, 2.2, 2.2 (أي)

quomodo, 1.3, 2.2 (كيف)

quoniam, 1.3, 2.3, 3.4, 4.3, 4.3, 5.3, 8.3, 9.1 (لأن)

   et illud ideo quoniam, 3.1, 3.2, 3.4, 5.1, 5.3, 5.3, 6.1, 6.2, 6.2, 6.3, 7.1, 8.1, 8. 2, 8.3, 9.2 (وذلك أنّ)

quoque, 1.2, 1.2, 1.2, 1.3, 2.1, 6.3 (أيضا)

quot, 2.3, 6.4 (كم)

radix, 8.1 **(5)**

raro, 8.3 (قليل)

rasceta, 2.1 **(145)**

ratiocinatio, 6.2, 9.2 **(344)**

receptio, 5.2 (قبول)

recipere, 5.2 (قبل)

recordari, 1.3, 1.3 (ذكر)

recurrere, 4.2 **(359)**

redire, 3.2 (عاد), 7.1 (راجع)

redundere, 3.1 **(288)**

regimen, 8.3, 8.3 **(131)**

relatio, 6.2 **(223)**

reliquus, 4.2, 6.4, 8.1, 8.4 (سائر)

remanere, 6.2 (بقي)

rememorari, 2.2

remotus, 4.3, 8.3 (بالبعد)

reperire, 2.2 (وجد)

res, 1.2, 1.2, 3.4, 4.2, 4.2, 4.3, 6.2, 6.2, 6.3, 6.3, 7.1 (شيء), 3.1, 3.2, 3.2, 4.1, 5.2, 5.2, 6.1, 7.3 (أمر)

resolutio, 3.2, 4.2, 4.2, 4.3, 4.3, 5.2, 5.2, 5.2 **(30, 89, 109)**

resolutus, 5.2 (استحالت)

resolvere, 3.2, 3.4, 4.2, 4.2, 4.2, 4.2, 4.2, 9.2 **(88, 105, 106, 107, 109)**

respondere, 8.1 **(133)**

resudare, 3.1 **(147)**

retentio, 4.3, 4.3 **(361)**

retinere, 7.1, 7.2 **(360)**

rubeus, 4.2 (أصفر) 9.1, (376) (صفراء) **(125)**

saliva, 6.3 **(367)**

sanatio, 3.2 (برء)

sanguineus, 1.2, 9.2 **(136, 417)**

sanguis, 3.2, 4.1, 4.1, 4.1, 4.1, 4. 1, 4.1, 4.2, 4.2, 4.2, 4.2, 4.2 , 4.2, 4.3, 4.3, 5.1, 5.1, 5.1, 5.1, 5.2, 7.2, 9.1, 9.1, 9.1, 9.1, 9.1 **(135)**

sanies, 3.2, 3.3 **(293, 374)**

sanitas, 3.2, 6.3, 6.3, 9.2 **(21)**

sanus, 6.3 **(205)**

scilicet, 4.1, 4.3, 5.2, 6.4 (أعني)

scire, 9.2 (علم)

scissura, 2.2 **(123)**

scorpio, 6.3 **(269)**

secare, 6.2 **(304)**

secundum, 1.3, 2.3, 2.3, 2.3, 3.1, 3.2, 3.4, 5.3, 6.1, 6.2, 6.2, 6.2, 7.2, 8.3, 9.2 (على), 4.3, 4.3, 7.2, 7.2, 9.2 (بحسب); 1.2, 3.3

sed, 1.2, 2.2, 2.2, 3.2, 3.2, 3.2, 3.3, 3.3, 3.4, 3.4, 3.4, 5.2, 5.2, 5.3, 6.2, 6.3, 7.1, 7.1, 7.3, 8.3, 8.3 (لكن)

sedari, 9.2 **(183)**

semita, 1.2, 6.2, 9.1 (طريق)

semper, 8.4 (دائما)

sensibilis, 8.1 **(82)**

sensibiliter, 8.1 (عيانا)

sensus, 2.2, 2.2, 5.3, 5.3, 8.2 **(80, 81)**

sentire, 5.3, 5.3, 6.1, 6.4, 6.4, 6.4, 8.1, 8.1, 8.1, 8.2, 8.3, 8.3, 8.3, 8.3, 8.3 **(78, 79)**

sequestrare, 2.1 (قسم)

sequi, 2.2, 2.3, 5.2, 8.3, 8.4, 8.4 (لحق)

sermo, 1.3, 6.2, 6.4, 7.3, 7.3 (قول)

si, 1.2, 3.3, 3.4, 4.1, 4.2, 4.3, 5.1, 5.2, 6.1, 6.2, 6.2, 8.1, 8.1, 8.1, 9.2

sic, 3.1 (كذلك)

siccus, 2.2, 3.4, 9.2 **(428)**

sicut, 1.1 (ك), 2.2, 2.2, 2.3, 3.4, 5.1 (كما) , 3.3, 8.3, 9.1 (بمنزلة), 6.3, 6.4 (مثل); 8.4

significare, 6.3 **(134)**

similari, 3.4 **(196)**

similis, 1.2, 2.2, 2.2, 2.2, 2.2, 6.1, 6.3, 6.3, 6.3, 6.3, 6.3, 8.1, 8.3, 9.2, 9.2 **(195)**

similiter, 1.2, 4.2, 7.3, 8.3, 8.4, 9.1 (كذلك)

similitudo, 3.2 (شبيه)

simplices, 1.2, 9.2 **(29)**

simul, 1.3, 1.3, 1.3, 1.3, 8.1 (معا), 3.1, 8.1, 8.1, 8.2 (جميعا)

singularis, 1.2 **(298)**

sinister, 5.1 (أيسر)

siphac, 3.3 **(209)**

sitis, 3.4, 3.4 **(264)**

sive, 9.2

sol, 1.2, 7.2, 7.3, 7.3, 8.1, 8.1 (شمس)

solus, 7.3

solutio, 3. 4, 6.2 **(307)**

solvere, 3.4, 6.2, 6.2 (فرق) **(303, 304, 305)**

sparsus, 8.2 **(15)**

spatium, 5.2, 5.2, 8.3 (مدّة)

species, 1.1, 1.2, 1.3, 1.3, 1.3, 1.3, 2.2, 2.3, 6.1, 7.1, 9.1 **(214)**

speculator, 5.3 **(396)**

spiritus, 4.2, 4.2, 5.1, 5.3, 7.3 **(156)**

spissior, 9.2 **(284)**

spissus, 4.2 (ثخين) **(42)**, 9.1 (غليظ) **(283)**

stare, 4.1, 8.1 (لبث)
stomachi, 3.3 **(388)**
sub, 3.3 (دون), 3.3 (تحت)
subito, 8.1, 9.2
submergere, 3.2 **(276)**
substantia, 3.4, 6.2, 6.2, 6.4 **(62, 304)**
subtilior, 4.2 **(366)**, 5.1 (أرقّ) **(153)**, ألطف
subtilis, 4.2 **(365)**, 9.1 (رقيق) **(152)**, لطيف
subtilissime, 9.1 (استقصى)
sufficere, 9.2 (كفى)
super, 5.3, 6.3, 8.1 (على)
superare, 1.2 (غلب)
superfluere, 4.2 **(299)**
superfluitas, 1.2, 1.2, 3.1, 3.1, 3.1, 3.1, 3.1, 3.2, 3.2, 3.2, 3.4, 4.3, 6.1, 6.1, 6.1, 6.2, 6.2, 6.2, 7.3 **(301, 302, 313)**
superfluus, 4.1, 6.1, 6.2, 6.2, 6.2, 7.2, 7.2, 8.3, 8.3 **(175, 300)**
supergrediens, 5.1 **(174)**
superhabundare, 4.3 **(281)**
synochus, 8.3 **(369)**

tamen, 8.3 (لكن), 8.3 (إلا); 1.2, 2.2, 8.3, 9.2
tantum, 1.2, 3.1, 3.1, 5.3, 7.1, 7.1, 7.3 (فقط)
tarde, 4.2 **(30)**
tempus, 3.4 (مدّة), 5.2 (زمان)
tendere, 1.2, 5.2 (صار)
tenuior, 4.2 **(153)**
tenuis, 4.2 **(152)**
terminus, 1.2, 5.2, 5.2, 5.2, 5.2, 5.2, 6.2, 6.2, 6.2 **(67)**
tertiana, 8.4 **(274)**
testiculi, 8.1 **(13)**
timor, 3.2, 3.2, 3.2 (خطر)
totus, 1.1, 4.1, 4.1, 4.1, 4.2, 4.3, 5.1, 5.2, 5.2, 5.2, 7.2, 7.3, 9.2, 9.2 (كلّ)
tranquillitas, 1.2 **(414)**
transcendere, 1.2 **(57)**
transmutare, 3.4, 3.4 **(289)**
tremor, 6.4, 6.4, 8.1, 8.3, 8.3, 8.3, 8.4, 8.4 **(399)**
tunc, 3.2, 5.2, 5.3, 9.2 (عند ذلك); 3.1, 3.3, 3.4, 3.4, 4.1, 6.2

ubi, 3.4 (حين)
ulcus, 6.2 (قرحة) **(331)**, 6.2 (قرح) **(330)**
ulna, 2.1 **(181)**
ultimus, 8.2 (آخر), 9.2 (غاية)
undique, 3.1 (من جميع جهاتها)
unguis, 2.1, 8.1 **(5,231)**
universaliter, 4.2, 4.2 (بالجملة)
unusquisque, 2.3, 3.4, 5.2, 6.4, 8.1, 8.2, 8.2, 8.3, 9.2, 9.2 (كلّ واحد)
usque, 6.1, 7.3 (حتّى)

usus, 8.3, 8.3 (**130**)
uterque, 3.1, 4.1, 8.1, 8.2, 8.4 (امرين)

vacuitas, 2.2, 2.2 (**381**)
vapor, 7.2 (بخار)
vehemens, 8.1
vehementer, 7.3
vehementissimus, 8.1 (شديد جدًا)
vel, 7.1
velle, 3.1
velocissime, 7.1 (**179**)
velociter, 4.2 (أسرع), 4.2 (بسرعة), 8.1 (سريعا) (**179, 186**)
velocius, 4.2 (**179**)
velox, 4.2, 4.2, 4.2, 4.3 (سريع), 4.3 (أسرع) (**178, 179**)
vena, 3.1, 3.1, 3.1, 3.1, 3.3, 4.2, 4.2 (**239**)
    vena pulsatilis, 2.1, 2.2, 3.1, 3.1, 3.2 , 3.3, 4.2, 5.2 (**240, 242, 243, 244**)
    vena non pulsatilis, 2.1, 2.2, 3.1, 3.1, 3.2, 3.3, 4.2 (**241, 242, 243, 244**)
venire, 4.3, 5.1, 8.1 (عمد)
venter, 1.3 (**32**)
ventositas, 4.3 (**157**)
ventriculum, 3.3, 3.3, 5.1, 5.1, 5.1 (**59, 60, 61**)
vere, 5.2 (بالحقيقة)
verificare, 2.2 (وضح)
vero, 3.1, 3.2, 3.3, 4.2, 4.2, 5.2, 6.4, 8.4, 9.2 (أما)
versus, 3.3, 3.3 (نحو)
verumtamen, 2.2, 5.2, 6.1, 6.2, 6.3, 6.4, 8.1, 8.3 (إلا أنّ)
via, 5.2 (طريق)
vicinior, 3.2 (قريب), 5.1 (أقرب)
vicinus, 5.2, 6.1 (**54**)
videre, 8.1, 8.3, 8.3 (رأى)
videri, 8.3 (أشبه)
villus, 2.2 (**370**)
vincere, 3.2, 3.2, 3.2, 3.2, 3.4, 5.1, 5.2, 6.2, 6.2, 7.3, 9.2 (**281, 285**)
violenter, 4.2 (**353**)
vipera, 6.3, 6.3 (**320**)
vir, 8.3 (رجل)
virtus, 6.4, 7.2 (**339**)
viscera, 3.3, 4.2, 4.3, 5.1, 8.3 (**83, 84**)
vitrum, 8.1, 8.3 (**160**)
vivere, 5.1 (حي)
vocare, 1.2 (عرف), 1.1, 8.3, 8.3, 8.4 (سمّى)

ydropisis, 1.1 (**182**)
Ypocras, 3.4, 6.2 (أبقراط)

C. Hebrew

The following glossary lists the principal words and phrases appearing in David Caslari's Hebrew translation of the Latin text. The number following each entry refers readers to the word's location in the numbered glossary, and will allow them to identify the word's Latin (and Arabic) equivalent in a given passage.

אבר 250 → פנימיות, פְּעָלָה

אבר אפושטומושא 254

האבר המתמגל 254

האבר העלול 253

אי זה אבר 251

אי זה אבר דומה החלקים 262

איברים 255

האברים אשר הם רבי הדם 84

אברים דומי החלקים <ה>פשוטים <ו>הראשונים 261

האיברים הכליים 260

האברים הפנימיים 83

האיברים הפנימיים המתגברים בדם 84

האברים הראשונים 258

איברים ראשונים דומי החלקים 256

האיברים הראשונים דומי החלקים 259

באברים אשר הם רביי הדם 83

בכל אחד ואחד מן האיברים אי זה שיהיה 252

אברי הגוף הראשונים 257

אֵד: איד 17

אָדֹם: אדומה 208, 377 → מרה

האדומ' 376

אדמי: אדומיית → לֵחָה

אודות: באו[דות] הנתוח 347

אוהב 66

(אות) ניאות 422

אויר 406

האויר המקרה 407

אחור → פעל

(אחר) מתאחר ההשתנות 107

איטיקא → קדחת, שִׁדָּפוֹן

איכות: איכויות 355

איכיות 357

שני האיכיות 356

איפיאלא 14

אִיפִילא/איפילא 14

אירִיסִיפָּלָא 101

איריששיפילא 401

איש 117

אישטיאומינוש 8

אֹכֶל → התמדה, רֹב

אסטומ[כה] → חלק

חזק 300, 340

יותר חזק 341

חֹזֶק: חזק 336

בחוזק 341

חי 116

חלה 10

חֲלִי: חולי 11, 270

ח(ו)ליים 271, 378 ← ספר

חלוק 45

חִלּוּק: חילוק רוע מזג מתחלף 189

חלל 59, 315

חללי החזה 316

(חלף) התחלף 127

מתחלף 105, 127, 128, 129

חלק 44 ← אבר, רפה

חלקים 45

חלקי האסטומ' 388

חלקי המוח 389

חלקי הצלעות 390

(חלש) יותר חלש 220

חַם 71, 176

יותר חם 71, 176

חֹם: חום 70, 72, 172, 211

ח(ו)ם חזק 73, 175

חום חזק מתגבר על הטבע 174

החום היוצא מהטבע 173

חום מופלג ביותר בתכלית 342

חום נח 74

החום העובר המנהג הטבעי 75

(חמם) חימם 170

מחמם 165

חומם 165

התחמם 165, 170

התחמ' מאד 167

התחמם מהרה 171

נתחמם 165 ← שְׁלֵמוּת

ניתחמם [בשיווי] 166

חסרון 321

טבע 225, 226, 227, 379 ← חֹם, תכונה

טבעי 227, 228 ← חֹם

(טוח) הטיח דברים לבזות אותו העניין 133

(יבש) התיבש 49

יבש 428

יד 429

(ידה) הודה 183

ידיעה 238

INDEX

INDEX CODICUM

9 781606 180457